DR GEORGE BEALE is Head of History at Stranmillis College. He h researched extensively in Irish social and economic history and h published articles in these fields. A keen student of the Celtic Church, he especially interested in the development of illuminated manuscripts and the impact of Irish monasticism on early medieval Europe. He has also written a range of school textbooks on Irish and local history.

DR EAMON PHOENIX is Senior Lecturer in History at Stranmillis College. A former Research Fellow at the Institute of Irish Studies, Queen's University, Belfast, he has written two books on modern Irish political history as well as numerous scholarly articles and a textbook for schools. He is a well-known journalist and broadcaster, contributing regular analysis on current affairs and historical issues to the BBC, RTE, the *Irish Times*, *Irish News* and *Belfast Telegraph*.

Stran

Stran

Stranmillis College
1922–1998

An Illustrated History

GEORGE BEALE & EAMON PHOENIX

BELFAST

STRANMILLIS PRESS

Stranmillis College would like to acknowledge
the Ulster Bank for its kind assistance.

The Stranmillis Press is an imprint of Stranmillis College Belfast
© Stranmillis College Belfast 1998

First published 1998

ISBN 0 903009 27 7

A catalogue record for this title is available from
the British Library.

Design by Dunbar Design
Printed by W&G Baird Ltd

Contents

Foreword

Ulster Bank is proud to be banker to Stranmillis and to be supporting its 75th Anniversary celebrations.

It is widely accepted today in business that, whilst physical capital and financial resources make things possible, it is people who make them happen. Equally, in education, it is the human capital – the teachers and the ancillary and support staff of all kinds – who determine how effective the system really is. As successive waves of change have swept through our schools, teachers have had to be adaptable and flexible in the management of its consequences.

Northern Ireland is fortunate in the calibre of entrant attracted to the teaching profession and Stranmillis has earned plaudits for its success in ensuring that this potential is fully developed. Those who emerge as qualified teachers have an understanding of educational needs, are committed to the achievement of high standards in the classroom and have a concern for the pastoral care of their pupils.

Good teachers recognize that the educational imperative is to assist the fullest personal development of those within their charge, to equip them to find satisfaction in work which matches their aptitudes and abilities and to enable them to discharge their responsibilities as citizens. Schools are privileged to have the earliest opportunity, at the most formative period, to stimulate creativity and a spirit of innovation and enterprise. In a world which is only on the threshold of the information age, pupils are being increasingly encouraged to regard their experience at school as the first few rungs on a ladder of lifelong learning.

Teachers and pupils relate to each other today in a world where many of the old certainties, in the shape of tight-knit families and traditional values, have dissolved. It is unreasonable to expect teachers on their own to resolve the resultant problems but the best teachers demonstrate what can be done by a partnership between the school and even the least promising of environments.

Whilst recognising the accelerating pace of recent change, we must not overlook that change, often radical in its nature, has been a characteristic of education and society throughout Stranmillis's history. The College's story, admirably told in this volume, is a record of its ability to respond vigorously to every challenge. It was not therefore surprising, based on its successful history, that the Dearing Report on Higher Education should in 1997 propose a role for the College in the provision of a wider range of higher education programmes.

Stranmillis can look back with pride and look forward with confidence. Ulster Bank, along with a host of well-wishers, has no fears for its ability to continue to carve a very successful future.

SIR GEORGE QUIGLEY
CHAIRMAN, ULSTER BANK

Introduction

It is now some twenty six years since Ronnie Marshall published his account of the first fifty years of the life and work of the community that is Stranmillis College. However, much has happened in the intervening period and it is also the case that Marshall's book was a child of its time. It was inevitable, then, that when the College was planning its seventy-fifth anniversary celebrations, the question of producing a new history would arise.

The College is fortunate to have on its current staff two historians of outstanding quality and I was delighted when Dr George Beale and Dr Eamon Phoenix consented to undertake the major task of producing a new history of the College, one which would reflect recent developments and place the early history of Stranmillis in the context of newly discovered source materials and recent scholarship. It was also intended that interviews with former students and the use of a large number of photographs would help to convey something of the flavour of life at Stranmillis in the past. When you have had a chance to read and enjoy the pages which follow, I am confident that you will agree with me that the authors have triumphantly achieved these objectives. The site's early history, the attractions of the

Professor Richard McMinn

campus and its buildings, the varied flora and fauna, the joys of student life, the seemingly endless changes in the structure and content of academic programmes, the wartime experiences of the College and its students, management issues and the contributions of the more colourful members of staff are deftly described.

Above all, the book gives the reader a real sense of what it is like in the present or what it was like in the past, to be a member of the 'Stran' community. Thus, the publication of this new account of the College's history provides a fitting postscript to the year of celebration to mark the seventy-fifth anniversary of one of Northern Ireland's finest and much-loved assets. This would not, of course, have been possible without the generous assistance of the book's sponsor, the Ulster Bank, and the personal interest taken in the project by its distinguished Chairman, Sir George Quigley. I would also want to acknowledge the assistance provided by designer, Wendy Dunbar and Bryan McCabe of W&G Baird Ltd, the printers of the volume.

Special thanks are due to those staff and students, past and present, who have made a significant contribution through their willingness to be interviewed or who have helped with the research in other ways. This volume is dedicated to them and to all of the other members of the Stranmillis community over the last seventy-five years. Truly, it is indeed the case that by teaching we learn.

RICHARD McMINN
PRINCIPAL

Acknowledgements

We would like to express our sincere thanks to a number of people whose assistance was invaluable in the preparation of this book. Professor Richard McMinn, Principal of Stranmillis College, Miss Shirley Magowan, Deputy Principal and Mr Norman Halliday, Director (Corporate Affairs) were most generous with their support. Mrs Cilla Wagner and the staff of the College's Learning Support Service, Mr Charles Reid and Mrs Ann Cairns of the Department of Computing and Information Technology and Mr Hugh Storey, Mrs Valerie Hamilton and Miss Cathy Brady all provided technical and administrative expertise.

We are also greatly indebted to many organisations and individuals who helped with archival material: Mr Wesley McCann, College Librarian, and his staff, Ms Carol Doherty, Mrs Lynne Dean and Mr John Erskine; the staff of the Irish and Local Studies Department of the South-Eastern Education and Library Board, Ballynahinch; Ms Linda Greenwood, Irish Studies Librarian, Belfast Central Library; Mrs Kathleen Bell, Librarian at the *Irish News*; the *Belfast Telegraph*, *Belfast News Letter*, *Northern Whig Ltd* and Miss Catherine McKinney of the Divisional Planning Office (DOENI) for permission to reproduce photographs from their collections.

Many former students and members of staff, both past and present, donated photographs and proffered a wealth of information. We thank them most sincerely: Mr L L Bell, MBE, Portadown, Mr G Blackwood, Mrs P Browne, Lisburn, The Lady Mairi Bury, JP, Mountstewart, Mrs S Callaghan, Mr J D Cameron, Mr K Craig, Belfast, Miss C J Crawford, Limavady, Dr R Cromie, Mr J Davidson, Mr H Fyfe, Dr J Greenwood, Dr H Grindle, Miss J Herbison, Mr H A B Lloyd, Mr J McBride OBE, Mr W J McClure, Mrs S E McDonough, Bangor, Mr J McDowell, Mrs S E Mawhinney, Broughshane, Mr C Mount, Dr G Patterson, Mr J Rutherford, Head Gardener, Miss M Shilliday, Bangor, Mr R Smith, Mr T Steele, Mrs M Steele, Mrs A M F Stevens, Buckinghamshire, England, Professor Sir William Taylor, CBE, and Mrs G H Thompson, Benoni, South Africa,

A special word of thanks is due to Colonel James Hughes CBE, KStJ, TD, DL, Deputy Principal of the College, 1970–82, for placing at our disposal his research findings on those former students who gave their lives in the Second World War.

Sadly, Mrs Ethel Beale, the esteemed mother of George Beale and a warm supporter of this project, died before its publication. The authors dedicate this volume to her memory.

GEORGE BEALE
EAMON PHOENIX

Back Gate-lodge, Stranmillis.
This 'dinky little brick building', with its pyramidal roof, central
chimney and copper-clad dormers dates from the late 1940s.
It was designed by Thomas Rippingham.

DR R CROMIE

'Stran'
The Early Days 1

The origins of the modern system of teacher education in Ireland can be traced to the *Society for Promoting the Education of the Poor in Ireland*, founded in 1811 by a group of Dublin businessmen, and more familiarly known from its metropolitan location as the Kildare Place Society. This body instituted a course of formal training for teachers based on the English Lancastrian system. Male and female model schools were organised at the Society's headquarters, and teachers were trained there for the Kildare Place schools. Able pupils in elementary schools were selected and served an apprenticeship as monitors, eventually becoming teachers themselves.

In 1878, the Church Education Society College was taken over by the General Synod of the Church of Ireland, and in 1884, the Church of Ireland Training College became a recognised denominational college for the training of National school teachers and received government aid.

In 1831, the newly-appointed Commissioners for National Education considered teacher training to be one of their aims. By the middle of the decade, they had set up model schools and a non-denominational training college at Marlborough Street in Dublin. Of 'Marlborough', one educational historian has observed:

> The amount of actual book knowledge acquired or the skill attained in the practice of teaching may not have been very extensive or profound, yet the intermingling of all denominations did much to give the teachers who were privileged to be trained there a national spirit and a breadth of outlook that could not have been developed or cultivated in any other college.[1]

In 1846, a scheme to establish 32 model schools throughout the country was proposed. Each of these was to have three divisions – infant, male and female with accommodation for 100 pupils. At the Commissioners' expense, boarding facilities were to be provided for three trainee teachers in the male school, and lodgings for one female candidate were to be found in the neighbourhood. Training was to last six months. Thus, annually, under such a scheme, a model school would produce six male and two female trained teachers. On completion of their work at the district model school, candidates were required to teach for two years. After passing an examination based on a thorough mastery of the Board's lesson books and the regulations governing the National teacher's work and behaviour, they were to proceed to the central model school in Dublin.

Teachers were forbidden to attend markets, fairs or political meetings and were expected to inculcate in their pupils 'a spirit of peace and respect for lawful authority'. The scheme was approved by the lord lieutenant and the first district model school was opened at Newry in 1848. Other early examples in Ulster were Belfast, Ballymena, Ballymoney, Coleraine and Newtownards. In the beginning the model schools attracted trainee teachers of every religious denomination. Typical was the Belfast Model, built in Divis Street in 1857, which in its architectural design and recreational facilities, was one of the most impressive buildings in the rapidly expanding industrial city. Model schools continued to be opened at intervals until 1865, by which date there were 30 throughout Ireland.[2]

It was originally intended to provide initial teacher training in these institutions with students proceeding to a college for final preparation, but the scheme proved impracticable.

By the early years of the twentieth century, a pattern had evolved by which bright pupils in Standard 6 of the elementary school were selected as 'candidate monitors'. They were obliged to study a number of subjects in addition to the regular school curriculum, and on passing an examination at the end of a year, they became monitors at age 15 and began a three-year course of training. The monitors received grants in successive years – £10, £15 and £20 for a boy, and £8, £12 and £16 for a girl. They were examined in the subjects they would teach, and were also required to prepare lessons and deliver them under supervision. In 1885, the Queen's Scholarship (later to become the King's Scholarship) was initiated and monitors sat this examination in their third year. Those who were successful were eligible for admission to a training college, but, many neither found, nor even sought admission there.

Schools recruited personnel from two additional sources: pupil teachers and junior assistant mistresses. The former were students, initially at model schools, and later at secondary schools, who spent three years as part-time teachers in selected elementary schools, teaching two hours a day for the first year and three hours in the second and third. They sat the scholarship examination and entered the training colleges under the same scheme as the monitors. As late as 1919-20, there were 1,400 monitors and 500 pupil teachers in Ireland. The second route into teaching in the Edwardian era was dictated by economy.

In those schools where the average attendance was perilously small the government was unwilling to employ trained staff. As a result, in 1906, it created a new grade of teacher – the junior assistant mistress. These

Pupils and teachers at Tullywest National School, Co. Down, about 1900.

ULSTER MUSEUM

The seventh Marquis of Londonderry, Northern Ireland's First Minister of Education, arguably 'the architect of Stranmillis Training College'.

THE LADY MAIRI BURY, MOUNTSTEWART, CO. DOWN

assistants were untrained and had to be at least 17 years old. They were selected by inspectors from promising pupils in elementary schools who were neither monitors nor pupil-teachers. Following a period of provisional recognition in schools, they could sit the King's Scholarship examination. Those who gained a pass in the first or second division, became recognised as junior mistresses without attendance at a training college.

Nevertheless, the numbers of teachers who undertook training at a recognised college increased significantly in the first decades of the twentieth century. In 1902, only 55 per cent of teachers had attended college, but by 1919–20 the figure had reached 80 per cent. Although several small colleges founded under the auspices of the Wesleyan Methodists and the Irish Missions' Society during the nineteenth century did not survive, by 1920 there were seven colleges in existence – the Church of Ireland College at Kildare Place, Dublin; Marlborough Street College, Dublin – a non-denominational institution and the only college availed of by Presbyterian students before 1922; and five Roman Catholic colleges throughout Ireland including St Mary's in Belfast, established as a women's training college in 1900.

When the Northern Ireland Ministry of Education was created in 1921, the Minister, Lord Londonderry, announced the establishment of a committee of inquiry under the chairmanship of R J Lynn, the Member of Parliament for West Belfast, to review the vexed question of educational reform. Lynn's brief was to examine the existing organisation and administration of education and to put forward recommendations regarding the future structure of that service in the new political entity. Teacher training was not included in the Commission's terms of reference; instead, the Committee for the Training of Teachers for Northern Ireland, under the chairmanship of the Minister of Finance, H M Pollock, was appointed by Londonderry on 19 May 1922, 'for the purpose of making arrangements for the preliminary education, training and certification of teachers for various grades of schools in Northern Ireland'.

The Pollock Committee was only too well aware of the widespread dissatisfaction with the pre-partition monitorial system and its teacher-centred approach. Moreover, there was a broad consensus among educationists and teachers' unions that future teacher training should be located in Belfast, either in association with Queen's University or in a separate third-level institution.

The committee set to work quickly. It held its first meeting on 25 May 1922, and determined to establish a training college for elementary teachers in co-operation with Queen's University and the Belfast Technical Instruction Committee. A site for this new college on the Stranmillis House estate, then the property of Queen's University, was procured in June 1922 and its purchase speedily arranged, though the deeds of transfer are dated January 1923.[3]

A temporary hostel for 30 men students was opened at Royal Terrace, Lisburn Road, in October 1922, while separate residential accommodation for women students was erected at Stranmillis. The 'Bungalow Hostels', as the residences came to be known, were occupied by 90 students from March 1924, and renovations to Stranmillis House to accommodate about 60 additional women students were completed in that autumn. According to a contemporary Ministry of Education report, each hostel afforded 'excellent accommodation' and left 'little to be desired from the point of view of comfort, convenience and healthful conditions'. A more candid view, however, can be gleaned from a male student's description of conditions in Royal Terrace on his arrival in Michaelmas Term of 1922:

> There is a look of expectancy on the newcomer's face as he anxiously looks forward to his arrival at his new abode. Great is his surprise as he sweeps through the pillars and past a portion of "No Man's Land" on each side of the carriage drive, and then draws up in front of a large three-storied building of the late Hanoverian period in line with several others.
>
> On entering the hall of this building a line of trunks indicates that other voyagers have arrived. The new Warden, of Welsh descent, is ready to welcome the newcomer. The sound of a workman's hammer from one of the front rooms makes it clear that the furnishing is not complete. Further incompleteness is noticed as the newcomer proceeds up the uncovered stairs, and the fear of not securing a bed grips him. His fears increase on looking at the first two or three dormitories, where all the available beds are already claimed. In haste and terror he rushes up the remaining flights of stairs, and is covered with perspiration by the time he reaches the top. On looking round the last scantily-furnished room he finds an unoccupied bed, which he claims. Thinking that his trouble is over for the day he proceeds slowly down the stairs wondering how he will get a shave the next

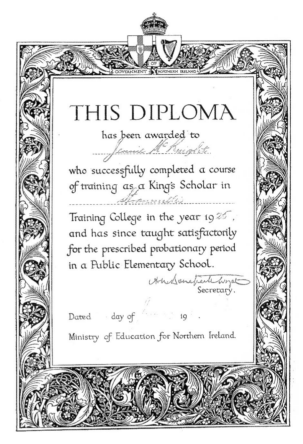

Jennie (Jane) McKnight was born in 1905 and entered Stranmillis in 1923. Her probationary teaching was carried out at Newtownards Model School. This certificate, awarded to her in January 1925, is signed by AN Bonaparte Wyse, Permanent Secretary of the Ministry of Education. He claimed descent from a brother of the Emperor Napoleon.

COLLEGE LIBRARY

The old 'Bungalow Hostels'. Built as temporary accommodation for women students on the site in 1924, these 'healthful' structures (to quote a Ministry report) remained in use until the late 1960s.

morning without a looking-glass, when he finds he has not paid the car driver, who kicks up a row for being kept waiting. Having finished this troublesome business our newcomer wends his way to the famed seat of learning of which Ulster is proud – "Queen's".[4]

The College opened in October 1922, but as there was at that time no building on the Stranmillis site where classes could be held, students were taught at the university and at the Belfast College of Technology. 'Academic' subjects were provided at the university, where teacher training students attended lectures and tutorials alongside 'mainstream' undergraduates, while those of a more practical nature – drawing, domestic economy, drill, chemistry and physics – were studied at the 'Tech'.

The staff of the College was initially very small. W J McCallister, Professor of Education at Queen's University, was responsible for its administration and management, but was not accorded the title 'Principal' until 1926. In addition to the salary commensurate with his Chair, Professor McCallister received a supplement from the Ministry of Education for College duties. A Banbridge man, McCallister had trained at Marlborough Street Training College and spent ten years in English schools before assuming the Queen's professorship.[5]

For the time being, several university professors and lecturers undertook to teach non-degree College students in various subjects: physical geography (Professor J K Charlesworth), history (Edward Hughes), English literature

(W H Semple), botany and nature study (Professor J Small and Miss M Duff). In 1922, the first appointments to the Training College, as distinct from those to the university, were mostly to the education department – J Ridley Thompson, Master of Method, Miss F Simms, Miss E L McCaughey, Miss M Brown and Mr James Dorwood. At that time, W H Lloyd of Methodist College, Belfast was appointed to teach mathematics and two part-time members of staff were employed – Miss E Matthews for 'reading' and W C Davison for music. W Ellison became Master of Method in 1924 on Thompson's appointment to Sheffield University.

When it opened, Stranmillis Training College as it was known, had 198 students, 64 of whom were entered on the College register as following the second year course. These students had been transferred after the successful completion of their first year of training at Marlborough Street College, Dublin, which was closed by the Irish Free State Department of Education in 1922, leaving only the voluntary or denominational colleges operative.

The Northern Ireland Ministry of Education had entered into a temporary arrangement with the Church of Ireland Training College in Dublin. Under this agreement the Kildare Place institution undertook to train a limited number of students from Northern Ireland for a period of two years from September 1922, pending the completion of the new Belfast college. The students trained at Kildare Place were instructed, partly in connection with Trinity College, Dublin, in a programme approved by the Northern Ireland Ministry, and their examination and certification as teachers were subject to its control. If students undertook to teach for five years in Northern Ireland on completion of training, they could expect a grant to be paid by the Ministry on their behalf to Kildare Place. Failure to comply with this undertaking resulted in students being required to reimburse £75 to the Ministry for each year of training. In all, there were 61 students from Northern Ireland in residence at Kildare Place during the 1922–23 session – four men and 26 women in their first year of training and five men and 26 women in their second year. However, under this north-south arrangement there were no fresh admissions in 1923, and from the commencement of the

The only escape route! Even if Miss Kyle, the Matron locked the doors religiously at 10 p.m., these inmates of the Bungalow Hostels in 1948 could still manage a smile!

MRS SE McDONOUGH

WOMEN'S HOSTELS.

HOUSE RULES.

(Approved by the Committee for the Training of Teachers)

1. The internal management and discipline of the Hostels are in the hands of the Lady Warden and students are required to conform strictly to these House Rules.

2. HOURS.

WEEK-DAYS.			SUNDAYS.		
Breakfast	-	7-55	Breakfast	-	9.
Lunch	-	12 to 1	Dinner	-	1-45.
Tea	-		Tea	-	4-30.
Dinner	-	6-30	Supper	-	8-30.

3. Cases of illness must be reported to the Matron at once. No student may remain in bed for any meal without notifying her.

4. Students must leave their rooms tidy with beds made at 9 a.m. weekdays and 10 a.m. Sundays

5. Students must be in by 6-15 p.m. each day exept Saturdays and Sundays when leave extends till 10 p.m. Special permission will have to be obtained for late leave on other occasions from Warden or Matron. Students who have permission to remain out after 6-30 must sign their names in the Hall Book and enter their destination before leaving and on their return must enter and initial the hour of return.

6. Students may receive visitors up to 5-15 p.m. in the common rooms only. No visitors may be received after this hour.

7. LAUNDRY.

Students must send to the laundry each week in a bag with list enclosed:

1 Sheet   1 Pillow-case   2 Towels

in addition to their personal laundry. For this the laundry charge is 1/11. Excess over 2/-, if any, must be paid by the students to the Matron.

NOTE. The under sheet only should be changed each week, the upper sheet taking its place.

8. Each student is supplied with the following for which she is responsible:

1 Bunch of Keys,	1 Under Blanket,
1 Tumbler,	2 Pillows and Covers,
1 Soap Dish,	1 Bed Cover,
3 Blankets,	1 Waste Paper Basket.

Losses and breakages and any damage or stains on furniture, blankets, etc. must be reported at once.

The pillows must not be taken out of the bedrooms, nails and pins must on no account be driven into walls or woodwork.

9. No dining-room crockery, cutlery or silver may be taken from the dining-room. A fine will be imposed if these are found in students' kitchens or rooms.

Flowers, tea-leaves, etc., should be left in the buckets provided in the students' kitchens.

10. Boots must be changed in the cloakrooms.

11. Lights will be turned out at 10-45 p.m. and students are requested to switch off their light, before retiring in order to prevent a waste of current when turned on next day. They are also requested to switch off lights when leaving any room unoccupied even for a minute or two.

A fine of 6d. will be imposed when lights are left burning unnecessarily.

12. At the end of each term all keys must be left in the letter pigeon hole. They may NOT be taken away.

At the end of the summer term all drawers must be left empty and pictures removed to facilitate cleaning.

13. No food may be kept in the bed sitting rooms. A cupboard is provided for this purpose in each students' kitchen.

14. Extreme quietness must be observed in the house after 8 p.m.

DO NOT BANG DOORS.

1924–25 session, it was anticipated that there would be in training in Belfast 'a sufficient number of students to provide for the needs of the public elementary schools of Northern Ireland'.

These needs would be met, in part, by the two training colleges in the city – St Mary's for Roman Catholic women, and Stranmillis, a non-denominational college for both men and women. In 1923, the management of St Mary's College which, initially, had not entered into any formal agreement with the Northern government, negotiated a settlement by which the college received a block grant from the Ministry of Education, while still maintaining denominational control. There was, however, no college for the training of Roman Catholic male teachers in Northern Ireland.

Traditionally, Catholic entrants to the profession had been trained in denominational colleges in Dublin or Waterford. However, the failure of attempts at cross-border co-operation in teacher education in the early 1920s meant that alternative arrangements had to be sought for Roman Catholic male students. Thus, Roman Catholic male students enrolled at Stranmillis for a brief period: in 1923, 25 out of a total enrolment of 42 first year students at the College were Roman Catholic; during the 1924–25 academic year Roman Catholic students numbered 32 out of a male student population of 72. Relations between students of both traditions at Stranmillis were most harmonious. 'There was never a discordant word', recalls Mr Lewis L Bell MBE, a member of the class of 1923–25.[6]

However, this expedient proved unsatisfactory for the Roman Catholic authorities, who insisted on separate denominational facilities in line with canon law. As a result, Roman Catholic teachers who trained at Stranmillis found themselves unqualified to teach in schools under Roman Catholic control, through no fault of their own. In 1925, the government offered to build a hostel for Roman Catholic men students if they would continue to attend Stranmillis, but the church hierarchy refused, demanding a separate college for men students, as well as a hostel. The Ministry rejected the church's request on the grounds that public funds could not be used for the endowment of a denominational institution and, in any case, there were too few Catholic men students to merit the establishment of a separate college. Eventually, arrangements acceptable to both the church and the Ministry were agreed in 1925 whereby male students would be trained at St Mary's

Mr Lewis Lloyd Bell, MBE, at 94 must rank amongst Stranmillis's 'elder statesmen'. Born on a farm near Gilford, Co. Down, he began his career as a monitor before securing the King's Scholarship and a place in the new training college. 'We were three days at Queen's and three at the Technical College', he recalls. Mr Bell spent his teaching career in Co. Armagh and now lives with his wife in Portadown.

The Main Building pictured on its official opening in 1930.

COLLEGE LIBRARY

College, Strawberry Hill in Middlesex, with their fees and maintenance paid for by the Northern Ireland Ministry.

A letter announcing this 'Concordat' was sent by Lord Londonderry to each Roman Catholic student at Stranmillis College in April 1925:

> The student from Northern Ireland accepted for training by the Training College at Hammersmith under arrangement with the Ministry … will be certified by this Ministry for recognition as teachers of public elementary schools in Northern Ireland …
>
> The course of instruction in religious knowledge given in the college is regarded as satisfactory by the Roman Catholic bishops in Northern Ireland and, consequently, the bishops will approve … the appointment of teachers trained therein …
>
> In order to remove the disabilities which at present prevent the appointment in schools under Roman Catholic management of teachers trained in Stranmillis Training College, the bishops propose to hold a summer course in religious knowledge open to teachers already trained in Stranmillis, or who will complete their training in that college this year, but to no others.[7]

As a recent historian of the Northern Ireland education system has observed:

While satisfactory to the church, this compromise was achieved at the price of ... local co-operation between the Catholic Church itself and the management of Stranmillis College which could have had profound effects for the training of northern teachers from the very beginning of the new system's existence.[8]

This arrangement continued until 1945, when, due to pressure of numbers, the Strawberry Hill management was compelled to ask the Irish Roman Catholic authorities to make alternative provision for the training of their men students. As a temporary measure, these students attended St Mary's College, Belfast, until St Joseph's College for Catholic men was opened at Trench House, Belfast, in 1961.

Group picture of the guests at Stranmillis House on 1 May 1930. Included are: front row, third left, Lord Charlemont, Minister of Education; fourth left, Lady Craigavon, seated alongside the Duchess of Atholl and Professor McCallister; second row includes (fourth and fifth left) HM Pollock and Viscount Craigavon.

MR WALTER McCLURE

CORDIAL RELATIONS WITH ST MARY'S IN THE 1920s

In spite of the educational controversies of the 1920s, Stranmillis College enjoyed a cordial relationship with the older Belfast training college, St Mary's, during these early years. In a portent of much later government policy, Lord Londonderry was instrumental in forging social links between students in the two colleges in the mid-1920s. Thus, in May 1924, the local press reported that 'three hundred young ladies and gentlemen, students at the city training colleges … were entertained at a garden party at Mountstewart by Lord and Lady Londonderry on Saturday'. The report conveys a flavour of the times:

> The guests consisted of 220 students from Stranmillis and 80 from St Mary's. The former were in charge of Miss F (Florence) Irwin, lady warden, Miss E Crockett, matron, Mr William C Parr, registrar of the college and Mr A R Rhys Pryce, warden, while the St Mary's students were in charge of Miss Murphy and Miss Gilmore. Special carriages were provided on the County Down Railway and on reaching Newtownards, the students were conveyed to Mountstewart in char-à-bancs …[9]

A year later, in June 1925, Lady Londonderry renewed the invitation to the students of both colleges. Amongst those present on this occasion were the Londonderry family, H M Pollock, the Minister of Finance, Professor Gregg Wilson of Queen's University, and, from the Stranmillis staff, Miss Florence Irwin, Miss Elsie Crockett, Miss E Hardy and Miss A McVea. The report concludes: 'Amidst the delightful scenery … and the wide stretch of Strangford Lough, the students found plenty to interest them … The guests returned to Belfast after a very happy visit'.[10]

From 1922 until April 1931, the Committee for the Training of Teachers exercised more direct control over Stranmillis College than over the voluntary college. Throughout this period, H M Pollock, Minister of Finance,

The ceremonial opening of the Main Building of the College on 1 May 1930: a party of Stranmillis girls in holiday mood await the arrival of the Duchess of Atholl.

NORTHERN WHIG

remained chairman, and all other members had some direct
involvement with education. These included Assistant
Secretaries from the Ministry of Education, the Principal of the
Municipal College of Technology, representatives from
Queen's University and school principals.

Relations between this committee and the College Principal,
Professor W J McCallister, were far from cordial. The volume
of work involved in his joint appointment with the university,
together with what he considered the excessive control of
affairs by the Ministry, eventually culminated in McCallister's
resignation in 1930. In its annual report for 1930–31, the
Ministry acknowledged 'the onerous nature of the duties'
inherent in the professor's dual position and recorded 'its appreciation of the valuable work he performed as Principal, at a
time when the college buildings had not been completed and
the full lecturing staff had not been appointed'.[11]

During the vacancy, W H Welply, the Ministry's Senior Chief
Inspector, administered the College until the appointment of a
new Principal in 1931.

Meanwhile, 1930 saw a major landmark in the history of Stranmillis with
the opening of the new Main Building amidst a fanfare of media attention.

The new building was opened officially on 1 May 1930 by the Duchess of
Atholl, MP, the former Parliamentary Secretary to the Board of Education
in the Conservative government, before an
invited audience of 600. This included the
Prime Minister, Lord Craigavon, the Minister
of Education, Lord Charlemont, H M Pollock,
Minister of Finance and Chairman of the
College Committee for the Training of
Teachers and the Principal of the College,
Professor McCallister. Other guests included
Lady Pirrie, widow of Viscount Pirrie, the ship-
ping magnate, Dr R W Livingstone, the
Vice-Chancellor of Queen's University, Rev
Principal F J Paul of Assembly's College and
the heads of Victoria College and Princess
Gardens School.

As her car swept through the College gates,
the Duchess was greeted by a cheering party of lady students and received a

The Duchess of Atholl arriving
with HM Pollock, Northern
Ireland Minister of Finance and
Chairman of the College
Committee for the Training of
Teachers.

NORTHERN WHIG

The Duchess viewing
the new building,
accompanied by
Professor
W J McCallister, first
Principal of Stranmillis
College and Professor of
Education at Queen's
University.

NEWS LETTER

bouquet of flowers from Miss Nan MacCormack, the Stranmillis head girl. There followed the formal opening ceremony. 'May sunshine', the *Northern Whig* reported, 'flooded the drive of the college grounds as the Duchess … was handed the golden key by Mr R Ingleby Smith, OBE, FRIA, the architect'. In her address, the Duchess of Atholl congratulated the Northern Ireland government on its constructive work in the educational sphere since 1921, and humorously suggested that the College's association with the Finance Minister was a major advantage.

> At Stranmillis everything seemed to show how thoroughly the Northern government understood the nature of the problem … It is quite evident that this building has been planned with great thought … and that it has enjoyed ample resources with which to provide the necessary funds. No doubt it has been happily placed as having the chairman of its Governing Committee someone who is in close connection with the national finances (a reference to H M Pollock, the Northern Ireland Minister of Finance).[12]

The Duchess urged those who received their training as teachers at Stranmillis to impress upon their pupils the dignity of all work and not merely that of clerical and professional occupations. 'Our teachers', she observed, 'could give a tremendous lot of help to employment in this country if they keep clearly before the eyes of their pupils the dignity of all creative work'. 'Education', she concluded, was 'an essential preparation for citizenship'.

In his speech, the Minister of Education, Lord Charlemont seemed to anticipate later 'outreach' programmes when he warned against the College adopting a narrow provincial outlook. While developing their own ideas they should be 'open to influences from elsewhere'. There should be a considerable interchange of ideas and personnel between Northern Ireland and Great Britain.[13]

In an allusion to the new building, the Vice-Chancellor of Queen's University reminded the audience that 'education was not a series of detached bungalows but one building with many rooms. It was impossible to exaggerate what Stranmillis and all it stood for might mean in the life of Ulster and what those training in it could do for her'.

The Belfast newspapers agreed that the opening ceremony had been a resounding success. 'Beatrix', the *Whig*'s social columnist, concluded:

> The afternoon was very jolly. Everybody was in the best of moods and the embryonic teachers learned something of the fine part they have to play in

'The belle of the ball': Miss Nan MacCormack, Head Girl at Stranmillis, presents a bouquet to the Duchess at the ceremony.

NORTHERN WHIG

the building up of Ulster, and the mothers and fathers amiably or with sighs regretted that in their young days youth had not such splendid advantages.

The local press was alive to the historic nature of the occasion. The *Northern Whig* expressed its delight 'that both teachers and pupils had the opportunity of working in such beautiful surroundings, with light air and everything possible for their comfort'. It was a far cry, it observed, from 'the conditions in which the old hedge-schoolmasters worked'.[14]

For its part, the *Belfast Telegraph* recalled the difficulties which the College had faced since 1922 owing to the absence of lecture facilities on the site. The editor felt that 'Stran's' affiliation to Queen's would make it easier for its students to gain academic degrees.[15]

Yet the students attending the College in the 1930s seemed less impressed by its educational and cultural advantages than the opinion-makers of the day. There were the predictable gripes about the boarding-school-type regime which prevailed in the Bungalow Hostels, the quality of the food, Teaching Practice and the lecturers. But, as a humorous ditty, penned by Evelyn Wilson in 1932 and preserved by her College friend, Mrs S E Mawhinney, conveys, there was a palpable sadness on leaving 'Stran':

> We hate the bell that wakes us in the morning
> And often too we grumble at our food,
> And we think Napier and 'Cherry' (Miss M Boyd) awful tyrants,
> Although they always say 'tis for your good.
> And we think the Bungalows most wretched prisons,
> And our teaching supervisors most unfair,
> And the lectures – simple torture!
> Years after, shall we think, I wonder, 'We were happy there'?[16]

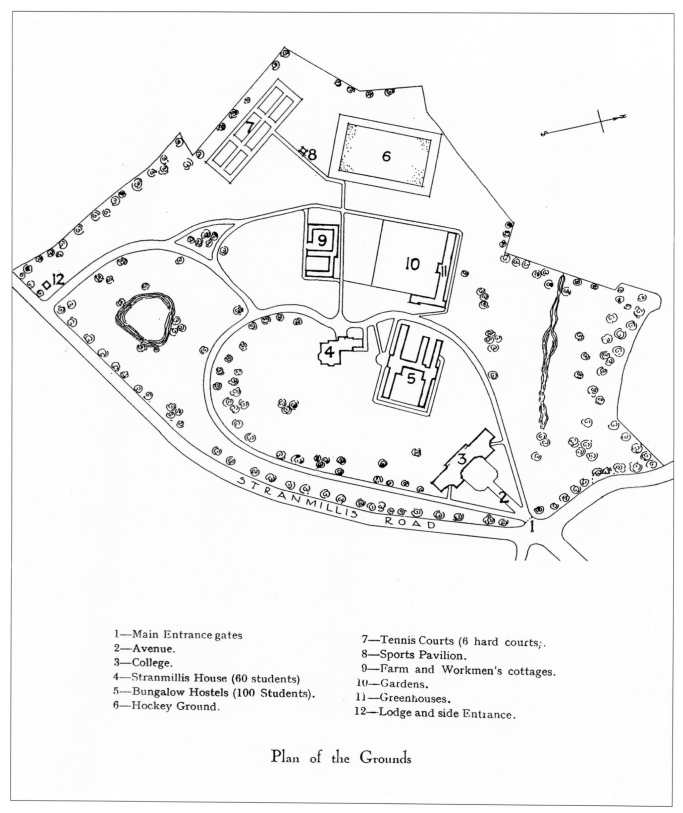

1—Main Entrance gates
2—Avenue.
3—College.
4—Stranmillis House (60 students)
5—Bungalow Hostels (100 Students).
6—Hockey Ground.

7—Tennis Courts (6 hard courts).
8—Sports Pavilion.
9—Farm and Workmen's cottages.
10—Gardens.
11—Greenhouses.
12—Lodge and side Entrance.

Plan of the Grounds

Plan of College Grounds, 1930

'The Battle
of Stranmillis' 2

The College could not hope to escape the educational controversies of the 1920s and early 1930s. The Londonderry Education Act of 1923 was religiously neutral, providing for a state secular system of primary schools based on a series of regional education committees. While the bulk of Roman Catholic schools opted for 'voluntary' status, Protestant church interests feared that the 1923 Act would lead to 'secularism' in state schools. During the period 1923–30 the United Education Committee of the Protestant Churches, backed by the Orange Order and led by Rev William Corkey, waged a vigorous campaign to have religious instruction included in the educational code.

The government's 'surrender' found lasting expression in the 1930 Education Act which granted concessions on Bible teaching and increased the influence of Protestant clergy on school management committees. Such a settlement overturned Lord Londonderry's earlier non-sectarian policy and ran counter to the religious safeguard in the 1920 Government of Ireland Act.

Against this background of church-state confrontation in the late 1920s, the Protestant Churches argued that, as the Roman Catholic community had its own teacher training institution, equity demanded a Protestant voice on the Stranmillis College committee of management. In July 1928, a deputation from the churches' United Education Committee to the new Education Minister, Lord Charlemont, demanded 'representation of educational and religious interests' on the Stranmillis governing board.[17]

This was elaborated in a resolution by the United Committee in February 1929:

> Without demanding a denominational training college, we ask as a matter of justice that the conditions under which teachers are trained, who are in the future to be entrusted with the education of Protestant children, be made as acceptable to the Protestant Churches as the conditions under which Roman Catholic teachers being trained are made acceptable to the Roman Catholic Church.[18]

At first, Lord Charlemont promised the Protestant churches representation on the Stranmillis governing body. Later, however, in April 1931, under intense pressure from cabinet colleagues, notably Pollock, he withdrew his offer, dissolved the Committee for the Training of Teachers and placed the College directly under the control of the Ministry. This extraordinary tactic was designed to remove the need for any intermediate management body on which clerical representation could be sought. At the same time,

Rev. William Corkey, Presbyterian minister and educational campaigner who took a keen interest in the fortunes of Stranmillis College.

MR JOHN ERSKINE

Charlemont appointed a full-time principal of the College in the person of H E Winn, a colourful figure and veteran of the Great War.

In his determination to evade his earlier pledge to allow church representation at Stranmillis, Charlemont was reflecting 'a newly-found conviction that it was wrong to allow the clergy to claim authority over secular education'.[19] Thus, in the spring of 1931, the Minister offered the Protestant churches places on an advisory committee which would be consulted on matters relating to the religious and moral education of students. The churches, however, were not to be satisfied with anything less than a direct voice in the direction of Stranmillis.

Official government papers on the 'Stranmillis affray', as it became known, reveal Lord Charlemont's view that the United Education Committee's

The Prime Minister of
Northern Ireland,
Viscount Craigavon (centre)
accompanied by Lady Craigavon
and Sir Robert Baird of
the *Belfast Telegraph* at
Stranmillis, May 1930.

NORTHERN WHIG

demand for representation at Stranmillis represented a further step towards
the 'denominationalism' espoused in the 1930 Education Amending Act.
Such a concession could not be justified, the Minister argued, since
Stranmillis Training College was in complete public ownership and thus
belonged to the entire community. This viewpoint was reinforced by the
Prime Minister, Lord Craigavon, in a forceful letter to Rev Corkey in August
1931.

Within a year, however, the combined pressure of Unionist public opinion
on the issue and the political crisis sparked by de Valera's electoral triumph
in the Free State induced a change of heart in government circles. In March
1932, the Minister of Labour, John M Andrews, commenced fresh negotiations with the United Committee of the Protestant Churches and an acceptable compromise was reached. The churches were to have three
representatives on the reconstituted college management committee of
nine, enjoying the full status and powers of the lay members. In May 1932,
Lord Charlemont agreed that lecturers in Bible-teaching should be appointed to the staff of Stranmillis 'in addition to the chaplains of different denominations'.[20]

Charlemont, as Minister of Education, had been absent during these crucial negotiations and regarded the success of the clerical campaigners with mixed feelings. His Lordship wrote to Corkey in May 1932:

> I feel that it would be hardly fair on my part not to give you my congratulations on your famous victory at the Battle of Stranmillis. Personally, of course, I think that had I commanded on the field in person, the results might have been different, but equally they might not.[21]

Despite the siren protests of the Ulster Teachers' Union and the Irish National Teachers' Organisation at what they saw as the Northern Ireland government's 'abject surrender' to clericalism, the change took effect in July 1933. The new Stranmillis management committee included three clerical representatives closely identified with the United Committee's agitation: the Anglican, Very Rev W S Kerr (later Bishop of Down and Dromore), the Presbyterian divine, Rev William Corkey and Rev W H Smyth, representing the Methodist Church.

The 'Stranmillis affair' may have been no more than a footnote to the wider schools controversy of 1923–30. However, it marked an important milestone in the evolution of the College as the major provider of teachers for the state sector of education in Northern Ireland.

Wartime Stranmillis 3

The outbreak of the Second World War marked the opening of a distinctive chapter in the history of Stranmillis College. At the opening of hostilities in September 1939 the College site and buildings were required by the military as a hospital and the training college was evacuated to a hotel in Portrush on the north Antrim coast. This unique situation continued until May 1944 when the students returned to the Stranmillis site.

It had been decided originally not to train men teachers during the war emergency but, as a result of pressure from the Stranmillis authorities and the teachers' unions, in October 1940, 17 young men were awarded King's Scholarships and admitted to the College in Portrush. One of these, a later headmaster, Thomas Henry Ellis, has left us a graphic pen-picture of 'Wartime Stranmillis' by the sea. The new College campus was Fawcett's Royal Portrush Hotel overlooking the harbour and commanding panoramic views of the Inishowen Peninsula and Scotland. T H Ellis recalls the scene with nostalgia:

> … the College at Portrush was really an ideal place for learning. Our professors lived in the hotel with us or lodged nearby, so that we met them

A wartime sketch of Fawcett's
Royal Hotel, Portrush,
by Mrs Iris Ellis.
TH ELLIS

much as medieval students would have done. The hotel was far more comfortable and convenient than any institution planned for students is ever likely to be. The lecture rooms, a small but adequate library, the common rooms, dining room and our bedrooms were all under one roof and we could walk to them, silently along carpeted corridors. There was a fine ballroom which was used for assemblies and as a gymnasium in addition to … dancing.[22]

In his first report on the evacuation, H E Winn reported that 'classwork proceeded normally in spite of the unusual conditions'. Fawcett's Hotel had proven satisfactory as a temporary home for 'Stran'. Owing to the reduction in student numbers, a smaller staff was retained for service in Portrush. This included D W T Jenkins, professor of history, W H Lloyd, professor of mathematics, Allan Murray, lecturer in geography and William Ellison, Master of Method. As the war progressed, however, both Jenkins and Murray were released to join the forces.[23] The loss of such experienced staff inevitably created problems for the College. The College committee was especially reluctant to dispense with the historical expertise of Professor Jenkins who had secured a post as an army lecturer. Indeed, at a meeting of the Stranmillis Training College Committee on 17 July 1941, the Dean of Belfast, Very Rev W S Kerr went so far as to declare 'that Professor Jenkins might be of greater service lecturing to students in the College than to H M Forces'.

For the hundred or so students at Fawcett's in the early 1940s, the college day began at around 5 am, since local time was two and a half hours earlier than official Greenwich Mean Time. The women students took turns at ringing a bell after which the student body joined the Principal, his family and the lecturing staff in the dining room. They stood reverently while the Principal, Herbert Winn recited the Lord's Prayer before sitting down to a breakfast of porridge, followed by a traditional 'Ulster fry' of eggs, bacon, sausages, potato bread and spam. 'As most food with a high protein content was strictly rationed, helpings were small, but the cooks did an excellent job with the materials at their disposal'.

Sexism was also a feature of the regime, however, with the male students enjoying waitress service while the hapless girls queued at the hatch for their porridge!

T H Ellis recalls a refined, animated atmosphere at communal mealtimes in Portrush:

Everyone was well dressed, even for breakfast. The men wore suits with fine shirts and ties. The women's clothes had many matching accessories which were used to vary the effect of a basic ensemble.[24]

Lunch was an informal meal but dinner at six o'clock was quite formal. 'Everyone was even more smartly dressed than usual and the women nearly all wore frocks'. On this occasion, the women students would sing grace, the assemblage standing behind their chairs until the Principal took his place at the table. The students of that frugal era were grateful for small mercies, especially the 'really good tea, served in pots … and plenty of good brown bread'. Jam, sugar and butter were carefully rationed while the butter was prized as a special delicacy to be eaten with potatoes. Supper consisted of hot or cold milk and slices of bread and butter, known to the students as 'doorsteps'.

Notwithstanding the novelty aspect of student life in Portrush, the academic programme was rigid, as T H Ellis recalls:

> From nine o'clock in the morning until one o'clock in the afternoon we had a succession of lectures each lasting an hour … By five o'clock we were free of lectures, but from seven until 9.15 we had a study period every evening except Saturdays and Sundays.

Lectures were suspended on Wednesday and Saturday afternoons. On Sunday mornings students attended their respective places of worship, the women students 'beautifully dressed', each wearing a hat, the men in their

'Between a rock and a hard place'. Margaret Shilliday and companions relaxing at Ramore Head near Portrush on 31 May 1941. Initially the College authorities frowned on the notion of men and women students 'walking out together'.

MISS M SHILLIDAY

Sunday best and 'well barbered'. Sunday afternoons might be spent on long walks round the headland or to the White Rocks, a local beauty spot. At first the College authorities frowned on the notion that men and women students should 'walk out together', but in the end the Principal and Warden were worsted. T H Ellis recalls :

> Looking back, I think the Principal rather enjoyed meeting a mixed party of students as he always raised his hat to the women while we, who were hatless, had to touch our forelocks in recognition of the salute. There were few social occasions then so awkward as having to acknowledge a salute without a hat. Nodding appeared rude and bowing … like a Nazi salutation, so we were compromised with a kind of civilian's version of the soldier's salute.[25]

The girl students, however, were less impressed by the apparent comforts of their new setting. There were complaints of 'insufficient bathrooms' (the hotel possessed only three baths) and, in the end, the women were allowed to visit the nearby Northern Counties Hotel for baths and a splash in its heated swimming pool.[26]

Moreover, Miss Margaret Shilliday, a Portrush 'trainee', recalls that the hotel had no central heating, making life unpleasant in the wintertime. The former hotel bar was converted into a lecture theatre but this did not prevent lectures being interrupted periodically by off-duty soldiers demanding

Halcyon Days! A happy group of Stranmillis girls enjoying the summer sunshine at their coastal retreat, May 1941.

MISS M SHILLIDAY

'a drink at the bar'. An awkward problem arose from the fact that the hotel proprietor was licensed to operate a public bar in the hotel over the summer months until the end of September. The Principal complained in September 1941 that, 'As the students came into residence on September 15th … this is very inconvenient in many ways and certainly very undesirable in others. I should like to urge that the bar be removed in future by September 12th'. For the students, such colourful incidents provided moments of light relief but provoked the unremitting ire of the staid female staff.[27]

The students made their own entertainment in the long winter evenings. Margaret Shilliday recalls how, during 1939-40, they produced 'Snow White', ostensibly a pantomime but, in reality, a 'skit' on the evacuation to Portrush in which North Antrim farmers rejoiced 'about not having to wash in the jaw-box or under the pump. We even had the Presbyterian minister (Rev J S Pyper) in it!'

Though the north coast was spared the horrors of the German air raids visited on Belfast in 1941, certain precautions were observed. The hotel was equipped with black-out curtains while outside air-raid shelters were built in front of the nearby LMS Hotel. The men students were soldiers during their spare time. As such, they formed a section of the Home Guard and went on military manoeuvres with the units of the regular army stationed near the town. As one former student-soldier recalls:

> During air-raid alerts we mustered on the roof (of the hotel) and prepared
> to fight fires or do rescue-work. As the main Allied shipping route to Great
> Britain passed just north of Portrush, long-range bombers would often pass
> overhead on their way to attack ships coming in under convoy and the low
> wail of the air raid warning frequently called us to duty during the night.

Yet, in spite of the fact that the men students in the Portrush 'college' were liable to be called out at any time to thwart an enemy invasion, the College rule that no student was allowed out after six o'clock, except at weekends, was strictly enforced. This 'curfew' was highly unpopular though it was an attempt by the 'powers that be' to safeguard the largely female student body from the unwanted attentions of the British and American troops based in the area. Since local time was half an hour later than Greenwich Mean Time and double summer time applied during most of the year, the rule meant that doors closed at 3.30 pm each afternoon!

'Breaking curfew' was a favourite pastime of the men students in the warm summer evenings of those wartime years. T H Ellis relates one daring escapade which almost ended in disaster:

> The unofficial way out was over a flat roof and along the edge of a steep

First Year students on the flat roof of Fawcett's Hotel, May 1941. 'Breaking curfew' by exiting unofficially across the roof was the favourite pastime of the men students at Portrush.

MISS M SHILLIDAY

cliff upon which the hotel was built. The cliff overlooked the harbour and at its foot there was a row of houses. I remember once looking over the edge and seeing down the chimneys of the houses below. One night after drilling in the main hall some of us went out to buy chips and lemonade. As these men were coming back over the flat roof, a woman lecturer looked out from an upper window and saw the uniformed figures. At that time our American allies had a tremendous reputation for womanising and the lady immediately had hysterics. She screamed out that the American army was coming over the roof to carry off the girls. She was quietened only when a few of us in the friendly, reassuring British uniform took up positions in the corridors. It was fortunate she made so much noise for had she merely raised an alarm, the men involved would have been caught and the secret of the hidden way revealed. As it was they gained the safety of the corridor and everyone, not knowing the true explanation, imagined she had had some sort of hallucination on awakening from a dream.[28]

Not all the women students beheld the proximity of 'the Yanks' with fear and trembling, however. The young Gwen Craig, who attended the College from 1943 to 1945, recalls the delight of her fellow students when American soldiers were billeted opposite Fawcett's: 'Forbidden messages passed between students and GIs from the room when we practised writing on blackboards!'

For Gwen (now Mrs G H Thompson of Benoni, South Africa), D-Day, 6 June 1944 'brought wonderful joy and relief. It was clear that the war would soon be over. We were sent home early so that the move to Belfast could be organised'.[29]

This ended a unique phase in the history of Stranmillis, emblazoned on the student memory as a collage of walks along the rocky headlands, daily cycle runs to rural schools, wartime rations and surreptitious signals to Allied troops or the Campbell College seniors, lodged in a nearby hostelry!

WORLD WAR TWO ROLL OF HONOUR

Stranmillis College, in common with Queen's University and other educational institutions, was well represented in the ranks of Northern Ireland servicemen during the Second World War. Since conscription did not apply here, those who joined up were volunteers. Seventeen former students of the College made the supreme sacrifice during 1939-45. They were :

Alfred Francis Beckett	1907–43
Maurice Watt Bell	1915–44
Henry James Christie	1915–44
George Arnold Exley	1918–45
Francis Wilson Galbraith	1915–42
John Malcolmson Gibson	1912–42
James Quinn Jamison	1917–45
Norman Harry Keel	1920–43
Adam Linton	1911–44
Hugh Larmour Magee	1911–42
William McCarroll	1918–42
Robert Getgood McCrory	1918–42
Albert McKee	1911–45
Charles Alexander McNabb	1913–42
Frederic James Perry	1911–44
John Molseed Scott	1908–45
Alan John Tait	1915–43

A Belfastman, A F Beckett attended the College during 1927–29 before entering the teaching profession in Belfast Model School. A member of the Royal Air Force Volunteer Reserve before the war, he joined the RAF as a fighter-pilot with 255 Squadron. He was killed on active service at Grottaglie, Italy, on 16 December 1943. He was just 36. He is buried in Bari

War Cemetery.

G A Exley had a similar profile, joining the RAF (27 Squadron) in 1939 after completing the post-graduate course at Stranmillis. A pilot officer, he died on active service on 28 June 1945 at the age of 26.

Two contemporaries of Exley's joined the RAF with him direct from College. William McCarroll, a Flight Lieutenant from Belfast met his fate on 21 November 1943 at Cromarty Firth in Scotland. He was just 24. Norman Keel left the College in 1940 to become a flying officer with the RAF. Tragically, he was killed in a training accident in Saskatchewan, Canada, on 7 May 1943, aged 23.

James Jamison, a Queen's graduate who attended the College in the 1937–38 academic year, and a pilot officer at RAF Rednal, was killed on 30 May 1945, aged 27. He is buried in St Andrew's Churchyard, Rasharkin, County Antrim.

Robert McCrory, a native of Portadown, left Stranmillis in 1938, becoming Principal of St John's School, Hillsborough, County Down. He joined the RAF, 115 Squadron, as a sergeant. He was killed on 29 July 1942 at Gemdine, Germany, aged 23, and was interred in Kiel War Cemetery, north of Hamburg.

Several other RAF casualties can be traced to Stranmillis College in the early 1930s. Adam Linton, a native of Belfast, died in combat at Wintzenbach near Strasbourg, on 20 October 1944. He was a pilot officer with 35 Squadron. He is buried in Wintzenbach.

Hugh Magee from Lisburn, a graduate of Queen's University and Trinity College, Dublin, as well as a Stranmillis alumnus, was teaching at Dunmurry Primary School when he enlisted as a Flight Lieutenant at RAF Feltwell. He was killed in action on 16 March 1942, aged 30. The exact details of his death are unclear. His remains lie in Victoria Cemetery, Carrickfergus.

Albert McKee, who attended the College in 1930–31 and taught at the Mariner's Church School, was an aircraftman with 130 AMES, RAF. He died on Christmas Eve, 1945, possibly as a result of wounds. A native of Castlerock, he is buried in Medjez-el-Bab War Cemetery, Tunisia.

A contemporary of McKee's at Stranmillis, Frederick Perry, a native of Londonderry, taught at the local Irish Street School prior to being gazetted a Flight Lieutenant in 28 Squadron, RAF. He was killed by enemy action at Tiddan, Tanzang, Burma on 27 March 1944, aged 33, and is buried in Singapore.

Another RAF fatality was Charles McNabb, a teacher in Elmgrove Primary School, Belfast, who attended Stranmillis during 1933–34. A sergeant in 24 CAOS, he died at Kabanga in Southern Rhodesia on 26 June 1942, aged 29. He is interred in Gwero Cemetery, Zimbabwe.

Two young men from the class of 1934-35 also gave their lives in the struggle against Nazism. Alan Tait from Derry was Principal of Ballygawley Primary School, County Tyrone, when he enlisted in the RAF as a Sergeant Navigator, 103 Squadron. He was killed on 3 October 1943 and is interred in Woodchapel Church of Ireland Cemetery, Londonderry. He left a young widow, Joy. His contemporary, Belfast-born Francis Galbraith taught at Edenderry Primary School, Belfast, before joining the RAF as a Sergeant Pilot, based at HMT Johann VO Barneveldt, South Africa. Sadly, this young man contracted malaria aboard ship on his way home after pilot training. He died off the coast of west Africa on 4 July 1942, aged 27, and was buried at sea. He is commemorated on the Alamein Memorial in El Alamein War Cemetery, Egypt.

Amongst those former alumni who joined the regular army were two close friends who attended the College in the early thirties. Henry Christie and Maurice Bell joined the Second Battalion, Royal Inniskilling Fusiliers together at the outbreak of the war. Maurice was a teacher in Euston Street School, Belfast, while Henry taught at Strandtown in the east of the city. Both were gazetted. Maurice Bell was a lieutenant and Henry Christie a captain. They were engaged in the heavy fighting at Minturno in southern Italy in January 1944 when they were killed. Captain Christie was awarded the Military Cross and DSO for valour in Italy shortly before his death. The two 'Stran' friends lie in Italian soil, Harry Christie in Minturno War Cemetery and Maurice Bell in Naples War Cemetery.

A contemporary of these brave men at College was Lieutenant John M Gibson of the Royal Artillery, a native of Newtownards who held a teaching post at Ballystockart, near Comber, County Down. He made the supreme sacrifice at Tobruk, Libya, during the desert campaign on 20 June 1942 and is buried in Knightsbridge War Cemetery near Tobruk. He was 30 years of age.

The final name on the Stranmillis roll of honour is that of John Molseed

Captain Henry J Christie (1915–44), killed in action in 1944. A student at Stranmillis between 1932 and 1934, Harry Christie taught at Strandtown Primary School before enlisting in the Royal Inniskilling Fusiliers. He was the most highly decorated of the 17 men from the College who lost their lives in the Second World War. He was awarded the DSO for gallant leadership at the Simeto River, Sicily, in August 1943 and the Military Cross for outstanding courage at the Garigliano River near Cassino, Italy in December 1943.

COLLEGE LIBRARY

Memorial tablet in
Stranmillis College.

DR R CROMIE

Scott, a native of Londonderry who attended the College during 1928–29. He secured his first post at First Derry School but moved before the war to become Principal of Darkley School, a small mill school near Keady, County Armagh. As an enthusiastic oarsman and leading member of the City of Derry Boating Club, it was hardly surprising that young Scott should be commissioned as a lieutenant in the Royal Navy on the outbreak of hostilities. During the war he was stationed at Alexandria on board a small vessel performing inshore and harbour defence duties. On 24 February 1945 Lieutenant Scott was part of the crew of HM Trawler *Ellesmere*, a Royal Navy escort vessel, performing convoy duties in the English Channel, when it was torpedoed by a German U-boat. The *Ellesmere* was lost with all hands. Scott, who was 37 years old, was engaged to be married at the time of his death. His sacrifice is commemorated on the Lowestoft Naval Memorial, Suffolk.[30]

The names of the Stranmillis war dead are inscribed on a memorial tablet in the Central Building of the College.

Another Stranmillis student from the thirties who served with distinction in the Second World War is Colonel James Hughes who went on to become Deputy Principal of the College in 1970. Born in 1917 and brought up in Greyabbey, County Down, Jimmy Hughes was commissioned in April 1940 in the Royal Artillery. Following defence duties in the south of England, the then Captain Hughes became adjutant of the 4th (Ulster) Light Anti-Aircraft Regiment and was detailed to support the Canadian landings on Juno Beach after D-Day, June 1944. From Normandy, Captain Hughes and his men helped to liberate Brussels before crossing the famous bridge at Arnhem. He was among the first British soldiers to witness the genocide perpetrated by the Nazis in the concentration camp at Belsen.

Colonel Hughes joined the teaching staff at his *alma mater* in 1948 and was attached to the general staff of the Territorial Army in Northern Ireland until 1965. Since then he has served as National Chairman of the Royal British Legion and has made a distinguished contribution to the community through a host of voluntary organisations including the Boys' Brigade, the St John Ambulance and the Ulster Cancer Foundation. He has been honoured by five nations and holds the CBE and the unique distinction of the Order of St John.

Reflecting on the Stranmillis contribution to the war effort more than half a century later, a wistful Colonel Hughes has an abiding sense of pride: 'These young men gave their lives – often in their twenties – to keep the world out of Hitler's grasp. I hope young people appreciate that fact today.'

Colonel James Hughes, CBE, KSt J, TD, DL, Deputy Principal of Stranmillis College 1970–82, pictured in the uniform of St John Ambulance (Northern Ireland), of which he was Commander. Colonel Hughes served with distinction in World War Two.

SOME COLOURFUL 'PROFESSORS'

The lecturing staff of the College in the thirties and forties was a blend of the scholarly and the colourful. Together they equipped their students with a sound intellectual training and a formidable knowledge of the theory and practice of teaching.

The Principal, H E ('Herbie') Winn, is fondly remembered as a gentleman and a scholar. A Yorkshireman, he had seen army service in Mesopotamia and India and was deemed 'considerate, fair, polite and painstaking' by his students. A 'bookish man' and an Oxford graduate, he specialised in history and poetry and was especially interested in the development of the British Empire. If he had a fault, it was his penchant for dilating on the military history of the Great War, to the chagrin of the girls in his classes. Winn died in 1985, aged 93.

The Principal, Professor McCallister with the lecturing staff at the opening of the Main Building, May 1930. The staff include: front row – Professor DWT Jenkins, (first left); second row– Professor WH Lloyd (third left), Captain TM Wright, Physical Training instructor (third right) and Allan Murray (second right).

COLLEGE LIBRARY

A most able, if eccentric, professor was William H Lloyd who taught mathematics at Stranmillis from 1922 until his retirement in 1945. A native of County Longford, Lloyd took first-class honours in mathematics at Trinity College, Dublin, in 1907 and was appointed head of department at Methodist College, Belfast. He was a noted mathematician with an original turn of mind, but had little patience for those less smitten with 'the great science'. Lloyd (nicknamed 'Piggy') was regarded by students as the archetypal absent-minded professor, complete with gown and permanently attached mortar-board. Often he would enter the common room, revealing by his vacant expression that he was not certain where to go. Such was his absent-mindedness that an unlikely story gained wide currency among the student population. T H Ellis writes:

> The story is told that he was walking along the pier at Bangor and absent-mindedly walked over the edge. He was fished out of the water by a young lady who was bathing nearby. She took pity on him, married him and lived happily ever afterwards, reminding him of his appointments and engagements. At least that is the story and the only reason for doubting it is that it is far too probable.[31]

Professor Lloyd was a fine bridge-player and represented Ireland at international competitions. On his retirement in 1945, his former students revelled in recalling his 'Lloydericks' at his presentation function in the Stranmillis Old Boys' Room in Great Victoria Street. An eye-witness records:

> When his turn came to speak, (Professor Lloyd) remained true to the tradition grown up around him. He lumbered to his feet … scratched his head and announced that he didn't know what to say. His voice became rich with a brogue that had always grown broader in moments of agitation … and … assured us that he would remember what he should say – when he got home.[32]

Professor Lloyd died in 1951. Few lecturers have enjoyed such deep affection, 'almost reverence', among their students.

Lloyd's contemporaries included Professor D W T Jenkins, a Welshman and an inspiring history lecturer and William (Billy) Ellison, who was responsible for Teaching Methods. Jenkins ended his career as Director of Education for Caernarvon. Ellison, who had the irritating habit of swinging his glasses as he spoke, regularly insisted that the good teacher never distracted his class! 'No mannerisms', he snapped, looking up from his notes and starting to swing his glasses. Yet, 'Billy' was renowned for turning out good teachers. He was particularly critical of any waste of class time. 'Wasting only a minute of the time of a class of thirty is the waste of half an hour', he used to say. A teacher must be incisive and give positive leadership to the class. Ellison was also a believer in traditional values in fashion. 'Ah! Miss, Miss! get an apron', was his injunction to a young lady whose rather short dress revealed a shapely leg as she stretched to write on the blackboard!

Professor William H Lloyd. An able, if eccentric figure, he taught mathematics at Stranmillis from 1922 until his retirement in 1945.

MR B LLOYD

During the Portrush sojourn, the College Warden was Allan Murray, a young Scots geographer and the author of several standard textbooks. Known as 'The Baron' from his seigneurial style as Warden of the men's hostel in the thirties, he left the staff to join the RAF during World War Two. Other lecturers during this period were Alan McKinnon, an acknowledged expert on Shakespeare, and 'Daddy' Davison, the music professor. Miss E K Abraham specialised in elocution while Miss A M Heaney taught handiwork and Infant Education.

The lady lecturers were very earnest. One, as T H Ellis recalls, 'dictated vast reams of notes in point form. She insisted in the exact replication of these points in every written answer to the consternation of her students'.

The Portrush episode ended in 1944 when the management committee was able to reclaim the Stranmillis campus. While the Main Building of the College and Stranmillis House – a naval convalescent home during the war – required major refurbishment, staff and students were able to avail of a new building in the College grounds in time for the 1944–45 session.[33]

The structure, later known as the Henry Garrett Building in honour of a former chairman of the College committee, was a typical example of wartime economy building. However, though far from ideal, it enabled a new beginning to be made. The Principal must have welcomed the return of his official residence which had served the Royal Army Medical Corps as an Officers' Mess during the military occupation.[34]

VE DAY AT STRANMILLIS

For the College students, many of them reoccupying the old 'Bungalow Hostels' in Stranmillis grounds, VE Day, 8 May 1945 was a deeply emotional experience. The official ending of the conflict in Europe, following the German capitulation, was greeted in Belfast by the pealing of church bells and a carnival-like atmosphere in the city centre. Gwen Craig, then a final year student, recalls the mood of excitement on the campus on that 'perfect summer's day':

> During our years in Stran, we were not allowed out late in the evenings …
> VE Day was different. We all set off on the tram to the city centre, joined
> in the wonderful excitement and celebrations and came home late. For
> weeks we had been practising a song, 'Let us all praise famous men', to sing
> at the end of the war and we could scarcely believe that the time had now
> come to sing it![35]

Management
and Change
1932–98 4

W ith the settlement of the 'Stranmillis affair' the management
committee could commence its work. Parliamentary Secretaries
to the Minister of Education chaired the committee from 1932
until 1944: J H Robb KC, MP during 1932–37 and Dame Dehra Parker during 1937-44. They were followed by two retired officials of the Ministry of
Education, Dr Henry Garrett 1944–51, and W H Smyth 1951–59. Colonel
M C Perceval-Price, the first chairman to be drawn from outside the educational community, or the Ministry of Education, took the chair in 1959.
Since then, the position has been held by Dr Stanley Worrall, a former
headmaster of Methodist College, Belfast, Dr R J Dickson, historian and
administrator, Mr Dermot Nesbitt, academic and more recently a prominent
politician, and Professor Don McCloy, former director of the Belfast
Institute of Further and Higher Education and previously on the staff of both
Queen's University and the University of Ulster. The remainder of the committee included two officials of the Ministry, one a Chief or Senior Chief
Inspector, one official of a Regional Education Committee, one primary
school principal, and three representatives of the three main Protestant
denominations.

The 'educational revolution' which followed the Second World War had profound implications for Northern Ireland society and for Stranmillis College in particular. An immediate problem in 1945 was the acute short-age of teachers owing to the virtual suspension of the training of men during the war. The government's response was two-fold. In September 1945 the Ministry of Education launched the emergency teacher training scheme for elementary school teachers. To meet the demands of the schools and church interests, it provided a special programme at Larkfield Emergency Training College, Dunmurry, for training ex-service personnel who held promise but lacked conventional qualifications. Some 405 former service-men and women were trained in this way between 1946 and 1949. The second response was to remove the restrictions on student numbers at Stranmillis.[36]

This situation was exacerbated by the passage of the Northern Ireland Education Act of 1947 which paved the way for major educational reform in line with the 1944 Butler Act in Great Britain. The 1947 Act provided for free post-primary education for all children and a new system of primary,

The College Staff 1954–55. Included are the Principal, Mr HE Winn (middle, front row), Deputy Principal, Major KGP Pomeroy, Miss C Macmahon, Mr W McClure, Head of Education, Col J Hughes and Mr JD Cameron.

MRS MAUREEN STEELE

secondary and further education, while generous university grants put real equality of opportunity within the grasp of every child, regardless of social background.

The introduction of new secondary and grammar schools ensured Stranmillis's place at the cutting-edge of the educational revolution. In response to the insatiable demand for more teachers, the College accepted 180 new students in 1948; in 1952, 300 came and a further 354 in 1953. The upshot was massive pressure on the College staff and buildings. Of these dramatic post-war years at the College, one historian has written:

> Outside the college precincts more and more students were in search of lodgings ... Inside, it was becoming a nightmare task for the timetable planners to find rooms for all the necessary classes. The college working-day could not be shortened and lunch hours had to be staggered. Even in the planning of teaching practice the alleviation of pressure on college accommodation had to be considered. All the new buildings (on the campus) had come at the last possible moment, if not too late.[37]

These post-war changes coincided with the final years of Herbert Winn's principalship. In 1956, he was succeeded by the Scots-born Alec Keith, a former lecturer at Jordanhill Training College, Glasgow. As Principal until 1970, Keith was responsible for the major building development of the late 1960s. In this he was assisted from 1949 by Stranmillis's first Vice-Principal, Major K G P Pomeroy, an Englishman who had seen service with the Royal Irish Horse during the war and later directed the short-lived Larkfield College.

In 1948, as a result of the Report of the Committee on the Recruitment and Training of Teachers (the Gibbon Report), the College management committee was reorganised. The number of members remained the same but there was a move away from Ministry of Education nominations towards the appointment of representatives from organisations with an interest in education, such as the Association of Education Committees and teachers' unions. The churches' representation was unchanged, although on a few occasions, laymen replaced clergy as members. As we have seen, the College, at its foundation, was closely linked with the university – the Professor of Education was its first Principal and the university was represented on the Committee for the Training of Teachers. However, this link had been severed by the resignation of Professor McCallister from his College position and by the creation of the new management committee on which the university had no representation. The question of a university representative replacing a Ministry nominee on the committee was raised unsuccessfully in 1951 and 1954, the chief obstacle being the Ministry's unwillingness to see its traditional representation reduced. One solution would have been the appointment of an additional committee member, but this was rejected by the churches who insisted on retaining their one-third of the membership.

Nevertheless, the matter was not forgotten and was tabled for discussion in 1960, again to no avail. On that occasion, the Ministry's representative argued that the committee dealt with administrative rather than academic matters and consequently, the work would be of little interest to the university. The issue was resolved finally in 1963, when the reorganisation of the committee was being considered. After discussions, the Ministry accepted a change in the status of its nominee from that of 'committee member' to that of 'assessor'. In future, he or she would not be one voting member among nine, but rather a representative of the College's ultimate controlling body.[38]

With the publication in 1965 of the Lockwood Commission's Report, which stressed that students in teacher training institutions should be afforded the opportunity to gain a university qualification, good relations with the university sector were vital. The Commission recommended that the university should be represented on the governing body of colleges, and that college Principals and some staff should be accorded full membership of the university. The Ministry of Education would continue to regulate admissions to Stranmillis and to provide funding, but the university was to control matters relating to the appointment and promotion of staff, the planning of courses, syllabus content and the setting and marking of examinations. In the wake of Lockwood's recommendations, a working party was set up to evolve new constitutions for the colleges of education, as they were now designated.

The result was the creation of a new a Board of Governors of sixteen members in 1967. Members, including three from the university, were nominated by representative bodies, but appointed by the Ministry, which retained its assessor. The present Board of Governors consists of 17 members, including the College Principal and two members of the College staff, the President of the Students' Representative Council of the Students' Union, representatives of the Education and Library Boards, the Queen's University of Belfast, the three main Protestant churches and the Department of Education's assessor.

In 1982, Stranmillis found itself at the forefront of the controversial proposals of the Higher Education Review Group (the Chilver Report). This report had advocated a sweeping reorganisation of teacher-training in Northern Ireland with the three colleges of education – Stranmillis, St Mary's and St Joseph's, together with the Queen's University Faculty of Education, amalgamating on a single site in a new Belfast Centre for Teacher Education. The report argued that such a 'consolidation' of teacher education provision was necessary in view of the reduction of intakes to teacher training in Northern Ireland. Chilver accepted the right of the individual colleges to retain their separate legal and administrative existence but was adamant on the advantages of a single site for the new venture. Such an arrangement, it stated, would 'encourage academic and practical co-ordination and the academic and social mixing of students while retaining safeguards for the distinctive educational ethos of each of the colleges of education'.[39]

Already, in its submission to the Review Group on 26 March 1979, the Board of Governors and Academic Board of Stranmillis College had favoured 'more formal inter-collegiate arrangements for reducing the degree of separation', adding that they would welcome an integrated approach to the training of teachers. 'Stran' had always enjoyed excellent relations with the voluntary colleges both at senior management level and on the joint subject boards, established in the 1960s to co-ordinate academic courses. However, the Stranmillis authorities made it clear to Chilver that any fundamental changes 'could only be arrived at by mutual consent... and there is no desire to try to force an unacceptable pattern on any institution'.

The Chilver recommendations evoked mixed feelings in the community with the two Catholic colleges anxious to maintain their distinctive denominational ethos. In a further response to Chilver in May 1980, Stranmillis accepted in principle the proposed creation of a single Teacher Education Centre but acknowledged the deeply-held views of the trustees of its sister institutions in west Belfast. As a possible compromise solution, the Stranmillis Board suggested that consideration might be given to a federation of the colleges on a split site.

In the end, however, the government abandoned the idea of a centralised institution. With the voluntary merger of the Roman Catholic colleges and the amalgamation of the New University of Ulster and the Ulster Polytechnic, the number of teacher-training institutions was reduced from six to four. The importance of Stranmillis was, therefore, enhanced.

An early EMU visit to the Ulster-American Folk Park, Omagh, 1990. Members of staff accompanying the group are Dr Richard McMinn (Stranmillis) and Dr B Feeney and Mr M Millerick (St Mary's).

Announcing the government's decision in December 1982, the Education Minister, Nicholas Scott, welcomed the decision of Stranmillis board of governors, in common with the trustees of St Mary's, to work for a much greater degree of co-operation in the future. He added: 'I think that is a big step in the right direction ... This co-operation is warmly welcomed by the government and its practical implementation will be watched with interest and given every encouragement'.[40]

1982 was a year of great uncertainty at Stranmillis, but there was widespread satisfaction that the College had emerged with its unique tradition intact and its academic and social links with its sister college strengthened. These events coincided with the principalship of James Pomfret who presided over 'Stran's' fortunes from 1970 to 1984. His successor was Dr R J Rodgers who was succeeded on his retirement in 1993 by his fellow-historian, Dr Richard McMinn.

In 1982 also, the Department of Education issued a circular which stressed that education for mutual understanding (EMU) was a duty and a responsibility of everyone engaged in education. And in 1987, the Department invited educational institutions to participate in a Cross Community Contact Scheme.[41] Stranmillis College, building on the foundations of friendship established over many years, was quick to join with St Mary's in the promotion of the two cross-curricular themes unique to Northern Ireland - EMU and Cultural Heritage. A series of attractive publications by members of the College staff and published by Stranmillis encouraged collaborative work by schools in the maintained and controlled sectors. In September 1986, the College appointed an EMU co-ordinator, Miss Shirley Magowan, to foster formal and meaningful links between student teachers at Stranmillis and St Mary's, and in November 1988 the Stranmillis College EMU group met for the first time. The following April, the Colleges' Joint Liaison Group commenced its work.

These efforts to build bridges between the two traditions earned the praise of the new Education Minister, Dr Brian Mawhinney, who stressed the role of the colleges of education in 'transforming community relations in schools'. In a speech at Stranmillis College on 26 November 1987, Dr Mawhinney told students: 'Nothing is more important in our schools than helping to promote community understanding and tolerance, and I am appealing to you to create a better Northern Ireland in the years ahead. For many reasons, former generations have not, manifestly, made a good job of building relationships across the sectarian divide, but I believe your generation can turn the tide of hatred, violence and destruction'.[42]

Stranmillis staff pictured in May 1998.

The Minister's visit was followed by the provision of special funding for the College's EMU programme. This has enabled student teachers from Stranmillis and St Mary's to meet informally and to engage in a whole range of cultural and educational activities. In addition to reciprocal visits between the colleges at all levels, students have participated in joint activities outside the province. These have included visits to the London Borough

of Newham to study multicultural education in Britain, cross-cultural exchange visits to Denmark and the 'Wider Horizons Project', based in the United States. This was first organised in the summer of 1989 when a partnership was established with Boston College, Middlesex Community College and the Lowell Public School System. Students from various colleges of education in Ireland, North and South, spend two months in

Massachusetts, working with young people from disadvantaged areas. In these ways, the College is playing a vital role in fostering inter-schools and cross-community contacts with a view to removing the barriers in Northern Ireland society.

During the 1980s and 1990s also, Stranmillis College has been at the forefront of research into the impact of the 'Troubles' on the lives of children and the need to address pupil under-achievement in schools. Another aim of the College has been to forge links between student teachers and the world of industry and business. 'Insight' courses have been provided, addressing such key areas as design and technology, economic awareness, inward investment and the implications of the Single European Market. The value of this programme has been acknowledged by government and the local business community.

Stranmillis marked its 75th anniversary by embarking on a new and closer relationship with Queen's University. In 1996, the then Vice-Chancellor, Sir Gordon Beveridge, entered negotiations with the Principal of the College, Dr Richard McMinn and the Principal of St Mary's College, Rev Martin O'Callaghan, to discuss possible changes in the academic and constitutional relationship between the colleges and the university. The desire on the part of both Principals for a radical review stemmed from the need to recognise the academic maturity and standing of Stranmillis and St Mary's and the changing relationship between colleges of education and their validating universities elsewhere.

In 1997, the Working Party, consisting of representatives of Queen's and the two colleges, formulated proposals for 'a confident, collaborative partnership'. Under this arrangement, Stranmillis will enjoy an enhanced 'university college' status from September 1998. It will retain its independent control, vested in its own governing body, but the College's academic provision will be fully integrated into the structure of Queen's University. The College has also established its right to extend its programme of academic diversification into courses additional to those providing eligibility to teach.[43]

Thus, Stranmillis can look forward to a new and challenging chapter in its history as it approaches the new millennium, confident in its great tradition and its academic excellence.

College Courses 5
Down the Years

At the beginning of the twentieth century, entrants to training colleges were drawn from two groups – monitors and pupil teachers. Changes in these arrangements took place after Partition when the recruitment of monitors was progressively reduced by the Northern Ireland Ministry of Education and ceased in 1929. Thus, the attempt to centre the preliminary training of teachers wholly in the elementary school was abandoned, and new rules for the appointment of pupil teachers were introduced. The underlying aim was to ensure that future primary school teachers enjoyed the advantages of a full secondary education. Junior pupil-teacherships were now awarded to the more promising pupils of public elementary schools on the results of an examination based on the Sixth Standard programme. These were tenable at any recognised grammar school. The age limits of 13½ to 15 years were lowered to 12 to 14 to fit in with grammar school arrangements, and to assist pupil-teachers with expenses, various allowances were paid.

In 1930, there were 580 applications for the 83 junior pupil-teacherships offered. These pupils were required to sit the Junior Certificate Examination at the end of three years and if they performed sufficiently well, they would

Group of First Year
students (Section 2),
1931–32.

MRS S MAWHINNEY

be awarded senior pupil-teacherships tenable for two years. During this period they would continue to attend grammar school in preparation for the King's Scholarship examination. Nor was practical classroom experience neglected: in each of these years the pupil-teacher was required to spend a month in an approved public elementary school and to undertake some teaching.

This system continued until 1939 when the King's Scholarship examination was abandoned in favour of the present system of a secondary school or FE college course followed by professional teacher training at a recognised institution. Admission to Stranmillis College was based on the results of the Senior Certificate examination of the Ministry of Education, and on satisfactory performance in an interview held at the College. There was also provision for university graduates to follow a one-year course in teacher training. Before the new regulations were enforced in 1939, graduates were admitted without having passed the King's Scholarship examination, provided that the Ministry was satisfied that they were 'in every respect suitable to undergo a course of training'.[44]

The 'ordinary' period of training for non-graduate entrants extended over two years. In 1922, a provisional arrangement was made with Queen's University by which certain students, selected by examination, were eligible for matriculation and, concurrently with their professional training, took

Group of First Year students (Section 3), 1931–32.

MRS S MAWHINNEY

two courses each year in the programme for the BA degree. This arrangement, as far as Stranmillis was concerned, was superseded in 1926-27 by a permanent scheme making it possible for students during their first two years in College, to obtain credit for three of the eight courses necessary for the pass degree in the Faculty of Arts. The remaining five courses could be pursued during the third and fourth years of training by attendance at lectures in the university. It was also possible for eligible students who preferred to obtain the university Diploma in Education without proceeding to a degree, to remain in residence for a third year and to attend the university for the Diploma course.

From the beginning, courses at Stranmillis aimed not only to prepare students to teach the subjects of the primary school curriculum, but also to extend their personal education, and the fact that classes on 'principles of education' were held alongside those on 'methods of education' reflects this balance. Subjects deemed to be particularly important were studied by all students throughout the two-year course. These were the principles and methods of education, English with speech training and reading, mathematics including arithmetic (women students were permitted to take arithmetic only), music, geography, physical education and, for women, domestic economy. A shorter time was spent on other subjects deemed less vital in professional importance.

During the first year, men studied British history, physics and chemistry (largely taught at a theoretical level), while women were able to add needle-work to their curriculum. In the second year, drawing became optional, and nature study and hygiene were introduced. Religious instruction was taught, not by members of the College staff, but by clergymen from the three main Protestant denominations, appointed by their respective churches and not by the College or the Ministry of Education.

Few changes occurred in the curriculum before 1929–30 when the Stranmillis building became available. At this time, students still spent 28 hours in class in Year 1 and 26 or 27 hours in Year 2 – there were even class-es held on Saturday mornings.

The completion of the new building on the campus offered considerable advantages to students and staff. For the first time since the foundation of the College, classes could be held under one roof, and practical subjects ben-efited particularly from the provision of rooms specially equipped and suited to their needs.

Whilst both personal and professional education gained in College were considered important for prospective teachers, it was in the classroom that most believed the art of teaching was to be learned. In 1922, 17 schools were used for teaching practice and after a short time this number was increased to 34. Among the first group were two schools under Roman Catholic management since in the early days it was hoped the College would attract students from all denominations. For teaching practice, students were divided into groups of five - all men or all women. During their first year, they visited schools on different days each week for 21 or 22 weeks. As the number of College lecturers was initially too small for effective supervision, school principals and teachers provided written reports on students' progress 'at the chalk face'. However, as additional staff were appointed to College departments, supervision by lecturers increased. Second year students were assigned to a two-teacher 'country' school within easy reach of Belfast. There, they hoped to gain experience in the organisation and management of the small rural school. In addition to this type of school experience, Stranmillis lecturers gave demonstration lessons at the adjacent Stranmillis Primary School.

The wartime evacuation of the College community to Portrush had implications for the curriculum, both in terms of accommodation and staffing. Science and woodwork were abandoned for a time, and when reintroduced were taught in school classrooms lent to the College. Other subjects suffered from a similar lack of facilities and students were unable to enjoy a full programme of activities. Also, a reduction in College staff resulted in the teaching of several subjects by non-specialists.

On the return to Belfast in 1944, there was no attempt to reinstate the pre-war curriculum or to introduce a new one, at least until the Gibbon Committee, established to review teacher training, had reported. When the Report was published in 1947, and its recommendations were considered, a radical reorganisation of College courses was introduced in time for the intake of students in 1948. In a portentous development the normal College course was extended from two to three years (such was not introduced in England until 1960), and four-year courses were now offered to enable students to specialise in selected subjects for teaching in the new secondary intermediate schools. A four-year course, by which selected students might qualify for a pass degree at Queen's University as well as for the Ministry's certificate, and a one-year post-graduate course were also in operation.

In the wake of the 1947 Education Act, with its introduction of training scholarships, the number of students and staff increased. For the first time, the College gained a full-time librarian, and full-time lecturers or senior lecturers were appointed in men's physical education, health education, science and woodwork.

Under the new three-year course structure, subjects could be studied in more depth and greater time could be allocated to teaching practice. From the academic year 1948-49, all first year students were required to take the following subjects: English language (including speech training), basic science, basic mathematics, religious education, physical education, and education (including observation and practice of teaching). They could choose either art or music, but the division between handicraft for men and needlework for women still existed.

Social studies, which now featured in the curriculum for the first time, involved students working in small groups with a member of the education, geography or history departments on selected projects. Another new subject was 'General Activities' involving debates and play-readings. In all this the emphasis was on group work and inter-personal skills as a preparation for a later teaching career.

In years 2 and 3, all students followed a 'common' course comprising five

A group of final year students,
June 1949.

MRS S E McDONOUGH

subjects – education, English language (including speech training), religious education, physical education and an 'opted' subject. Those who had chosen the course for primary teachers (the 'A' course), mostly women, studied additional subjects – art, music and environmental studies (geography, history, nature study). Domestic science was taken by women, whilst men chose one of general science, rural science or woodwork. Students wishing to teach in the secondary sector ('B' course students) might specialise in secondary school subjects. A special 'infant-nursery' programme (the 'C' course) was offered to women wishing to teach the under 5s.

In the late 1940s and 1950s there was a growing emphasis on 'hands on' experience. Year 2 included six weeks' teaching practice, and in year 3 the complete second term was spent in schools.

Some modifications to these courses were introduced during the ensuing decade, one of the most important being that, from 1959, entrants to College were asked to decide whether they wished to train for the primary or secondary school.

Although there had been some provision in the immediate post-war years for a small number of students to continue their studies for a third year,

A happy group of 'Stran' girls from 1954. Included are Maureen Logan (now Mrs Thompson Steele), Thelma Leckey, Sadie Hall, Hilda Jennings, Margaret Lyttle, Maureen Twinem, Beth Watt, Evelyn Dunbar, Margaret Kernohan, R McBride, Edna McDowell, Winifred Twyble and Iris McBride.

MRS M STEELE

Fourth Year General Science Group 1957–58.

BACK ROW (L–R): Willie Dorman, Ian Magowan, Willie Rafferty, Albert Nixon;

MIDDLE ROW (L–R): Thompie Steele, Gerry Wright, Roy Leinster, Jim Hewitt, George McBride, Tom McAuley.

SITTING (L–R): Lucy McNair, May Phillips, Betty Black and Marshall Markey.

MR T STEELE

specialising in art, science and domestic science at the Belfast College of Technology and in physical education at a college in England, such courses terminated in 1951–52. From that time, on the recommendation of the Gibbon Committee several years earlier, the staffing needs of the new secondary intermediate schools were met, in part, by the introduction of four-year certificate courses in 1951.

By the mid-fifties there were fourth-year courses in English with drama and speech training, general subjects, 'with special reference to the teaching of backward children', art, music and science.

Provision was made for students to take fourth-year courses outside the College: commercial subjects and domestic science were both studied at the Belfast College of Technology, and those wishing to specialise in physical education could undertake courses in England – the men at Loughborough and the women at a college in Liverpool.

From 1956, a physical education course for men was offered at Stranmillis, and a similar one for women began the following year. During the 1956–57 session, women were sent to the newly-opened Ulster College of Physical Education at Jordanstown. When the Stranmillis courses got under way, they were attended for a time by students from St Mary's and St Joseph's Training Colleges, until the latter were in a position to organise their own PE courses.

In order to meet the needs of schools, two new fourth-year courses commenced in 1961. These were in mathematics and religious education. For religious education as a subject, 1961 was an important milestone as a new undenominational course replaced the three separate denominational courses which had operated since the College's foundation. A new religious education department was created and College staff took responsibility for a subject which had long been the domain of visiting lecturers, appointed by the churches.

Although personal education was an important feature of all of these courses, the professional aspect was not neglected, and students usually spent one day each week in schools, practising their newly-found knowledge and skills in the classroom.

UNIVERSITY COURSES

Courses by which Stranmillis students could study for a degree from Queen's University had existed from the College's foundation. During the war years,

Fourth Year Physical Education students 1958–59 outside Stranmillis House.

BACK ROW (L–R):
KW Webster, HE Gourley, MSA Wright, G Brock, HW Chambers, WJB Murphy, JR Mulligan, D Mulligan D Carroll, B. Burns.

MIDDLE ROW (L–R):
SD Allister, R Ashe, WG Compston, R Smyth, J Bogan (lecturers), Dr J MB Donaldson, TE McCreedy, AW Moore, JBH Hill.

FRONT ROW (L–R):
S McKinney, A Thompson, H Millen, S Campbell, J McKeown, CA Montgomery (now a lecturer in the Education Department).

COLLEGE LIBRARY

however, these were abandoned, with the result that students who had successfully completed their first year of the degree in 1939 were compelled to change to the ordinary course of training. This was due to the fact that the College had released for wartime service those members of staff who were responsible for this work. Students in their third and fourth years were able to continue their degree studies as they had already transferred to the university. Opportunities for students to read for a pass degree of the university were reinstated when the College resumed classes in Belfast in 1944.

By the following year, the three 'professors' who taught degree courses at Stranmillis had relinquished their posts, and their successors in charge of English, mathematics and history had no responsibility for teaching university courses, which were undertaken at the university by its own staff. Under this new system, all students followed a common course in their first year. Those who had matriculation qualifications might opt to study either for a BA or a BSc degree.

A restructuring of the 'combined' course on the recommendations of the Gibbon Committee enabled students to study for a degree in arts or science, as well as the Ministry's Teacher's Certificate. For those accepted by the university, the option of completing an honours degree was provided. For the first three years (four years in the case of those taking an honours degree),

The final conclave! Students sitting an examination in the College Hall in 1970.

COLLEGE LIBRARY

these students attended lectures at the university in their degree subjects while at Stranmillis they undertook courses in religious education, physical education and six weeks practical teaching annually. In the final year of professional training taken at the College, all students studied education (including the practice of teaching), English (with speech training), religious education and physical education. Some students who wished to teach in the expanding grammar school sector chose to complete their professional training at the university itself.

Links with the university were strengthened in the 1960s with the introduction of the four-year Bachelor of Education degree, awarded by Queen's University and taught at Stranmillis by staff who had been granted the university's 'recognised teacher' status. In 1967, Queen's established a Faculty of Education to co-ordinate and supervise the BEd degree and an Institute of Education to oversee the courses for the Certificate in Education (Cert Ed) which replaced the Ministry's Teacher's Certificate.

From 1967, undergraduate entrants to the College could follow either the three-year course leading to the Certificate, or the four-year BEd degree course. The study of education, which included a period of school experience, formed a significant part of each course. While all students also chose a main subject such as English or history, those hoping to teach in the

A Commerce class at Stranmillis in the early 1970s.

primary sector attended classes on the teaching of the subjects of the primary school curriculum, and for some years were also required to select a subsidiary subject. Students bound for secondary schools studied education, a main and subsidiary subject, as well as English, religious education and health education.

As the years progressed, courses in all subjects taught in the College were validated by the university for inclusion in the BEd programme. Moves towards making 'teaching' eventually an all degree profession came a step nearer in 1977 when an honours BEd degree was introduced and the certificate course discontinued. From 1977–78, students followed a two-year common course, and, on the results of examinations, elected to complete the BEd general degree, or the honours BEd which required two further years. From 1988, all students were able to pursue courses leading to the BEd honours degree. Unfortunately, due to rationalisation in the 1980s, courses at the College for prospective secondary school teachers have been restricted by government to three areas – business studies, religious studies and technology and design.

The year 1991 marked the end of the College's long tradition of promoting the French language, pioneered by Gordon Skingle and Miss Eleanor Houston. Ironically, at a time of increasing European integration,

Stranmillis was compelled by a change in government policy to withdraw French as a subject for the BEd degree. Under the new Northern Ireland curriculum, which became law in 1990, the teaching of modern languages was not compulsory in primary schools. The decision came as a shattering blow to the College's active French department which had already interviewed candidates for the forthcoming academic year.

At present, all BEd students follow a four-year modular course, which includes the study of education, school-based work and a main subject. Those intending to teach in primary schools (the vast majority) also take curriculum studies as an intrinsic part of the degree. Students who have opted to teach in the post-primary sector, are required to study a subsidiary subject during the first two years of their course. In addition, all students are equipped with the necessary skills in information technology to enable them to meet the demands of the accelerating technological revolution.

One-year professional training courses for graduates have been a feature

'Teachers for the new century': a group of BEd graduates at Queen's University, July 1997, with the authors, Dr George Beale and Dr Eamon Phoenix.

throughout the history of the College. Similarly, in-service work, including summer schools, has formed an important part of the Stranmillis programme. In recent years, the College has been involved in the teaching of award-bearing courses leading to the Advanced Certificate in Education, the Diploma in the Advanced Studies in Education, and the Master of Education degree of the Queen's University, the Certificate of Professional Development of the Open University, the Stranmillis Certificate in Professional Development and the Advanced Certificate in Science. Courses in the teaching of English as a foreign language (TEFL) and teaching English to speakers of other languages (TESOL) have been introduced under the direction of Dr Jim Ferguson. In 1996, as part of its plans for diversification into areas cognate with education, the College initiated the BA degree in Early Childhood Studies of the Queen's University. This is taught by College staff at Stranmillis and, with the help of modern technology, simultaneously at the university's out-centre at Armagh. Highly successful, it is seen as the harbinger of a whole range of undergraduate and post-graduate degrees in such areas as

Above:
'Adieu le français!'
Mrs Laurence Siberry with a group of French students during its heyday at Stranmillis.

Right:
School-based work remains an integral part of the BEd degree programme at Stranmillis.

NICLR

Arts in the Community, Health and Leisure Studies, Heritage Management, Performance Studies, Education Studies and Peace Studies.

Over the years, Stranmillis has been the main provider of in-service courses in Northern Ireland. This began in the wake of the 1947 'education revolution' when the then Ministry of Education utilised summer courses at Stranmillis to provide a reservoir of teachers for the rash of new intermediate schools.

By the early 1960s, Stranmillis College had acquired a high reputation for professionalism throughout the British Isles and the Commonwealth. It was no surprise, therefore, that in 1960, 'Stran' was selected as one of the United Kingdom colleges to provide courses of intensive training for Commonwealth students. Consequently, during the 1960s, students came to

Principal Alec Keith and staff with a group of Ugandan teachers in 1969.

COLLEGE LIBRARY

Erasmus students from Sweden and Finland celebrating the Scandinavian 'Festival of Light' at the time of the winter solstice, December 1996.

MR M BLEASE

Stranmillis from the West Indies, Aden, the Bahamas, Brunei, Cyprus, Gambia, Malaysia, Malta, Mauritius, Saint Helena, Tanzania and Zambia. In the period 1960-68, 36 students from these countries came to Stranmillis to pursue one-year teaching courses in music, physical education and crafts.

Stranmillis was also one of five United Kingdom institutions asked to provide a special two-year course planned to meet the needs of teachers from the emergent new states of Nigeria and Uganda. The course was designed to prepare qualified, experienced Commonwealth teachers to undertake the work of teacher training in their own countries.

Today, Stranmillis is very much attuned to the new position of these islands within the European community and fruitful contacts have been made with its sister colleges on the continent. Since 1994, as part of several Erasmus networks, students from the College have had opportunities to study at various colleges and universities in Europe, while, in turn, students from those institutions have spent a semester at Stranmillis. As a result, Northern Ireland student teachers now have the opportunity to interact with their peers from third-level colleges in a host of EU states including, Denmark, Finland, France, Germany, the Netherlands, Spain and Sweden. Students from these member states also avail of the opportunity to teach in local schools and engage in the study of conflict resolution, Irish Studies and Anglo-Irish literature at Stranmillis.

Social and
Sporting Life
at 'Stran' 6

I n the early years of the College's existence, the occasional dance was the
highlight of the social calendar, and any additional social life was centred
in the hostels. Rag Day did not impinge on the consciousness of
Stranmillis students until the 1960s, though some recall an unofficial 'tug of
war' between 'the Stran men' and a 'raiding party' from Queen's in the mid-
fifties to the chagrin of a hapless Mr Winn! In spite of strict discipline and
relatively frugal living conditions, an *esprit de corps* did exist. Various con-
tests were arranged at Balmoral Hall between boarding students of different
years. Billiards, table-tennis, handball and badminton were played, with
classes in ballroom dancing a popular diversion. Meetings of student organisations were held in the hostels: the men's Literary and Debating Society,
the men's and women's Student Christian Movement, the League of Nations
Union in the inter-war years and the Girl Guides. Contact sports such as
men's and women's hockey, rugby and soccer were also popular.[45]

From 1938, a Students' Representative Council emerged to play a significant part in student affairs and College life in general. This body owed its
existence to the interest and enthusiasm of Professor D W T Jenkins who
had come to Stranmillis a decade earlier and who was keen to foster a more

friendly and informal relationship between staff and students. While much smaller than its modern counterpart, the early SRC was representative of men and women students of all four years and and included members of the College staff. It had few, if any, powers, apart from making representations to the Principal. However, since the Principal was not even a member of the powerful controlling committee of management, the SRC made little impact on decision-making.

During the Portrush interlude, the council ceased to function. When the College returned to Belfast after the war, the SRC was revived under a formal constitution with a chairman, vice-chairman, secretary and treasurer, and 18 members representing the various years. Today's students would hardly consider the old SRC a democratic forum, however. The Principal was its President until 1951 when the office was entrusted to a student for the first time. At the same time students gained greater freedom in the discussion of College affairs.

In the decades since the 1950s, the growth in the numbers of students at the College demanded changes in the council to ensure representation from

all sections of the student community. By the early 1970s, in addition to representation from each year group, the first and second years of the Commonwealth course each returned one member to the council, 'mature students' elected two members and there were representatives from the postgraduate course, the Student Games Committee and the Student Societies Committee. Additional members with 'observer status' included a student representing the Halls of Residence and representatives from the College Magazine Committee and the College Radio. At that time, the 'Union executive' consisted of the President and the Vice-President (who was not to be of the same sex) elected by members of the Union. The higher profile now accorded to the SRC was reflected in the creation of the new post of Administrative Officer and the admission of the President to the College Board of Governors.

When Stranmillis House was assigned to students as a Union building in 1967, the Stranmillis College Club was formed. Extensive renovations were carried out and a bar installed. Refurbishment of this area which now includes a snack-bar for both staff and students and is known as Scholars,

A group of male students with staff including Allan Murray, warden, and his daughter at Balmoral Hall in 1934.

COLLEGE LIBRARY

was completed in 1996.

Over the years, the Charities Committee has raised funds for voluntary causes and co-operates with the university in Rag Day activities, and Stranmillis Union members have participated in events on the wider student scene in Ireland and the United Kingdom.

Throughout the history of the College, student interests have found expression in a variety of clubs and societies. These have ranged from the traditional, long-established, socialising associations found in all third-level institutions, to the more novel groups which fluctuated with student enthusiasm. However, the popularity of religious societies, a music society, drama groups and sports' clubs, some of whose teams have achieved significant successes, has remained consistent throughout the history of the College.

RELIGIOUS SOCIETIES

The Student Christian Movement was established as a branch of the nationwide organisation at a meeting in the men's hostel in October 1922. This was followed by the formation of a parallel society for women in 1923. Membership during the years before 1939 was large with as many as 69 out of 70 men, and 70 or more women joining the movement. Sunday meetings, which tended to be hostel-based, consisted of an act of devotion and an address by members or visiting speakers and there were also Bible-study sessions during week-nights.

From their foundation, the College branches maintained close contacts with the national body, with delegates attending the movement's annual conferences until these were discontinued in the mid-1960s. In order to generate finance, an 'Open Day' was held annually in the summer term. Tennis tournaments, cricket matches between past and present students and afternoon tea served in Stranmillis House were features of these occasions. Indeed, throughout the pre-war years, this day was a red-letter date in the College calendar, and the SCM was, undoubtedly, the most important Stranmillis society.

Despite the large membership of the two branches, concerns were expressed, most forcibly in 1929, that many students were 'materialistic in outlook', with 'some going so far as to deny any special importance to the Bible'. At the same time, it was alleged, somewhat paradoxically, that the more evangelical students did not attend SCM meetings. Consequently, a College branch of the Bible Union was formed in 1945. Like the SCM branch, it was affiliated to a national body, the Inter-Varsity Fellowship, and catered for those students who were more conservative in their faith. Initially, the two groups co-existed but in the 1970s the SCM folded. Since then, the Bible Union, or Christian Union (CU) as it came to be known, has been a vibrant organisation with a present membership of just over one hundred. Through its weekly meetings, Bible study groups, Sunday-night epilogues and 'weekends', it has been a seminal influence on the lives of many students.

SOCCER

The Association Football Club was founded on 4 October 1922 within a few days of the opening of the College, and its first game was played three days later. In the 1923-24 season, the newly-named King's Scholars Football Club played in the Northern Amateur League. The name reflected the official designation of training college students at that time. As the club had no ground of its own, the Grove or Ormeau Parks were the usual venues for home matches. From the following season until 1932, when new grounds were purchased at Shrewsbury Gardens, the Stranmillis club used its own field at Finaghy.

During the years at Portrush when the intake of male students was drastically reduced, it became increasingly difficult to field a team and some years it proved impossible. In 1944 there were just enough men to form a soccer side and friendly matches were arranged against local teams.

On its return to Belfast, the College could boast some 30 potential players who were able to undertake a larger number of friendly games. For some time, the team was compelled to play its home matches at Monkstown, as the rugby club, whose ground had been used for allotments during the war, had been granted use of the soccer pitch. In the 1946-47 season, the club re-joined the Amateur League and in the fifties enjoyed some notable successes, winning successively the Antrim Junior Shield and the Amateur League Division 1.

The opening of the College Sports Centre at Shaw's Bridge in 1966 saw an increased enthusiasm for soccer and by the late 1960s, the club fielded three, and for a time, four teams. The first XI played in Division B of the Amateur League and was placed fourth in 1967-68. In 1970, the team played in the closed competition of Irish Universities and, as runners up, won the Collingwood Shield. In that same season, it participated for the first time in the Northern Ireland Universities and Colleges League and won the cup.

Friendly matches were played against local teams and against visitors to

The College Soccer team travelled to Holland in 1996.

BACK ROW (L–R): J Hanna, D Titterington, N Irwin, N Megaw, A Manning, S McGonagle, B Leslie

FRONT ROW (L–R): K Qua, D Massey, J McCourt, D Hutchinson, D McFarlane, W Shirlow.

MR B LESLIE

Northern Ireland, including those from Brasenose College, Oxford and from Southampton University, and, on tour, the team has played in Dublin, Glasgow, Kent and the Netherlands.

During the same period, the second XI played in Division C of the Amateur League, having competed for the Cochrane Corry Cup and for the Junior Shield. In addition, this team participated in Division 2 of the Northern Ireland Colleges League and played a number of friendly matches each season. The third XI also played friendly matches and for a time was in the Saturday Morning League, Division 3. Between 1968 and 1970, a fourth XI, known at first as the 'Stranmillis Casuals', played 'friendlies'. Such was the popularity of the game in College that an Old Boys' team was formed in 1971 and in its first season was at the top of the Second Division of the Amateur League.

The 1980s and 1990s have seen mixed fortunes for the soccer club. Members took part several times in the Collingwood Cup reaching the final on one occasion; several 'Stran' players were selected for the Northern Ireland universities team to play in the British Universities Sports Federation competitions; several represented the all-Ireland universities; and the team progressed through the Amateur League and reached the 'B' division of the Irish League. Unfortunately, as with other sports, the dwindling numbers of male students has posed problems for soccer at College; nevertheless, keen players have still been able to field teams and to undertake several successful tours.

In August 1980 members left for the United States where they visited universities and colleges. At Pennsylvania State University, the 'A' team struggled in the hottest part of the day to win 2–1, but the 'B' team won easily 6–1.

In subsequent years, despite some difficulties raising funds, tours were arranged to Palma Nova, Majorca, in the 1988–89 season, and more recently to the Netherlands in 1996. Here the 'Stran' boys demonstrated their skills by defeating the local teams very respectably.

RUGBY

In 1925, there was sufficient interest among students to form a rugby club. The team played its first matches during the 1925–26 season and, like the soccer club, rejoiced in the historic title King's Scholars. Progress was steady and in the 1927–28 season the club reached the final of the competition for the Harden Cup. In 1929 with a club membership of 40, it was able to field two teams, the first XV playing in the Junior League and the seconds in the Minor League. A third XV which played mainly friendly matches was active during the thirties. During that decade the firsts and seconds acquitted themselves well but the most notable achievement by 'Stran' was the winning of the YMCA Seven-a-side Trophy in 1934.

Until 1930 the club had no ground of its own, but that year a field was

The birth of a great tradition: the first ever King's Scholars Rugby Football Club XV, 1925–26.

King's Scholars Rugby Football Club First XV, 1936–37.

BACK ROW (L–R) Prof Jenkins, J Malone, J Frost, R Blair, WJ Heuston, R Johnston, J Hughes, GCH Siggins.

FRONT ROW (L–R) G Power, H Brown, C Wylie, WE Halliday, WJ Patterson, F McCarroll, C Wilson, S Neill, S Cosby.

MR N HALLIDAY

acquired on Balmoral Avenue opposite the men's hostel, and in 1932 new grounds in nearby Shrewsbury Gardens became the venue for home matches.

Like soccer, rugby activities were curtailed during the war years, but on the return to Belfast these soon recommenced. The firsts and seconds once again played in the Junior League and in the Minor League respectively, while the thirds played friendlies.

Enthusiasm surged during the 1950s when it is reported that frequently upwards of 70 turned out to play! In that decade the first XV lifted some glittering prizes. They headed the league in 1955–56 and were runners-up in four other seasons. They performed well, too, in the Junior Cup, winning that trophy in 1954–55 and again in 1970–71, reaching the semi-final in 1955–56, 1958–59, and 1967–68, and playing in the final in 1966-67 and 1969–70. The Scholars also competed for the McCrea Cup which they won on eight occasions, in 1954, 1955, 1956, 1958, 1962, 1968, 1970 and 1971. Teams took part in Seven-a-side competitions at Omagh for the Campbell Cup which they won in 1954, 1955, 1957 and 1959, and in similar tournaments at Jordanstown in 1963 and Deramore in 1968.

As well as league and cup matches, the 'Stran' team played several friendlies each season. These included fixtures against visiting sides from Christ's College, Cambridge (1959), St Edmund's Hall, Oxford, Battersea Tech. and Guinness RFC in 1964, and Nottingham University in 1965. On tour, they played Liverpool University and Nuneaton (1958), teams in Glasgow (1966) and in 1970 had a most successful tour of Canada. By the late 1960s

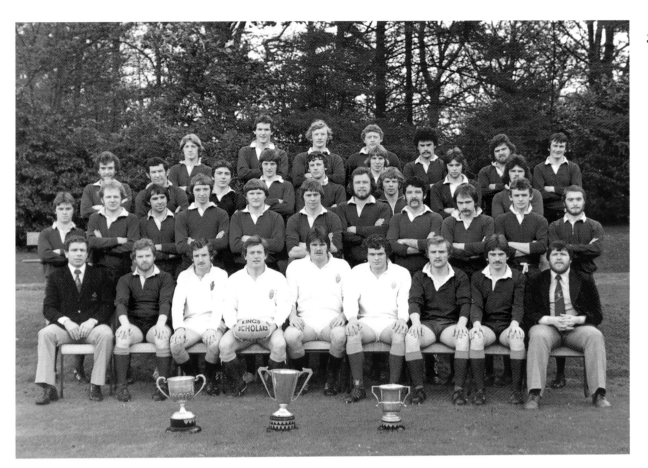

the standard of College rugby was so high that the team began to play friendly matches against senior clubs and was, in effect, 'virtually a semi-senior club'.

The seconds played in the Minor League and managed to maintain a creditable league record, being placed regularly high in the tables and winning the League Cup (Section 2) in 1969–70.

Despite occasional difficulties the other club teams had some successes. One of the third XVs played in Section C of the Fourth Division League and rose to Section A in 1958-59. An enthusiastic 'Freshers' team fielded in the 1960s won 13 out of 16 games in 1963–64, and two third XVs toured the Isle of Man in 1971. In 1970–71 the King's Scholars club won four out of the seven trophies for which it competed – the Junior and McCrea Cups were won by the first XV; the Fourth Division Championship and the McCamley Cup were won by the third 'A' XV; and the seconds were defeated finalists in a fifth competition for the Forster Cup.

The contribution that King's Scholars Rugby Football Club made to Ulster rugby, however, is best measured not so much by cup or league success, but rather by its role in the development of all aspects of the game at school, club, provincial and international level.

King's Scholars RFC 1976–77. The First XV were winners of the McCrea Cup.
Flanking four junior Ulster representatives are Jimmy Davidson (now Head of PE at Stranmillis and former Ulster and Irish coach) and Billy Tate (present Principal of Aughnacloy Primary School).
In the third row (second left) is Ed McCann, former lecturer in Education and now practising law in Calgary, Alberta.

COLLEGE LIBRARY

'Farewell Scholars Team',
1979–80.

BACK ROW (L–R)
Arthur Topping,
Kenny Graham, Mervyn
Moore, Ray Cromie,
Philip Vance,
Terry Annesley, Michael
Snoddy, Bill Connor,
Stephen Snoddy.

FRONT ROW (L–R)
Gary Jackson,
John McIlmoyle,
Charlie McAleese,
Gary Clegg, Bill Foreman
(Capt.) Gary Hunter,
Roderick Geddes,
Stephen Allen, David Beattie.

COLLEGE LIBRARY

Guided from the earliest days by enthusiastic College staff such as Bob Porter, Jos Lapsley, Norman Nesbitt and Ed McCann who believed emphatically in the principle of self-government by students within the club, the Scholars' undergraduates acquired skills in playing, teaching, coaching, refereeing, selection and administration during their period at College and as graduates, many rose to the highest positions in the game in Ireland.

On the playing field Ken Armstrong, Jim Stevenson, Ronnie Lamont, Roger Clegg, Ian McIlwrath, Ronnie Hakin, Stewart McKinney and Willie Anderson all gained international honours with Ireland, indeed Anderson was appointed captain of his country in 1989–90. Ronnie Lamont was selected on the 1970 Lions tour to New Zealand and Stewart McKinney toured in South Africa with the successful 1974 Lions.

Senior Ulster clubs have been well served by capable administrators with Ernie Davis rising to become President of the Ulster Branch IRFU and W J (Paddy) Patterson serving a long and distinguished period with the Irish

Rugby Football Union. The versatility of the Scholars' rugby academy is perhaps epitomised by internationally respected rugby commentator, Jim Neilly.

It would be no exaggeration, however, to claim that the professional teaching and coaching skills that were first developed among the students in the College laid the foundations for the development of rugby football coaching in Ulster and Ireland. Ulster Schools rugby is indeed indebted to Dawson McConkey and Ken Armstrong. Armstrong was the first official coach to the Ulster provincial team; Jimmy Davidson (now Head of PE at Stranmillis) coached the Ulster team that defeated the 1984 Australian Grand Slam team and later became the Irish national team coach from 1988-90. In the new professional era Willie Anderson was appointed as full-time coach to English premier league team, London Irish.

As a result of a policy decision taken by the Department of Education in Northern Ireland to reduce the numbers in secondary training at Stranmillis, King's Scholars were forced to consider their future as a Junior League club. Rather than suffer the indignity of demeaning defeats because of a lack of players, the club elected to withdraw from the Ulster League in 1980. A 'Farewell Scholars' match to announce the decision and celebrate the proud traditions of the past was played at Ravenhill on 30 April 1980.

The club has always remained affiliated to the Ulster Branch of the IRFU and the student body has fought valiantly to play friendly fixtures in the intervening years, keeping alive the 'spirit and ethos' of King's Scholars by arranging tours to Holland, Spain, England and the Republic of Ireland.

The outstanding coaching tradition of former King's Scholars is well reflected in schools and youth rugby. Alan McGonigle is the current manager of the Ulster Schools team, Stephen Graham the Ulster Schools coach, Charlie McAleese is presently the Irish Under 18 coach and Keith Patton is Irish Schools coach.

HOCKEY

Hockey for both men and women was played from the earliest days of the College's history. A women's hockey match took place on 25 November 1922, probably between two student teams, and a club was founded that same term. From the following autumn, various teams were fielded and games were played somewhere at Stranmillis. There were two teams in 1924 and again in 1925-26 when the firsts played in the Junior League of the Ulster Women's Hockey Union.

During 1927-28, three teams were coached by a Miss Charters, an Irish

international player, but in the 1931-32 season the number of teams had fallen to two. In 1937, the first XI won the Ulster Junior Cup and were finalists in the all Ireland White Cup played in Dublin. However, by 1938-39, the club was well-established having three teams in Intermediate and Junior Leagues and two others playing. During this season, Miss Kathleen Watson, who had joined the College staff, presented a cup to be awarded annually to the team which won the most matches.

The Portrush sojourn limited the activities of this club, as it had the others, but when students and staff returned to Belfast in 1944, the game became increasingly popular. By 1950, four teams were playing competitive matches, the firsts in the Qualifying section of league competitions, the seconds and thirds in the Intermediate section and the fourths in the Junior one. Although the firsts ended this season in second place in their section, the other teams were less successful, apparently suffering frequent defeats. This was due in many cases to teams having to play at less than full strength, 'owing to the persistent habit of girls going home for weekends as often as college rules allowed'. In addition to league fixtures, matches were also arranged between college sides.

There was only one pitch on the campus, the level ground below the old stable buildings, as the area behind Stranmillis House was reserved for other sports. There were, therefore, considerable demands on the ground before two blaize pitches, the first of their kind in Ireland, were laid in 1956.

Two years earlier, Miss Catherine McTavish joined the staff of the PE department and became deeply involved in the hockey club as coach, player and umpire – an association which lasted until her retirement 30 years later. From the second half of the 1950s, the teams were generally successful in their respective leagues and competitions. In the 1956-57 season the firsts began a series of tours to Scotland which subsequently continued. Dublin was visited in 1966 and that Easter, a team travelled to Germany and won the Wiesbaden Tournament.

During the 1970s, the number of teams fluctuated between three and four. In 1972, the club marked its golden anniversary by travelling to Canada with members of the Pegasus Ladies Hockey Club, and subsequent tours were undertaken to Hong Kong and Bermuda.

The reduction in the numbers of students at the College in the 1980s had a significant effect on the hockey club with the number of teams varying between two and three. Nevertheless, teams went 'on tour' to Spain, Portugal and the Irish Republic. Regrettably, in the latter years of that decade the fall in numbers resulted in the relegation of the first XI from Senior League hockey after 22 years.

The club began the 1990s in the Qualifying League Section Two. However, the firsts gained promotion in two consecutive years and reached Section Two of the Senior League in 1995. The previous year, members

Stranmillis v
Greenock Ladies:
Hockey Tour 1959–60.

raised £12,000 to go on tour to Canada. Also in 1995, they won the Ulster Women's Hockey Union Qualifying Plate. The team played in Senior League until 1997, but again, falling numbers necessitated the first XI's move to the Qualifying League, Section One.

Throughout the first 75 years of 'Stran's' existence, many members of the club have represented Ireland, Ulster, and British universities teams and several have succeeded in becoming top level umpires and have held important positions in the Ulster Women's Hockey Union.

A men's hockey club was founded in 1924 and although initially only a few 'friendly' matches were played, by 1927 the team had been admitted to the 'A' Division of the Minor League and captured the McMeekin Cup in 1930. A second XI was fielded in 1927 and a third in 1930. Sadly, before the mid-thirties, the club ceased to exist and was not revived until after the war.

Following the return from Portrush, the club was refounded in 1946, and played most of its home matches on a pitch at Shrewsbury Gardens. League matches were played, with teams competing for the McMeekin, Minor and Junior Charities Cups, as well as playing friendlies against schools and the university. In the early 1960s, two teams were again in existence, one playing in the Intermediate and the other in the Junior League. However, by the end of that decade, only one team was fielded, playing in the Intermediate League and ending the season in the middle of that League's premier table.

At Easter 1970, a team travelled to Germany and gave an impressive account of itself. Out of nine games, the students won six, drew two and lost one: a very commendable performance! The following Easter, the club visited Dublin to take part in the Leinster Festival which attracted teams from all over the British Isles. At this event, out of five games, the team won two, lost two and drew one.

The College team struggled during the 1974-75 season. Some good hockey was played but points were not gained and eventually the team was relegated from Senior 2 to Intermediate League. However, the following season was much more successful. The team was undefeated in the league, notching up numerous victories and gaining promotion to Senior League. In April 1976, after much fund-raising, 14 students travelled by minibus to Mechelen in northern Belgium for an eight day tour. The hockey was competitive and the team finished fifth in the tournament. In the final game the opposition turned up in the same colour of shirts and, as a result, 'Stran' played shirtless. This was a memorable tour which left an impression on Mechelen both on and off the field. The Belgian hosts even became word-perfect in the 'Stran Medley' !

The next two seasons saw the team consolidate its senior status, but as numbers at College decreased, it became exceedingly difficult to field a senior team and at the end of the 1977–78 it was decided to disband the men's team and withdraw from Saturday hockey.

NETBALL

In October 1949, a College netball club was founded with an initial membership of 35. As the game was new to most students, much time was spent on coaching and practice, with sessions being held in the Henry Garrett Building. By the late 1960s, three teams played at competitive level in the Senior 'A' and 'B' and in the Intermediate sections, competing for the Margaret Shaw, Betty Richmond and Mona Baird Shields against a variety of teams - former pupils from schools such as Park Parade and Larkfield, university groups, and clubs from the Civil Service and the business world. Tours to Great Britain were organised every third year and students from the club gained places on Northern Ireland's Under 21 and Senior 'B' teams.

'Smiles all round!': the Stranmillis Netball Team, 1977–78.

BACK ROW (L–R):
Wendy McCoo, Barbara Capper, Heather Johnston, Hilary Boyd.

FRONT ROW (L–R):
Moya Megaghey, Stephanie Duncan, Pauline Sergeant, Leslie Kirk.

MRS S CALLAGHAN

Mrs Sheila Callaghan, former lecturer in PE, with the College Netball team, Easter Tour 1994.

BACK ROW (L–R) Joanne Crooks, Joanne Somerville, Barbara Kerr, Laura McAuley, Nuala O'Hare, Heather Wallace, Nichola Bailie, Rosemary Hughes.

FRONT ROW (L–R) Wendy Newell, Ruth Galbraith, Leslie Thompson, Elaine Hassin, Gillian Mathers, Mrs Sheila Callaghan.

MRS S CALLAGHAN

The netball players also accompanied the College hockey club on their tour to Hong Kong in 1982.

Until the mid-eighties netball was very strong and several 'Stran' players were selected for Northern Ireland teams. But by that time the club had dropped to Section C of the league and, sadly, league fixtures had to be abandoned for a few years. However, in 1992, a group of very enthusiastic students revived interest in the sport. They relaunched both the College team and the former students' team which is, at present, vibrant and performing exceptionally well at league level.

Closer links with Queen's meant that the netball students were eligible for membership of the Northern Ireland squad which participated annually in the prestigious British Universities tournament. Over the years, many players, under the expert tuition of Mrs Sheila Callaghan, a lecturer in the PE department and a Northern Ireland coach, were selected for that team and travelled to university campuses in Great Britain, gaining silver medals at Newcastle-upon-Tyne, Strathclyde, Swansea and Oxford and gold at the

University of Ulster at Jordanstown. In 1985, Mary Lavery became the first ever Northern Ireland student to be a member of the British Universities Select team - a great honour for the 'Stran' club.

MUSIC AT STRANMILLIS

Music has been intrinsic to the life of the College since the appointment of the first full-time lecturer in the subject in 1934. Concerts were organised jointly by the staff of the music and speech departments and two men students, one in the pre-war and another in the post-war years who recruited and trained male-voice choirs from among their fellow students. Unfortunately these choirs faded away as their founders moved into the world of work.

After 1945, as student numbers increased, musical activities became more adventurous. Choral concerts continued to be given and these often included substantial works by composers such as Benjamin Britten and Purcell, the

Gilbert and Sullivan at 'Stran'. From the 1960s Stranmillis was renowned for its annual Gilbert and Sullivan productions.

MR J MCDOWELL

Choir rehearsal under the direction of Dr Harry Grindle, in the recital room, Stranmillis College, 1995.

performance of whose *Dido and Aeneas* aroused considerable interest from Belfast's musical fraternity. A member of the music department founded a girls' choir which was successful in competitions at Belfast Music Festival. But, there was no music society until 1954, although for a brief period there had been a student 'gramophone society'. In 1955, with some financial assistance from the SRC, the Music Society purchased instruments and scores, and on 1 June that year, the choir gave its first broadcast on BBC radio. At Christmas the following year, members of the Student Christian Movement combined with the choir and by that time with a College orchestra, to perform a Mystery Play.

When the new Hall/Refectory was opened in 1954, the Music Society seized the opportunity to stage a series of Gilbert and Sullivan operas. The first of these, *Patience*, was performed with some outside help in 1959. This was followed in 1963 by *Trial by Jury*, entirely a College production, by *Princess Ida*, which ran for three nights in February 1964, and by *The*

Sorcerer, in 1965. In March 1966, a concert included Bach's *Cantata 79* and part of *Cantata 21*, and recitals were given by various choirs, soloists and orchestral groups.

The buzz and excitement of the annual performances of Gilbert and Sullivan operas resumed under the musical direction of Michael Richards, with choreography by Miss Maureen Annesley.

The vitality and diversity of the Music department's activities has continued during the past two and a half decades under the direction of John McDowell, Dr Harry Grindle and Alex McKee. In addition to regular lunchtime recitals by both music students and visiting artistes, choral and orchestral concerts have been an important feature of the department's programme of events. These concerts have been presented in the College Drama Theatre as well as at such venues as the Harty Room, Queen's University, and Belfast Cathedral. Works performed have included Handel's *Messiah*, Mozart's *Requiem*, Bach's *Christmas Oratorio*, Haydn's *Mass in B flat* ('The Theresa'), and Britten's *Ceremony of Carols* for ladies' voices and harp.

Orchestral ensemble in the Music Department, 1995.

A wide-ranging selection of orchestral items has included music by Cimarosa, Vivaldi, Bach, Handel, Mozart, Vaughan Williams, Flor Peeters and Bryan Kelly. Outstanding student soloists have appeared with the orchestra in various concertos and such works as *Carnival of the Animals* by Saint-Saëns.

The Stranmillis choir and instrumentalists have, for many years, provided the music for the annual Christmas Carol Service held in Fisherwick Presbyterian Church, Malone Road, and have delighted congregations of students, staff, parents and friends with their professional performance of seasonal music. A miscellany entitled *Music for a May Evening* has in recent years proved to be a very popular event both musically and socially.

The Stranmillis Singers, a chamber choir founded in 1970 by John McDowell, further enhanced the already-high reputation of the College's music students, many of whom remained members after graduation. This 'select' group performed music ranging from sixteenth century madrigals and motets to twentieth century compositions and folk-song arrangements. Recitals were given at many venues throughout Northern Ireland as well as in Dublin, Galway and St Giles' Cathedral during the Edinburgh International Festival. The Singers broadcast regularly and appeared several times on television. In the 1970s they were three-times winners of the Northern Ireland heat of the BBC choral competition, *Let the Peoples Sing*, and on one occasion were United Kingdom runners-up.

The quality of their choral work was recognised in their repeated success at various musical festivals and competitions over the years. Unfortunately, in the mid-1980s, the lack of male singers made it impossible to maintain the professional standard to which the choir had always aspired, and in 1985 the decision was taken to disband.

DRAMA

The Dramatic Society began just after the war and since then its members have performed successfully both on the College campus and farther afield. Initially, students, and indeed some members of staff, staged one full-length play or a group of one-act plays each year. These were selected for their entertainment value and included 'West End' type farces or comedies such as Priestley's *Laburnum Grove*, although some short plays by Yeats and Thornton Wilder also featured.

In due course drama became a subject in the College curriculum, and in 1949 a full-time lecturer was appointed. During the 1950s, the prestige of the subject increased and for the next 20 years works by 'classic' authors were performed. Shakespeare's *As You Like It*, Sheridan's *The Rivals* and Ibsen's *Hedda Gabler* have taken their place alongside plays by Sartre, Arthur Miller, Becket, Shaw and Yeats. The society also made a significant contribution to the College events commemorating Shakespeare's Tercentenary.

The Stranmillis society was the first group from a college of education to be accepted as a member of the Irish Universities Drama Festival and, in 1958, when Queen's hosted the event, the College company was invited to stage a performance of Ustinov's *Romeo and Juliet*. This production won a premier award and from that time the Stranmillis students were invited to participate in subsequent competitions at which they gained some notable successes.

From the early years of the society, plays were entered for drama festivals across the province. At Larne in 1962, the Larne Times Cup was won for a performance of Ibsen's *Medea*, and a prize for décor was gained – a success which was repeated the following year when a member of the team also won the cup for the best actress. On several occasions the Shakespeare Cup was won at Belfast Musical Festival.

The 1970s and early '80s were particularly rich times for the College theatre, a studio space whose potential resources were demonstrated to an eager audience in a performance of *Everyman*, the medieval morality play, directed by Mrs Gladys Black, a lecturer in the drama department. This was the first production to be mounted in the new theatre shortly after the opening of the Central Building.

There was much interest and involvement in drama at this time and the enthusiasm was due in no small part to Miss Mary Morrison, another member of the drama staff. Until her tragic and untimely death in a road accident, Mary organised a week-long drama festival each year, mainly, she claimed, to encourage first year students, especially those not studying English with dramatic art, to gain experience in acting and directing and to learn something about theatre arts. It was a competition which was one of the highlights of the College year, adjudicated by invited members of the College staff, and a social event which brought staff and students together.

In 1972, Dr Gertrude Patterson of the English department directed T S Eliot's *The Family Reunion* with a group of students from Stranmillis and Queen's. This was a collaborative production which benefited from the advice of Maureen Annesley and Patricia Calderwood, with haunting music composed by Michael Richards and performed by music students and a wonderful set, designed by Derek Kinnen. This was memorably furnished with antiques borrowed from friends, a carpet which the College Principal, James Pomfret, had been persuaded to lend from the Board Room, and a huge cake,

A scene from a student production of the morality play *Everyman* in the Drama Theatre, 1971.

prepared by Miss Kathleen Strawbridge and students from Home Economics.

The early '80s were dominated by Sam McCready, best known and loved for the fun of his impromptu performances in the theatre foyer and for his love of Yeats's plays. Shortly before he left the staff to take up an appointment in the United States, he and Gertrude Patterson jointly directed *Calvary*, *The Resurrection*, and *Purgatory* with a group of student players from Stranmillis and Queen's – a production which later transferred to the Lyric Theatre. These plays were esoteric but deeply moving, with dance and movement directed by Helen Lewis, a most gifted professional dancer who, at that time, regularly taught dance to students of English and dramatic art.

In November 1984, the Stranmillis Theatre Company was formed and participated in the Belfast Festival with a celebrated performance of *Our Day Out* by Willy Russell. On that occasion the 'Festival' used the College Drama Theatre for the first time, and for over a decade companies as varied as the Royal Shakespeare Company, the Royal National Theatre and the Belfast Theatre for the Deaf have performed at Stranmillis.

Several College productions won acclaim during the 1980s. 1985 saw a performance of *Caritas* by Arnold Wesker, and the following year, the Stranmillis Theatre Company combined with Queen's Drama Society to perform Berthold Brecht's *The Caucasian Chalk Circle*. A largescale production of Adrian Mitchell's version of *The Pied Piper of Hamelin* attracted significant audiences in 1988. For this event, schools participated in a poster competition which resulted in considerable publicity for the show.

STRANMILLIS THEATRE COMPANY
with
SPEECHPLAY
present

THE PIED PIPER

Stranmillis College Theatre
Wednesday 19th February at 2.00pm & 7.30pm
Thursday 20th February & Friday 21st February at 7.30pm
Saturday 22nd February at 7.30pm

The winning poster for
The Pied Piper of Hamelin,
produced at Stranmillis,
1988.

MR H FYFE

The 1990s have been years of significant achievement for the College's drama students. In 1991, the Stranmillis Theatre Company was among the finalists in The Sunday Times National Student Theatre Festival. Their play *Making the Number Up* was devised by the company and painted a harrowing picture of lives led in Ulster's rural isolation. It won more awards for a single production than any other play in the history of the festival. Robert Hewison, drama critic of *The Sunday Times*, was unstinting in his praise:

'Here, for once, in its synthesis of word and image, of speech and song, of precise local detail and wide cultural reference of the natural and the symbolic, was a complete piece of theatre'.

The financial rewards of the play's success allowed it to transfer to the Edinburgh Festival where it was shortlisted for The *Independent* Newspaper Theatre Award and gained a 'Fringe First'. Early in 1992, the play won a number of awards at the Irish Student Drama Festival in Belfast.

The year 1992 was, undoubtedly, one of the most enterprising in the history of drama at 'Stran'. In October, the Stranmillis Theatre Company, led by Hamish Fyfe, joined students from St Mary's College in a production for the World Festival of Theatre hosted by the Indian government. The play, which was a re-working of the *Cúchulain* legends of the Ulster Cycle, was very well received in Delhi, Chandigarh, the Punjab and the United Provinces. The visit proved to be an extraordinary experience for the students. Travelling during a time of heightened tension in India was especially unnerving. In Srinigar, the company's performance was the only exception to an eight o'clock curfew in the locality; and that evening, the students' coach was the only vehicle on the streets of a very eerie city.

But the fame of the drama students did not end there. In 1995, the Theatre Company toured Edinburgh and the Scottish Borders with *Away from Home*, a 'Theatre in Education' production for primary schools, and the following year saw the ground-breaking physical theatre performance of

Stranmillis and St Mary's drama students at the World Festival of Theatre, India, 1992.

MR H FYFE

Ramblers Club at
Knockbarra, Co. Down,
May 1957.

MR T STEELE

Metamorphosis, in an adaptation by Steven Berkoff.

For many years the College pantomime has proved a useful link between the College and schools in the province. Students from all departments utilise their talents to present a humorous and professional performance each December.

All of these efforts have added, and continue to add, an extra dimension to life in the College. They have produced a great deal of public respect for the work at Stranmillis and have furthered its local, national and international reputation. It is also notable that so many young people who were first enthused by and initiated into the thrill and magic of the theatre on the College stage, like Alex McClay of the present English department staff, went on to distinguish themselves in the professional theatre.

THE FIELD STUDY SOCIETY

One of the most vibrant societies for those who attended 'Stran' in the fifties and early sixties was the Field Study Society which drew on the expertise of Stanley Skillen, Louis de St Paër and Clare Macmahon of the Science Department. Stanley, a keen biologist with an infectious love of the countryside and local history, led parties of intrepid naturalists on field-trips to the Antrim Glens, the Mournes and even the Norwegian fiords in the late 1950s. Owing to the popularity of rambles in the Glens, the Society's members in 1957–58, under the chairmanship of Thompson Steele, declared themselves (with apologies to Percy French) 'the Ballyvoy Mounted Fut'. On their weekend excursions the members were entertained in traditional style by Norman Nesbitt, a lecturer who played the tin whistle and organised impromptu *ceilis*. But tragedy struck at Easter 1957 when Tom Finlay, a third year student, was drowned during a trip to Ballycastle, an event still recalled with sadness by his contemporaries.

In the winter months the society organised an impressive programme of talks by eminent experts. The 1957–58 series included contributions by the leading geographer, Professor E Estyn Evans on 'Folklore in the Field' and the Antrim-born Celtic scholar Professor Hamilton Delargy on the work of the Irish Folklore Commission. In October 1962, Richard Hayward, the noted Ulster writer, spoke on 'The Humour of the Ulster Dialect'.

The society, with its distinctive curlew symbol, had a significant impact on the cultural formation of many 'Stran' students. For David Hammond, folksinger, later BBC producer and film-maker, it fostered a lifelong interest in the music and folklore of his native province. For Thompson Steele, teacher and local historian, the Field Study Society opened a door through local studies to Irish history which was not as yet offered as a formal subject in the College.

One of the most remarkable things about the society has been its longevity, symbolised by an annual reunion for former Field Club enthusiasts.

Reunion of the 'Ballyvoy Mounted Fut' at Castleward, 1996.

(L–R)
M Markey, T Steele,
Mrs B Beattie, D Wallace
(Vancouver Island),
Mrs I Zammet (Toronto),
Mrs D Wallace, J Hewitt,
Mrs U McKitterick
(Bermuda) and
S McKeown.

MR T STEELE

Donegall Estate map 1770
PRONI

From Castle to College 7

The Site and its Buildings

When the first Northern Ireland government acquired the Stranmillis estate as the site for the new state training college in 1922, it ensured that the College would enjoy a setting of great historic interest as well as one of unspoiled natural beauty.

The place-name 'Stranmillis' is derived from the Irish *struthan milis*, meaning 'the sweet or pleasant stream', a reference to the River Lagan which was described by seventeenth century travellers as well-stocked with trout and salmon. The present College grounds occupy a spur of the Malone Ridge, an esker deposited by the melting ice-sheet and forming the main line of communication southward from Belfast since early times. On a 1570 map of the Belfast area, predating the establishment of the town, Stranmillis lies deep in the dense forest of Cromac Wood, stretching from the modern city centre southwards towards Malone and Lisburn. Belfast is marked by a crumbling Anglo-Norman castle while the nearest settlement to the present College site is 'Freerstone' or 'Friar's Town' – the medieval monastic foundation of 'Kilpatrick' ('Patrick's Church'), now Friar's Bush graveyard, designated by three single-storeyed houses.[46]

There were, however, a number of early Christian raths or ring-forts –

'Sir Moses's Cellars':
The Victorian Farm
Buildings below Stranmillis
House are built on the
foundations of the original
Plantation Castle.

DR R CROMIE

essentially farmstead enclosures – in the district including one near Stranmillis House. When excavated in 1969, this site yielded traces of the rath ditch and sherds of decorated souterrain pottery, dating the fort to the ninth or tenth century, AD.[47]

The documented history of Stranmillis, however, does not begin until the early seventeenth century. At the outset of the Plantation of Ulster in 1606, Sir Arthur Chichester, first Earl of Donegall and founder of Belfast, leased the lands of Stranmillis and Upper Malone to Moses Hill for 61 years. Hill was to build two Plantation castles on his estates, one at Malone and the other on the site now occupied by Stranmillis College. The Stranmillis castle was probably designed to guard the ancient fording point on the Lagan, close to the present King's Bridge. The *Report of the Plantation Commissioners* in 1611 describes it as follows :

> Within a mile of Hillsborowe (probably the site of the present Malone House) by the River Lagan, where the sea ebbs and flows in a place called Strandmellis, we found the said Moyses Hill in hand with the building of a strong house of stone, 56 feet long, and (he) entends (sic) to make it two stories and a half high … and to build a good bawn (fortified enclosure) of lime and stone about it.

This first manor house would appear to have stood on the site of the old farm buildings, on the slope below the present Stranmillis House. George Benn, the historian of Belfast, says that the ruins of the 1611 house existed 'almost within living memory and were known as Sir Moses's Cellars'. Tradition records that the remnants of this first building can still be seen in the arches and vaulted roofs underlying the later farm buildings in the old stableyard. Certainly, this labyrinthine structure was designed as the foundation of a substantial residence.

Sir Moses planted his lands with tenants from Lancashire and Cheshire and by 1635, was drawing a handsome rental of £1,000 per year from his Stranmillis estate. The area was described as 'good ploughing land which is now clothed with excellent corn'. Stranmillis Castle would seem to have escaped the ravages of the 1641 Irish uprising which saw the destruction of Hill's other seat at Malone.[48]

The Hills moved before their lease expired, establishing themselves at Hillsborough, Co Down, and the Stranmillis property reverted to the Donegall family to become the Countess of Donegall's Deerpark. Some impression of the surrounding area in the late seventeenth century can be gleaned from a description by Richard Dobbs, written in 1683 :

> From Lambeg the way leads direct to Belfast, which is all along for the most part furnished with houses, little orchards and gardens and on the right hand, the Countess of Donegall hath a very fine park well stored with venison and in it a Horse Course of two miles, and may be called an English road.

A Donegall document of 1692 more precisely defines the Deer Park: '100 acres were then enclosed in a Deer Park and called Strandmellis Park'. The demesne included the whole area now enclosed by the Stranmillis and Malone Roads and the horse course seems to have followed its perimeter, possibly formed by the roads themselves. Of these, the Malone Road was of prime importance as the main route to Dublin. But the section which became Stranmillis Road in Victorian times was as yet little more than a country lane through the still extensive Cromac Wood. Stranmillis demesne itself was still a good two miles from the small Plantation town.

From 1770, the Donegall family divided their Stranmillis demesne into small parcels of land and leased them to farmers. About this time a prominent Belfast mercantile family, the Blacks, leased forty acres on the southern part of the 'Deerpark' – comprising the present College grounds. The Blacks built a summer residence, somewhat grandiosely described as a 'gentleman's seat' by a writer in 1777. In 1794 they renewed their lease and in 1801 built an elegant mansion, the predecessor of the present Stranmillis House.[49]

Detail on the walls of Stranmillis House. This curious figure below the oriel window may represent Sir Moses Hill, the estate's 17th century occupant.

CROWN COPYRIGHT

STRANMILLIS HOUSE AND THE BATTS

The Blacks later acquired a freehold and in 1857 they sold their property to Thomas G Batt, a director of the Belfast Bank who had lived previously at Purdysburn. Within a year Batt had rebuilt Stranmillis House. The new mansion was designed in Jacobean revivalist style by the leading Belfast architects, Sir Charles Lanyon and W H Lynn. A wildly asymmetrical building with a square corner tower surmounted by an open belfry and ogee spire on top, the house was multi-gabled in a romantic style which owed much to English Elizabethan houses. Impressive details still visible include mullioned windows and a large oriel window while the walls are decorated with curious stones and gargoyles. These include a strange figure with branches and

Stranmillis House (1858) in its late Victorian splendour, as designed by Lanyon and Lynn.

COLLEGE LIBRARY

foliage below the oriel which may have been an allusion to Sir Moses Hill or, alternatively, an Elizabethan 'Green Man'. The two heraldic lions (now standing on each side of the front steps) were originally positioned above the entrance porch gable. Their shields still bear the initials of the house's first owner, 'T G B' – Thomas G Batt.

Despite later alterations, the ground floor of Stranmillis House remains largely intact. Nineteenth century features still extant include the tiled floor, fine vaulted ceiling, plasterwork and the original fire-place.

In its mid-Victorian splendour, Stranmillis House was guarded by two gate-lodges. At the foot of the hill, near the present main gate, stood a very picturesque Gothic Revival gate-lodge with Tudor-style gables and mullioned windows. In what one writer has described as 'a piece of official van-

The Victorian house: a rear view.

COLLEGE LIBRARY

The original Tudor-style Gate-lodge at the main entrance to the College. Sadly, this picturesque essay was demolished in the 1930s.

dalism', this 'architectural gem' was demolished in 1933 in favour of a more functional structure. Until the 1920s the main avenue to the house was from the back gate further along the Stranmillis Road (almost opposite Richmond Park) and a second lodge stood there. (The only other approach was by means of a foot-path from the present main entrance past the Principal's House). Stabling was provided by the old farm buildings in front of Stranmillis House.[50]

The first owner, Thomas Batt, did not live to enjoy Stranmillis House for long; he died in 1861. The house then passed in succession to William Murphy, a linen manufacturer, Sir Daniel Dixon, a leading timber merchant and Unionist politician who took possession in the 1880s, and by the end of the century, to Walter Henry Wilson, a director of Harland and Wolff's shipyard. Its final occupant was James McConnell, a brick and tile manufacturer, who remained in residence from 1902 until 1922.[51]

But Stranmillis's long history as a gentleman's seat was drawing to a close. In 1919, the estate was purchased by Queen's University for £13,500. When the University bought Queen's Elms a year later, however, it was decided to sell off the Stranmillis Estate. Finally, in October 1922, the new Northern Ireland Ministry of Finance, bought it for £15,000 as the site of the proposed Teacher Training College.[52]

THE NEW TRAINING COLLEGE

The opening of Stranmillis Training College necessitated major reconstruction work on Stranmillis House. The house was extended in Elizabethan style for use as a women's hostel by R Ingleby Smith (1882–1942), the chief architect of the Ministry of Finance. This work, carried out during 1922–24, involved the removal of the original entrance porch and service wing. The extension is still clearly distinguishable by the lighter colour of the stone, but this junction between the old and the new was handled sensitively. The temporary single-storey 'Bungalow Hostels', erected in 1924 to provide female accommodation, continued to supplement that available in the refurbished house for the next forty years. Smith's alteration endured until 1967 when the house became the Students' Union building. At this stage, Smith's

Stranmillis House undergoing reconstruction during 1922–24 to meet the needs of the new Teacher Training College. Ingleby Smith, the architect, removed the original entrance porch and service wing and extended the building for use as a women's hostel. The blend of old and new was delicately handled.

COLLEGE LIBRARY

The house as extended by Ingleby Smith in the early 1920s.

entrance was changed and a modern stairway inserted.

To accommodate some 80 male students, temporarily housed in Royal Terrace, Lisburn Road since 1922, the Ministry bought Hampton House in Balmoral Avenue. Formerly a 'Female Industrial School', the new hostel – renamed Balmoral Hall – evinced an elegant façade but was less than comfortable inside. It served as a student residence from 1928 until 1965 when it was demolished to make way for the Public Record Office. Its situation, a mile and a half from the College, was considered an advantage in keeping the men well away from the women's hostels but, as an earlier historian of the College notes :

> The journey between hall and College was only partially served by the tramway system along the Malone Road, and to have to make it four times a day … was burdensome. It also made a long luncheon break unavoidable and this, in turn, gave some reason for running lectures as late as 5.30 p.m. Few, indeed, could sentimentalise over it when the time eventually came for its closure.[53]

The elegant façade of Balmoral Hall which served as a men's hostel from 1928–65. Its distance from the College was rated an asset in maintaining a *cordon sanitaire* between the male and female students.

COLLEGE LIBRARY

THE MAIN BUILDING

As the *Belfast Telegraph* pointed out in 1930, Stranmillis Training College began life without classrooms or offices and it was not until the completion of the Main Building in September 1929 that these became available on the site. The College had already been open for seven years.

The prestigious new building, constructed during 1926–29, has been officially attributed to Ingleby Smith though the design may well have been the work of his able chief assistant, T F O Rippingham, described by a recent authority as 'the unsung hero of the Stranmillis site'.[54]

An impressive neo-Georgian edifice, the Main Building was cast in the style of a French château with a crescent shape and forward projecting wings. These are joined to the main block by curving bays with elaborate doorways and recessed columns. An aesthetically pleasing feature was the addition of 'a precious little tempietto' or Roman temple lantern, perched eye-catchingly on top as a centrepiece. The building is composed of walls of purple Cornish brick with Portland stone dressings and is roofed with red pan-tiles. The regular bays of windows, glazed with small panes, introduced a new serenity into local architecture.

Doors in the angles lead to the corridors and staircases while the main entrance hall is reached by a central doorway. In the early years, access to

TOP RIGHT:
Plan of the First Floor, Main Building, 1930.
COLLEGE LIBRARY

BELOW RIGHT:
Plan of the Ground Floor, Main Building, 1930.
COLLEGE LIBRARY

BELOW:
The prestigious new Main Building, constructed during 1926–29.
NICLR

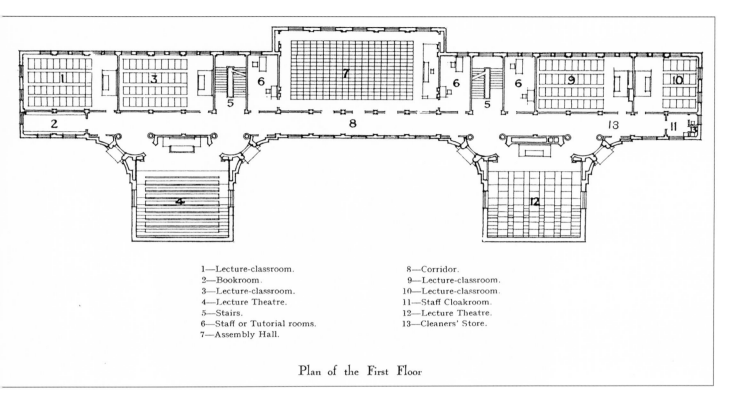

1—Lecture-classroom.
2—Bookroom.
3—Lecture-classroom.
4—Lecture Theatre.
5—Stairs.
6—Staff or Tutorial rooms.
7—Assembly Hall.

8—Corridor.
9—Lecture-classroom.
10—Lecture-classroom.
11—Staff Cloakroom.
12—Lecture Theatre.
13—Cleaners' Store.

Plan of the First Floor

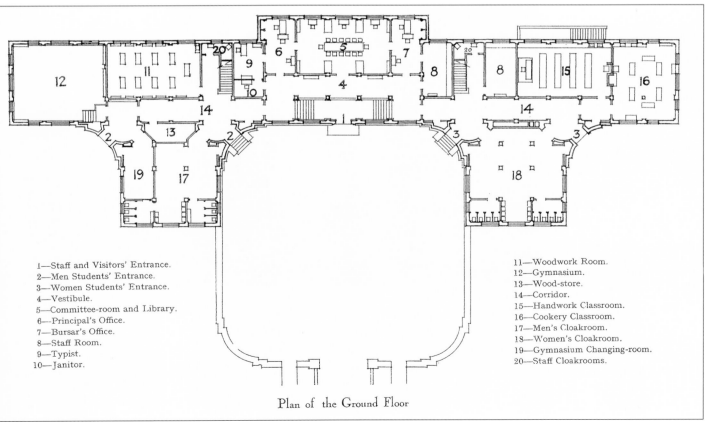

1—Staff and Visitors' Entrance.
2—Men Students' Entrance.
3—Women Students' Entrance.
4—Vestibule.
5—Committee-room and Library.
6—Principal's Office.
7—Bursar's Office.
8—Staff Room.
9—Typist.
10—Janitor.

11—Woodwork Room.
12—Gymnasium.
13—Wood-store.
14—Corridor.
15—Handwork Classroom.
16—Cookery Classroom.
17—Men's Cloakroom.
18—Women's Cloakroom.
19—Gymnasium Changing-room.
20—Staff Cloakrooms.

Plan of the Ground Floor

The splendid Tuscan columns on the ground floor of the Main Building.

COLLEGE LIBRARY

the College was carefully regulated. Staff and visitors might use the main entrance in the middle of the façade, but men and women students were allocated separate entrances in the angles and, once inside, were guided to the upper floors by segregated staircases!

LEFT:
An art class in the new Art Room, 1930.

BELOW:
The Library in the Main Building in the 1930s.

COLLEGE LIBRARY

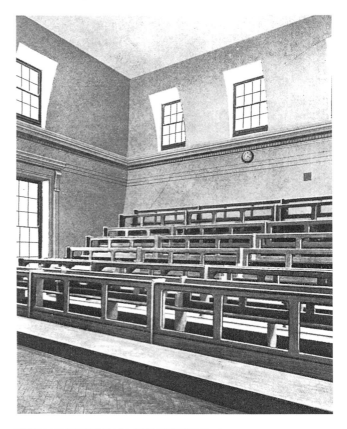

The new clerestorey lecture theatre, Main Building, 1930. Until the erection of the Main Block the College had no on-site teaching facilites and was forced to avail of lecture rooms at nearby Queen's University and the Municipal College of Technology.

COLLEGE LIBRARY

OPPOSITE RIGHT:

The Principal's House (now Lagan Lodge) was built in 1934 to Thomas Rippingham's design. During World War Two it served as the Officers' Mess for the RAMC.

CROWN COPYRIGHT

RIGHT:

The Henry Garrett Building. Designed by Thomas Rippingham, 'the unsung hero of the site', the 'Henry Garrett' combines wartime economy construction with a unique double height entrance porch.

COLLEGE LIBRARY

A rare aerial view of the Stranmillis campus in the 1950s. Note the expanse of the Bungalow Hostels between the Main Building and Stranmillis House.

COLLEGE LIBRARY

A striking feature of the building on its official opening in May 1930 was the colour scheme used in the entrance hall: this included Tuscan columns in a vivid Pompeian red, with shining black bases set against cream walls. The ground floor plan included a gymnasium, the Principal's office, a Committee Room which housed the library, and specialist rooms for Needlework and Domestic Science. On the first floor was the Central Hall (now the Conference Room), flanked by lecture theatres and staff rooms while the upper storey contained a science laboratory, art room and a 'Cinema Projection Room', designed for projecting films to the Central Hall. On the top floor the long corridor was lighted by two spectacular ocular windows, a unique feature of the overall structure.[55]

The visitor to the Main Building at Stranmillis cannot fail to be touched by its architectural beauty. As the leading architectural historian, Dr Paul Larmour has observed: 'All in all, this is a building of some quality, particularly in its exterior treatment, and must rank high in the inter-war architecture of Northern Ireland'. The cost of constructing and equipping it was £179,025. A year later the College acquired an 18 acre site near Balmoral Hall for £5,000 and a rugby pitch and pavilion was provided.

In 1934, the 'Principal's House' was built up the hill from the main block. This two-storey white-walled residence was given a slightly Mediterranean look by its designer, the eclectic Thomas Rippingham. To complete the approach to the Main Building, Rippingham also designed the present front lodge, a low rustic brick bungalow behind a curved screen wall. This was a far cry from the original picturesque building with its Tudor-style gables. The new entrance of Portland stone pillars with moulded capstones and ceremonial urns was the work of Ingleby-Smith.

No further alterations were made to the Stranmillis buildings or grounds until 1939 when the College uprooted to Portrush and the buildings on the site were adapted for use as a military hospital. Balmoral Hall was also pressed into wartime emergency service and its playing fields transformed into allotments and leased to the Garden Plots Association. When restored to the College in 1946, these fields were reconditioned to include pitches for rugby, soccer and hockey, as well as three tennis courts.

POST-WAR DEVELOPMENTS

The post-war years saw a major physical expansion of the College with the erection of new buildings in the grounds. The first of these was the Henry Garrett Building, designed in 1944 by Rippingham and named in honour of a former chairman of the College Committee. Owing to wartime shortages, the 'Henry Garrett' was built without using wood and was capped with a concrete roof. Originally the building centred on a two-storey gymnasium, flanked by lower wings of lecture rooms and joined to art and handicraft rooms by means of short covered passages. The whole structure, skilfully added to by Rippingham in 1953, was plain yet subtle. A noteworthy feature is the double height entrance porch, set in a gracefully bowed wall.

Rippingham's hand is also evident in the back gate-lodge dating from 1949, and replacing the Victorian lodge. This 'dinky little brick building', with its pyramidal roof and copper-clad dormers, has been compared to the lodges at Parliament Buildings, Stormont.

In the immediate post-war years, the dramatic rise in student numbers, along with the continued use of Balmoral Hall by the civil service, necessitated the extension of student accommodation. By 1945, two houses had been acquired in Beechlands Avenue for use as a men's hostel and, for a time, accommodation for male students was provided at the Presbyterian Memorial Hostel, Howard Street, in the city centre. Stranmillis House and 'the Bungalows' continued to service the women students and were augmented by the Beechlands houses once Balmoral Hall re-opened as the men's hostel in the late 1940s.

The introduction in 1948 of three-and four-year courses of training underlined the need to expand the campus still further. In 1952–53, the structure known as 'The English Building', (later the Orchard Building) was erected on the slope leading to 'Sir Moses's Cellars'. Built of aluminium and of a design then widely used in school construction, the 'Orchard' remains an interesting, if rather uninspiring, relic of 1950s' 'austerity' architecture. Over the years it has housed a number of departments, amongst them English, Music, Geography and Art, but its main claim to posterity must be as the first home of the Students' Representative Council. The new building, however, did not solve the problems caused by ever-increasing student numbers and local church halls at Fisherwick Presbyterian on the Malone Road and St Bartholomew's Church of Ireland at Stranmillis had to be adapted as classrooms and gymnasia.

THE 1960S AND 1970S

To meet the challenge the College's Management Committee drew up a comprehensive development plan which envisaged the total transformation of the site over a ten-year period. This phased rebuilding programme won the approval of the Northern Ireland government. In March 1960 the

A cricket match at Stranmillis Sports Centre, *c.* 1967. Despite the short playing season, the move to Shaw's Bridge gave cricket a presence in the College sporting calendar.

COLLEGE LIBRARY

BELOW:
The Dining Centre and Halls of Residence, 1970.

COLLEGE LIBRARY

Minister of Education, Morris May assured parliament that 'no time will be lost in seeing that the needs of Stranmillis are adequately met'.

As a result of this commitment Stranmillis experienced the most dramatic expansion in its history. In 1966, a new 33-acre Sports Centre was opened at Shaw's Bridge, two miles from the campus. In the following year, Stranmillis House was converted from a women's hostel to its present role as a Senior Common Room for staff, and Students' Union Offices. This required the alteration of the entrance and the re-modelling of the staircase.

One of the first priorities of management was the establishment of modern Halls of Residence to replace the outmoded 'Bungalow Hostels', erected as temporary dwellings 42 years earlier. The site chosen for the new halls was on the hill slope below the farm buildings, overlooking the hockey pitches. Fortunately, the planners rejected the current vogue of tower-blocks in favour of a series of low-rise buildings, designed to blend more harmoniously into the rustic landscape. Because of the marshy condition of the land, an enormous amount of piling was necessary before construction work could

Laying the foundations of the Music Block in 1969. This unique, almost free-standing, circular building is a minor architectural triumph. The panels of mosaic pebbles relieve the flat concrete finish of the rest of the structure.

Central Building with the circular Music department in the foreground, 1970.

begin in 1966. A side-effect of this project was the laying down of what was to become a permanent ring-road around the Malone end of the campus, erected initially for the transportation of earth and building materials.

Finally, in February 1968, the six halls, together with a new dining centre were opened to students. Each hall was named after an important historic or archaeological site in one of the six counties of Northern Ireland: for Tyrone, Arboe, celebrated for its magnificent tenth-century High Cross; for Londonderry, Culmore, with its Plantation fort; for Fermanagh, Devenish, with its monastic round tower; for Armagh, Navan, the ancient capital of Ulster; for Antrim, Dunseverick, the ancient capital of Dal Riada; for Down, Nendrum, with its Celtic monastery once sacked by the Vikings. The new halls had accommodation for 450 men and women students.

The new dining block was designed as the focal point of social life for the student body and remains so today. It includes both a large self-service canteen and a formal dining room as well as television and games rooms and a student laundry.

Meanwhile, 1968–69 saw the clearance of the 'Bungalow Hostels' to make way for the Central Building. Completed in 1970, the new four-storey structure became the main teaching block for many departments including Mathematics, Science, History, Geography, English and Music as well as a spacious College library. The Central Building included a 'state-of-the-art' Drama Theatre with seating for 350 and an almost free-standing circular building for the Music Department. This amphitheatre, containing studios and a recital room, stands out as a minor architectural masterpiece. The building is an illustration of the versatility of concrete construction. As the architectural historian, Hugh Dixon, observes: 'Concrete rarely looks attractive, but here it is concealed behind applied panels of mosaic pebbles. Between these, windows, like facets, catch the light and give the whole building a lively extra dimension'.[56]

Another novel feature is the central quadrangle with its shrubs and trees, ensuring that every room in the block enjoys a view of the sylvan beauty of the surroundings. The cost of the Central Building was £750,000.

A PRICELESS HERITAGE

Throughout the dramatic expansion of the 1960s, the College authorities took care to preserve the attractive woodland setting of Stranmillis. The result has been to conserve what has been justly described as 'a priceless heritage of well-wooded landscape and some very fine buildings'.[57]

The unique history and hidden beauty of the College grounds is now officially recognised with the Department of the Environment's incorporation of the site in the Stranmillis Conservation Area. Under the 1991 Planning (Northern Ireland) Order, the campus has been designated part of 'an area of special architectural or historic interest, the character of which it is desirable to preserve and enhance'. This special status should ensure that the last vestiges of Lady Donegall's Deer Park and Sir Moses Hill's demesne survive to be enjoyed by future generations of students and visitors alike.[58]

'By the Pleasant Stream' 8
The Natural Environment

LANDSCAPE

The attraction of the College grounds lies not only in their extensiveness and quintessentially 'rural' atmosphere. They are also unique in the richness of their topography spanning marsh, woodland and stream. 'Stranmillis Hill', which provided a superb setting for Stranmillis House, is a summit on a long sinuous ridge of glacial drift which stretches from the university in a south-westerly direction to the The Maze beyond Lisburn. The section skirting the river from Stranmillis to Barnett's Park, is known as 'Malone ridge'.

The uneven spread of the drift deposited by the melting ice-sheet, some two million years ago, accounts for the undulating nature of the present College grounds. The ridge is composed of glacial sands and gravels, giving rise to sandy soils on the higher parts of the grounds and heavier boulder clay at lower levels.

The depressions on the estate, particularly 'the Pond' near the rear driveway, and the 'Marsh' to the north of the Orchard

The 46 acre site retains a unique rural quality in its blend of woodland, meadow and marsh.

Building, are interesting. They were undoubtedly formed by the melting of isolated blocks of ice covered by a veneer of glacial debris. As the ice slowly melted subsidence occurred and the College Pond is a 'kettle-hole' formed in this way.

It would seem that post-glacial meandering and erosion by the River Lagan against the base of the ridge, prior to the building of embankments and local roads, could partly account for the steep gradients from the Main Entrance to Stranmillis House. The deceptively level ground fronting the Main Building is an artificial landscaping feature dating from the establishment of the College in the 1920s.[59]

WILD PLANTS: NON-FLOWERING PLANTS

The shady damp micro-climate of Stranmillis woods provides suitable conditions for several species of moss, for the common Liverwort, and for at least one species of fern, the Male Fern, a large coarse-growing plant that dies back to a root stock in winter. Most of the tree trunks and branches have patches of green on their bark, due to the growth of the powdery green alga, Pleurococcus; other patches are grey-green due to growth of smooth powdery lichens.

Small ferns also grow on the old walls near the stableyard. In the mortar of these walls are rooted two species of fern common to this situation, Wall Rue and Maidenhair Spleenwort.

In early autumn, rotten tree trunks and dead branches come alive with interesting fungi. There is a short spell of a few weeks when it is possible to see quite a wide variety of fungus types.

FLOWERING PLANTS

The grounds offer a variety of habitats for flowering plants, so that the common types found in woodland marsh, grassland, and stone walls may be found.

In the wood, the flowers found in the largest numbers are the yellow Lesser Celandine, followed by white Wood Sorrel and Wood Anemones. In the wood between the Henry Garrett Building and the old stable yard, sizeable patches of Winter Heliotrope scent the air in early February. The Common Helleborine can be found widely throughout the grounds.

On the stone walls, the dominant plant is the Ivy-leafed Toadflax, covered with delightful mauve flowers in May and June. The boundary walls are also festooned with Wall Lettuce.

On the lawns, as well as the ubiquitous Daisy, there are carpets of blue

during the summer, the flowers of the creeping Speedwell.

Associated with the flowering plants is the usual range of nectar-seeking insects, but the insect population of the grounds has never been surveyed in detail, and much interesting work remains to be done.

THE MARSH AREA

The marsh on the north-west side of the grounds is a botanist's delight. It has been kept moist over the centuries by the outflow from the Vice-Chancellor's lakes adjoining the Stranmillis estate. The area is bounded on three sides by trees. This sheltered and warm location ensures a luxuriant flowering of marsh plants in the spring and summer. Plants which immediately catch the eye are the flat, strong, tall grey-green leaves of the Reedmace (often commonly called the Bulrush): the clear green of the water Horsetail, and at the west end large tussocks of Padicled Sedge. Creeping Buttercup and the Cuckoo-Flower or Lady's Smock abound, alongside Dandelion, marsh thistles and grasses such as Sweet Vernal and Meadow Foxtail.

In at least two places in the marsh, badger walks wind their way from the setts in the woods to the reedy area below the north driveway.

The number and variety of trees in the College grounds are a tribute to the

The approach to Stranmillis House from the Dining Centre is a blaze of colour in summer. On the right is the Victorian residence of the Head Gardener.

vision of the Victorian planners of the estate. Very little timber has been lost because of building developments and much has been added, so that there is a pleasant mixture of 'garden' trees, which delight the eye with their blossoms in spring and summer, and 'wild' trees, including most of the common species found in Ireland. Significantly, even during the severe timber shortage of the Second World War, the Principal, H E Winn, rejected a proposal for a large-scale felling of Scots Pine. As the minutes of the Stranmillis Training College Committee for October 1942, note: 'the Principal ... felt that the Spanish Chestnut, which is the only one in the grounds, should not be cut down, and that only two beech, two sycamore and one elm should be cut'.[60]

The sylvan beauty of the College grounds.
CROWN COPYRIGHT

Probably the finest tree in the grounds is a Turkey Oak which is, perhaps 150 years old, and stands opposite the Warden's houses. It is a native of southern Europe and Asia Minor and is widely grown in estates and gardens. The acorn-cups are mossy, unlike those of the Common Oak. The Copper Beech, near the former Principal's House, is also an impressive tree even if it is showing signs of ageing.

Most trees common in Ireland have been introduced from other countries. Some, like the Sycamore, have become naturalised, while others such as the Spanish Chestnut do not seem to have become well established except in certain areas. The Spanish Chestnuts at Stranmillis in most years produce only very small fruits due to the local climate. Generally, however, the grounds offer a suitable environment for growing trees and shrubs with both soil and climate appealing to widely different species. For example, the Arbutus (Strawberry Tree - native only in County Kerry as far as the British Isles are concerned) flowers and fruits in the wooded area between the Main Building and the former Principal's House. A mature specimen of the Tulip Tree (native to North America) grows at the back of the College Hall. From Australia come Eucalyptus trees and from New Zealand the evergreen Griselina or New Zealand Broadleaf. A handkerchief tree near the pathway up the 'hill' produces its 'handkerchief'-like flowers in May.

Many of the trees are marked by unusual blemishes called galls. These growths look rather like birds' nests but are commonly known as Witches Brooms. A number of large Willow trees border the path running from the tennis-courts to Beechlands.

THE BADGERS

Because very few people have actually seen them, it is hard to believe that there are badgers living inscrutably in the College grounds, a mere three kilometres from the centre of Belfast, and only a hundred metres or so from the College buildings. Badgers are known to have lived in these grounds for over a hundred years.

The badger is a large animal, about one metre in length, though low on the ground because of its short legs. Its coat of coarse hair is grey-fawn in colour, and on its head it is strikingly marked with black and white. Badgers are normally not seen in the grounds, because they are nocturnal animals, remaining underground in their burrows or 'setts' in the daytime, and emerging only at night, when they come out to hunt for food.

The College badger setts can be seen at the foot of the wood that lies between the marsh area and Riddell Hall grounds. The mounds of earth excavated by the badgers are sandy, and remain as large humps at the mouth of the setts. This is a typical site for badgers, well-drained ground on a steep slope, backed by woodland. In Spring, the hay and leaves used for bedding can be seen outside the sett, thrown out, to be replaced with fresh bedding later. The sett is kept very clean. The

One of Stranmillis's hidden delights: the tree-lined walk from the tennis courts to the Dining Centre.

badgers' 'latrine' is always some distance from the sett, a shallow hole specially dug for the purpose.

From the setts, badger tracks, like narrow footpaths, can be traced through the wood, some into Riddell Hall grounds, some through the marsh, and some can also be seen in the trees between the Halls of Residence and the grounds of Northern Ireland Electricity. Sometimes paw-marks can be found in muddy places.

Near these tracks, there are often signs of scratching or digging in the earth. A badger's food consists largely of grubs and other insects – earthworms, bulbs and fleshy roots. In the woods at Stranmillis are plenty of tuberous roots of the Lesser Celandine and some Bluebell bulbs, for which badgers dig. Occasionally the eggs and young of ground-nesting birds may be taken.

Badgers have few enemies, and fear only humans and dogs. To watch them, the observer must take up a position some metres away from the sett, just before dusk. Eventually the badger may emerge from the sett, look about him, and then amble off along one of the tracks. In early summer, the family of young may come out to play in front of the sett. During winter, however, the badger can remain underground completely during periods of severe weather.

OTHER MAMMALS

Other mammals found 'on campus' include the red fox. Like the badger, it is secretive but an early morning or late evening walk anywhere in the grounds can be rewarded with a sighting.

Rabbits abounded until the mid-1980s but have died out due to myxomatosis. Around that time red squirrels first visited Stranmillis, possibly having spread from Belvoir Park Forest. They are seen frequently now, along with their close relative, the grey squirrel.

Bats may be observed, swooping low on summer evenings, while the woodland shields wood mice and the pygmy shrew.

BIRDS

The wealth of the College grounds in natural history terms stems largely from the relative stability of the site and ecosystem since the earliest times. Its pleasant non-urban character is reflected in the bird population today.

Given terrain which combines parkland, generous tree cover, (deciduous

and coniferous), considerable shrub growth and a pond, it is not surprising to find the list of birds include Mallard and Moorhen, Woodpigeon, Collared Dove as well as many of the common resident small birds, such as the Robin, the Goldcrest, the Tits and Finches. Also found at Stranmillis are some of the larger species such as Hooded Crow, Jackdaw and Magpie. The Hooded Crow nests, somewhat noisily, in the trees near the Central Building. Migrants are represented by the Blackcap, Willow Warbler and Chiffchaff in the spring and summer, while in winter Redwing and Fieldfare are common. Another occasional visitor, presumably from the Lagan, is the Kingfisher, which often stays at the pond for lengthy periods. The Jay is now resident all year round.

The pond has always been a unique feature of the College grounds. Here Biology students record the plant life on an autumn day in the early 1970s.

HORTICULTURE

The regional climate and the relatively sheltered position of Stranmillis grounds make it possible to grow a very wide range of plants from all over the world. There are trees and shrubs from Australia and New Zealand, the Americas, and the Himalayas, as well as from all over continental Europe. Most of these have been raised from seeds, sown by students or members of staff, or by cuttings gathered from other Irish gardens; only a few have been bought in from nurseries. Of particular interest are two 'fossil trees', the Maidenhair Tree and the Water Fir. These are now growing between Stranmillis House and the College Hall. The Maidenhair Tree is of older lineage than the Water Fir and is one of the connecting links between flowerless and flowering plants. The Water Fir is considered to have grown in the Mesozoic Age – about 130 million years ago. It was discovered in China in 1945.

'The Vice-Chancellor's Lakes', adjoining the College grounds, provided Belfast's early water supply.

CROWN COPYRIGHT

THE COLLEGE POND

The Pond lies like a basin-like depression. For many years the area was left untouched but in recent decades Mallards, Moorhens, and Dabchicks have nested there while small birds use the bushes for cover.

A glimpse of paradise: the
parterres of flowers and herbs in
the shadow of the Victorian
stables and farm buildings.

THE VICE-CHANCELLOR'S LAKES

While not part of the Stranmillis estate, no survey of the natural environment would be complete without some account of the 'Vice-Chancellor's
Lakes' which adjoin the campus on its north-western side.

From the roadway to the north side of the Orchard Building, the Vice-
Chancellor's lakes can be glimpsed through the trees. The lakes are two
quiet and attractive stretches of water, covering an area of over an acre. An
overflow from the larger lake runs into Stranmillis grounds and feeds a small
stream which traverses the marsh area.

The lakes had a unique role in the development of Belfast's early water-
supply. Until 1840 the Belfast Charitable Society was responsible for sup-
plying the growing industrial town with water. In 1794 the Society was

advised to inspect the Malone Springs and also a spring at 'Strand Miles' or Stranmillis. In 1806 they decided to use the Stranmillis supply. The 'Strandmile Dam' is today the Vice-Chancellor's lake. The spring fell into the dam on the west side and the water course went completely round the dam on the western side, then in a northerly direction under the Stranmillis Road to the Botanic Park, after which it emerged at the Rugby Road end of the Botanic Gardens and curved-eastward and northward. As a result of complaints about the bad taste of the water, ascribed to decaying vegetation in the dam, the lake had to be emptied and deepened in 1819.

There was further trouble in 1826, when the reservoir still proved unsatis-factory, and as the level was not rising sufficiently to fill the water course, pumps had to be used. In 1831 an engineer was dismissed because the water course had been neglected. The Spring Water Commissioners reported: 'The pipe which conveys the water across Strand Mills road near Mr Black's entrance (Stranmillis House) was nearly closed up. We found in it an old tea-kettle and a mass of vegetable substance …'[61]

By 1840, the use of the lakes for Belfast's water supply had been discontin-ued. It was not until 1901, however, that the first Mourne water was pumped to the city.

Towards the Future 9

Throughout the first seventy-five years of its history, the greatest achievement of Stranmillis has been to produce teachers of quality, commitment and vision. As the eminent educationist, Sir William Taylor observed in his lecture to mark the College's seventy-fifth anniversary in September 1997: 'The quality of the teachers in our schools remains the single most important factor in providing each and every child with opportunities to develop his or her talents to the full'.[62]

The impact of 'Stran'-trained teachers has touched large sections of Northern Ireland society through the primary and secondary schools system. Many have plied their skills overseas in Canada, the United States, the African continent and Australasia, as well as in Great Britain and the Republic of Ireland.

Over the years many Stranmillis graduates have made their mark in other fields apart from education. A number have become ministers of religion in the Presbyterian Church, Church of Ireland and other denominations. Several have gained prominence in the media. Amongst these are Dr James Hawthorne, former Controller of BBC Northern Ireland,

Professor Sir William Taylor CBE delivering the 75th anniversary lecture, September 1997.

COLLEGE LIBRARY

Jim Neilly, the well-known sports broadcaster and Alastair Jackson of RTE. In the field of politics former 'Stran' alumni include two Westminster MPs, Ken Maginnis and Roy Beggs of the Ulster Unionist Party, Dermot Nesbitt, Unionist Assembly Member and a signatory of the 1998 Belfast Agreement, and Oliver Gibson, a Democratic Unionist Assembly Member.

Over the decades since 1922 the influence of Stranmillis College on Northern Ireland society and culture has been wide-ranging and profound. But the dawn of the new millennium, the College's new relationship with Queen's University and the changing context of politics and society in Northern Ireland itself, will bring their own challenges. Having celebrated three quarters of a century of excellence as a teacher education institution, Stranmillis College now aspires to a different future in which teacher education will remain a core activity but will be matched by a whole spectrum of undergraduate and post-graduate courses, often unrelated to the teaching profession. Not only will the College's title hopefully reflect its new university-level status, but it is anticipated that student numbers will expand to over a thousand. All of this will entail a change in Stranmillis's cultural ethos.[63]

Stranmillis College can have no direct political role. However, as Sir William Taylor has observed, the College's 'principal and indispensable contribution is as a source of the knowledge, competence and understanding essential for a solution of the problems that stand in the way of a happier future for all the people of the United Kingdom and of Ireland'. Thus Stranmillis sees itself responding positively both to the new political arrangements and opportunities arising from the Good Friday Agreement of April 1998 and its provision for a devolved partnership administration in Northern Ireland.

The new strategic and academic partnership with Queen's University will bring its own challenges and rewards. But Stranmillis, as a university sector college, will not rest content as a mere 'outpost' of the university. 'Stran', while integrated academically with Queen's, will retain its proud identity and organisational autonomy. The College's past record of excellence will be maintained and extended to a whole new range of academic courses. At the same time, the College will endeavour to make a vital contribution to a solution of the problems of this society through Education for Mutual Understanding and other initiatives, while building bridges to our sister colleges within these islands and the wider European Community.

The aims of Stranmillis for the coming decades are perhaps best expressed in the College's proposed new Mission Statement: 'to promote excellence in the education of its students through teaching, scholarship and research of the highest quality, and to help meet the professional needs of the community'. As Sir William Taylor reminded the College in his anniversary address: 'It is by building on the work of the first seventy-five years, and by responding to the challenges of the next, that the best hope lies for staying ahead in what H G Wells described as the race between education and catastrophe'.

Facing the future: (from right) Professor Richard McMinn, Principal, Stranmillis College, with Right Rev Dr Samuel Hutchinson, Moderator of the Presbyterian Church in Ireland and Rev Professor Martin O'Callaghan, Principal of St Mary's College, at the 75th Anniversary service in St Bartholomew's Parish Church, September 1997.

DR R CROMIE

Appendix 1

COLLEGE PRINCIPALS

1922–30	Professor W J McCallister
1931–55	H E Winn
1956–70	Alexander Keith
1970–84	James Pomfret
1984–93	Dr R J Rodgers
1993–	Professor J R B McMinn

Appendix 2

COLLEGE VICE PRINCIPALS / DEPUTY PRINCIPALS

VICE PRINCIPALS

1949–69	Major K G P Pomeroy
1964–82	Miss Clare Macmahon

DEPUTY PRINCIPALS

1970–82	Colonel James Hughes
1982–85	Miss Clare Macmahon
1985–91	James Greenwood
1991–94	Alan Dinsmore
1994–98	Miss S E Magowan

References

1   John A McIvor, Popular Education in the Irish Presbyterian Church, (Dublin, 1969), p. 149; Susan M Parkes, *Kildare Place: the history of the Church of Ireland Training College 1811–1969*, (Dublin, 1984), pp. 17-85.

2   John Magee, in E Phoenix (ed), *A Century of Northern Life*, (Belfast, 1995), 'From National Schools to National Curriculum', p. 103; D H Akenson, *The Irish Education Experiment: the National System of Education in the Nineteenth Century* (London, 1970), pp. 258-9, 326-7; J W Musson, 'The training of teachers in Ireland from 1811 to the present day', Ph D thesis, QUB, 1955, pp. 44-65, 264–280.

3   Ronald Marshall, Stranmillis College Belfast 1922–1972, (Belfast 1972), pp. 4-7.

4   *The Blue Bird: The Chronicle of the King's Scholars in the Northern Training College, Belfast*, No. 1, Michaelmas Term, 1922, (Stranmillis College Library).

5   T W Moody and J C Beckett, *Queen's, Belfast 1845-1949: The History of a University*, vol. II (London, 1959), pp. 587-8.

6   Marshall, *op.cit.*, pp.6-9; Interview with Mr L L Bell, MBE, Portadown, June 1998.

7   *Irish News*, 19 April, 1925.

8   Sean Farren, *The Politics of Irish Education*, (Belfast, 1995), p. 52.

9   *Irish News*, 11 May 1924; *Newtownards Chronicle*, 17 May 1924.

10   *Ibid.*, 7 June 1925.

11   Report of the Ministry of Education for Northern Ireland, 1930-31, p. 26.

12   *Northern Whig*, 2 May 1930.

13   *Belfast News Letter*, 2 May 1930.

14   *Northern Whig*, 2 May 1930.

15   *Belfast Telegraph*, 1 May 1930.

16   Interview with Mrs S E Mawhinney, Broughshane, County Antrim, 28 October 1997.

17   D H Akenson, *Education and Enmity: The Control of Schooling in Northern Ireland 1920–50*, (Belfast, 1973), p.125; Farren, *op. cit.*, p.132.

18   Akenson, *op. cit.*, p.125.

19   Akenson, *op. cit.*, p.126.

20   Akenson, *op. cit.*, pp. 131-2; Marshall, *op. cit.*, p. 12; Farren, *op. cit.*, p. 132.

21   Cited in Akenson, *op. cit.*, p.132.

22   T H Ellis, *Noisy Mansions* , (Lisnaskea, 1980), p. 29; Minutes of Stranmillis Training College Committee, 7 September 1939.

23   Principal's Report for 1939-40; Minutes of Stranmillis Training College Committee, 7 September 1939, 20 September 1939, 17 July 1941 (Stranmillis College Archives).

24   Ellis, *op. cit.*, pp. 32-3.

25   Ellis, *op. cit.*, p. 35.

26   Letter to authors from Mrs Adelaide Stevens (née Bell), Buckinghamshire, 25 April 1995; Minutes of Stranmillis Training College Committee, 14 November 1939.

27 Interview with Miss Margaret Shilliday, Bangor, May, 1998; Report of Principal (to Training College Committee), 30 September 1942.

28 Ellis, *op. cit.*, p. 30.

29 Letter from Mrs Gwen Thompson (née Craig), Benoni, South Africa, June 1995.

30 Information based on research by Col. James Hughes, CBE, DL, (former Deputy Principal of Stranmillis College) and Commonwealth War Graves Commission.

31 Ellis, *op. cit.*, pp. 38.

32 *Ulster Teachers' Union Bulletin*, October 1945; information from Mr Barry Lloyd, June 1995.

33 Minutes of Stranmillis Training College Committee, 27 April 1944.

34 Minutes of Stranmillis Training College Committee, 18 April 1940.

35 Letter from Mrs Gwen Thompson, *ibid.*

36 Akenson, *op. cit.*, pp. 151, 261.

37 Marshall, *op. cit.*, p. 31.

38 Marshall, *op. cit.*, pp. 14-21.

39 The Future of Higher Education in N. Ireland: Report of the Higher Education Review Group for Northern Ireland (Chairman: Sir Henry Chilver) (HMSO, Belfast, January 1982). Submission to the Higher Education Review Group on behalf of the Board of Governors and Academic Board of Stranmillis College, 29 March 1979 (College Library). Stranmillis College Board of Governors' response to the Interim Report of the Higher Education Review Group, May 1980 (College Library).

40 *Irish News*, 23 December 1982.

41 DENI circular 1982/ 21, 1 June 1982; DENI circular 1987/47, 13 October 1987; DENI circular 1988/ 2, 22 January 1988; *Education for Mutual Understanding: A Guide*, (Northern Ireland Council for Educational Development, 1988).

42 *Belfast Telegraph, Irish News*, 27 November 1987.

43 Report of the Working Party to review relationships between QUB and St Mary's and Stranmillis Colleges (1997).

44 This account is based on Marshall, *op. cit.*, pp. 41-97; Stranmillis College Prospectuses 1928-97; interviews with Mr J D Cameron, (former Senior Tutor (Schools), Stranmillis College, June 1998), and Mr W J McClure, (former Head of Education), June 1998.

45 This chapter draws on Marshall's account and information kindly provided by Mr Jimmy Davidson, Mrs Sheila Callaghan, Mr George Blackwood, Miss Judith Herbison, Dr Gertrude Patterson, Mr Hamish Fyfe, Mr Charles Mount, Dr Harry Grindle, Mr John McDowell, Mr Hugh Storey. We are indebted to Mr Thompson Steele and Mrs Maureen Steele who provided the Minutes of the Field Study Society, 1957–62.

46 E Phoenix, *Two Acres of Irish History: Friar's Bush and Belfast 1570–1918*, (Belfast, 1988), pp. 7–9.

47 *A Guide to the College Grounds*, (Stranmillis College, 1974), p. 4.

48 S T Carleton, 'The growth of south Belfast', MA thesis (QUB, 1967), pp. 5–15.

49 Marshall, *op. cit.*, pp. 23–4.

50 Marshall, *op. cit.*; J A K Dean, *The Gate Lodges of Ulster: A Gazetteer*, (Belfast, 1994), p. 29.

51 *Adair's Belfast Directory 1860–61* (Belfast, 1860), p.215; *Belfast and District Directory for 1878* (Belfast, 1878); *Belfast and Ulster Directory for 1890* (Belfast, 1890); *Belfast and Province of Ulster Directory for 1897* (Belfast, 1897).

52   Marshall, *op. cit.*, p. 24.

53   Marshall, *op. cit.*, pp. 24–26.

54   Anniversary Lecture by Dr Paul Larmour, QUB, at Stranmillis College,
      21 April 1998.

55   P Larmour, *The Architectural Heritage of Malone and Stranmillis*, (Belfast, 1991),
      pp. 164–170; H Dixon, *An Introduction to Ulster Architecture*, (Belfast, 1975), p. 79.

56   Dixon, *op. cit.*, p. 87.

57   P Larmour, Anniversary Lecture, 21 April 1998.

58   *Stranmillis Conservation Area*, (DOENI, 1996), pp. 2–8.

59   *A Guide to the College Grounds*, *op. cit.*, *passim*. The authors are grateful to Dr Julian
      Greenwood (Head of Science) and Mr Jim Rutherford (Head Gardener) for
      their assistance.

60   Minutes of Stranmillis Training College Committee, 14 October 1942.

61   R W M Strain, *Belfast and its Charitable Society*, (Oxford, 1961), pp. 195–211.

62   'And gladly teache'; a lecture to commemorate the 75th Anniversary of the founding
      of Stranmillis College, by Professor Sir William Taylor, CBE, 17 September 1997.

63   Stranmillis College Strategic Development Plan, 1998–2001, *passim*.

Bibliography

PRIMARY SOURCES

Donegall Estate Map 1770, (Public Record Office of Northern Ireland,
L'Estrange and Brett Collection, Map 18, Ref. No. D835/1/3/18)
Minutes of Stranmillis Training College Committee of Management
(Stranmillis College)
Minutes of Stranmillis Training College Field Study Society (Stranmillis College)
Reports and Minutes of College Clubs (Stranmillis College)
Annual Reports of the Ministry of Education for Northern Ireland
Report of the Working Party to review relationships between The Queen's University
of Belfast and St Mary's and Stranmillis Colleges (Stranmillis College)
Stranmillis College Prospectuses (Stranmillis College)
Stranmillis College Strategic Development Plan 1998-2001, 1998 (Stranmillis College)
*The Blue Bird: The Chronicle of the King's Scholars in the Northern Training College,
Belfast*, No 1, Michaelmas Term 1922, (Stranmillis College)

Adair's Belfast Directory 1860–61 (Belfast, 1860)
Belfast and District Directory for 1878 (London & Belfast,1878)
Belfast and Province of Ulster Directory for 1884 (Belfast, 1884)
Belfast and Ulster Directory, 1890 (Belfast, 1890)
Belfast and Province of Ulster Directory for 1897 (Belfast, 1897)

DENI Circulars,1982/21, 1 June 1982; 1987/47, 13 October 1987;
1988/2, 22 January 1988
Report of the Gibbon Committee, (Belfast, 1947)
Report of the Lockwood Committee, (Belfast, 1965)
Report of the Working Party on Higher Education (Chilver Report, Belfast, 1982)
Education for Mutual Understanding: A Guide, (Belfast, Northern Ireland Council
for Educational Development, 1988)
'And gladly teache', Address by Professor Sir William Taylor, CBE, Stranmillis College,
17 September 1997

Stranmillis College: A Guide to the College Grounds, 1974
Stranmillis Conservation Area, (Belfast DOENI, 1996)
Ulster Teachers' Union, *Bulletin*, October 1945

Belfast News Letter
Belfast Telegraph
Irish News
Newtownards Chronicle
Northern Whig

Interviews with Mr L L Bell, MBE, Mr J D Cameron, Mr W J McClure,
Mrs S E McDonough, Mrs S E Mawhinney, Miss M Shilliday, Mr T Steele

Correspondence from Miss C J Crawford, Col. James Hughes, CBE, KStJ, TD, DL, Mr Barry Lloyd, Mrs Adelaide Stevens, Mrs Gwen Thompson

SECONDARY SOURCES

D H AKENSON, *The Irish Education Experiment: The National System of Education in the Nineteenth Century*, (London, 1970)

D H AKENSON, *Education and Enmity: The Control of Schooling in Northern Ireland 1920–50*, (Belfast, 1973)

NORMAN ATKINSON, *Irish Education*, (Dublin,1969)

S A CARLETON, 'The growth of South Belfast', MA thesis, QUB, 1967

JOHN COOLAHAN, *Irish Education: history and structure*, (Dublin,1981)

J A K DEAN, *The Gate Lodges of Ulster: A Gazetteer*, (Belfast, 1994)

HUGH DIXON, *An Introduction to Ulster Architecture*, (Belfast, 1975)

T H ELLIS, *Noisy Mansions*, (Lisnaskea, 1980)

SEAN FARREN, *The Politics of Irish Education*, (Belfast, 1995)

PAUL LARMOUR, *The Architectural Heritage of Upper Malone and Stranmillis*, (Belfast, 1991)

J A McIVOR, *Popular Education in the Irish Presbyterian Church*, (Dublin, 1969)

RONALD MARSHALL, *Stranmillis College Belfast 1922–1972*, (Belfast, 1972)

T W MOODY & J C BECKETT, *Queen's, Belfast 1845–1949: The History of a University*, Vols. 1 & 2, (London, 1959)

J W MUSSON, 'The training of teachers in Ireland from 1811 to the present day', PhD thesis, QUB, 1955

S M PARKES, *Kildare Place: the history of the Church of Ireland Training College 1811–1969*, (Dublin, 1984)

EAMON PHOENIX, *Two Acres of Irish History: Friar's Bush and Belfast 1570–1918*, (Belfast, 1988)

EAMON PHOENIX, *A Century of Northern Life*, (Belfast, 1995)

RWM STRAIN, *Belfast and its Charitable Society*, (Oxford, 1961)

Keep it Cleaner (KIC) is a leading health and fitness app that delivers a holistic wellness program to your pocket. Through movement, mindfulness, nutrition and community, we help people find their personal recipe for a healthier, happier lifestyle. We believe that fitness can and should be enjoyable. It's not about looking a certain way; it's about how it makes you *feel*. Our philosophy is to empower people from all corners of the world to be confident in their skin. The app we've created together has everything you need, including yoga, Pilates, HIIT, strength, boxing, run programs, pre- and postnatal Pilates, guided meditations, dietitian-approved recipes and more!
Every journey is different, but no matter where you are on yours, KIC is here to support you.

You Take Care

You take Care

Laura Henshaw & Steph Claire Smith

murdoch books
Sydney | London

Contents

Welcome to *You Take Care*

Our lives have been enriched by some incredible people and the lessons they've taught us. Now, it's time to pass what we've learned on to you.

Keep it cleaner

We're the proud co-founders of Keep it Cleaner (KIC), and creating expert-led content about health and fitness is something we are passionate about. In our business, we team up with an outstanding line-up of fitness, wellness and nutrition experts from across Australia to help build and grow our KIC program and community. Since its inception, we've been incredibly fortunate to experience first-hand the knowledge and advice from each of our experts. We've learned so much over the years, and this book is the perfect opportunity to pass our learnings on to you. These pages go far beyond the two of us; we're sharing the words of wisdom and tools from those who've inspired and educated us in the hope that it will do the same for you.

Throughout this book, we'll be opening up about the vulnerabilities, challenges and experiences that we've faced, and we'll also be coming together, as KIC, to explore our mutual learnings. The purpose of this book is to encourage you to find zest for life and love for yourself in your day-to-day. Health and wellness go beyond sleeping well,

6

eating nutritious foods, exercising and meditating, and though we'll be touching on each of those pillars in this book, we'll also be digging deeper to offer holistic support. *You Take Care* has three parts: Mind, Body and Connection. We believe that to not only survive but truly thrive, we need to nurture all three.

We're KIC'ing things off (sorry, couldn't resist) with Mind, which is packed with practical tips to challenge, nourish and empower your mind. Together, we'll dive deep into the damage done by comparison, and explore forms of anxiety that so many of us struggle with. We'll also talk to experts about how to move past these and explore the freedom waiting for you when you let go of the need for external validation.

Body confidence is something the two of us have struggled with, and we've worked hard to come out the other side. We share a passion for helping others learn to accept and appreciate their body for the amazing things it does, and this is the underlying message of the second part of the book, Body. We are big believers that moving your body shouldn't be a chore nor a punishment, and throughout this section we've shared the tools that have helped us fall in love with the way healthy living makes us *feel*.

The final third of the book is dedicated to connection because strong connections – at work and at home – are key to a fuller, happier life. We'll explore the many ways we connect with others: at work, in our platonic and romantic relationships, online and finally, with ourselves. We hope this part of the book will be a reminder to surround yourself with people who celebrate your uniqueness and bring out the best in you, and to say goodbye to those who don't.

You Take Care **has three parts: Mind, Body and Connection. We believe that to not only survive but truly thrive, we need to nurture all three.**

Although we've split the book into three parts, each one is leading towards one big overarching goal: encouraging you to take small, sustainable steps to prioritise yourself. We recognise that each of us is dealing with our own unique challenges; these might include issues with poor mental health, past trauma, a serious or chronic illness or a disability. There's no such thing as a one size fits all, step-by-step guide to happiness, so it's all about finding what works for you and letting go of what doesn't. Keep that in the back of your mind as you're reading this book. There may be tips and stories that truly resonate with you and other areas that don't, and that's okay. We hope that as you move through the different chapters of your own life, you can reflect on what you've read here or even come back to particular areas that are now relevant to you.

Take motherhood, for example. This has become a huge part of Steph's life since she fell pregnant with Harvey in 2020. Organically, Steph's experience helped us grow and flourish as a company in this brand-new space. Because of that, we've sprinkled helpful tips on pregnancy and new motherhood throughout this book, but we realise that this information won't be relevant to every reader. You may not be at this stage, so perhaps parenthood isn't even on your radar right now, or maybe you've experienced a loss and find the topic triggering. Whatever your situation, how, when and what you read is entirely up to you. *You Take Care* will be here for you whenever you're ready. We hope that you close this book feeling empowered to tune out the noise of how you 'should' live your life and tune in to your inner, truest self and live the life you want and deserve.

Laura

I've always had this desire to inspire and teach others how to live
a healthy, active and balanced lifestyle. I was lucky to grow up in a
family that was educated about health, but even that didn't protect
me from the toxic diet culture on social media. That, combined with
the pressures of working in the modelling industry, led to me spending
a big chunk of my early twenties struggling with disordered eating and
a negative body image. Thankfully, my mindset around healthy living
eventually changed, and I learned that it was about so much more than
just movement and nutrition. This is what drives me to speak up and
educate others on how to feel comfortable in their own skin. I want to
help others resist or reset that damaging mindset and focus on balance
in their health journey.

I started small by sharing my favourite healthy recipes on a blog.
That soon snowballed into an ebook, then a website, and then a fitness
program. Together with my best friend, business partner and co-author,
Steph, we expanded our passion project into Keep it Cleaner, which is
now one of Australia's leading health and wellness apps.

Behind the scenes, I live with my husband, Dalton, and my cheeky
golden retrievers, Bill and Ben. As a business and law graduate, one
of the things I'm proudest of is the way I've been able to learn to
juggle my studies with the demands of running a global business. I'm
incredibly grateful that I get to pursue other interests while having a job
that empowers hundreds of thousands of people on a daily basis. It's
honestly a dream come true.

As proud as I am of being able to juggle these two worlds, recent years
have taught me that I can't do it all. The last half of 2020 and the start
of 2021 were, for me, some of the hardest months in my life so far with
how I felt about myself. The spark I once had was lost. The light inside
of me switched off, and I didn't know where the switch was. I hadn't
had to search for the switch before to turn it back on, and searching for
it again was a really confronting experience. I think one of the biggest
reasons for this was that I couldn't pinpoint the exact reason the light
had gone off. In my studies, I learned to problem solve: I'd locate the
problem and then apply the relevant legislation or solution. But when
I tried to apply this same approach to my life, I found it really difficult

because the problem wasn't clear. I knew I didn't feel like me. I had lost my confidence and felt less motivated, but I didn't know why. Originally, I thought it was due to the space the pandemic had given us to think. Without my commute, events and normal life things going on, there was a lot of quiet and a lot of time for thoughts to ring loud.

Looking back, while I do believe the feeling of numbness and hopelessness caused by the pandemic contributed to the way I was feeling, I think the main factor was that I'd been putting my self-worth into the hands of others and forgetting the importance of believing in myself first. I'd become so reliant on validation from others that I forgot what I was truly capable of.

There is no way that the 'me' of 2020 could have written these words. Not because I didn't have them in me or because I wasn't good enough, but because I did not believe I was good enough to write another book. I didn't feel I had anything to share that mattered. I was lost.

The thing about losing yourself is that there is no one-size-fits-all approach to finding yourself. We each have to do our own work to get back to a good place. I turned to podcasts, books and to some of the people around me who'd been there all along but had no idea of what I was going through. Steph and Dalton were my rocks, and I found the more I reached out to those people in my network for advice, the more I realised that self-doubt is a part of life. It's how loud we let that voice echo through our minds that truly matters. Everyone feels it, and it doesn't mean that we are flawed or that we can't take back control and our power if we speak about it.

There is no handbook or easy solution when life gets tough, but in these pages, we have shared some of the things that we have learned along the way – approaches and tips that have helped (and are still helping) us to take care of ourselves. Some of the thinking that got me through is in here, and if you are feeling lost or sucked into the vortex of self-doubt, first, I am so sorry, and second, it's my hope that some of the information collected here helps you the way other people's words have helped me. I hope we can help you reflect and see that you are exactly where you need to be right now and that you do, in fact, have the answers you are looking for. We want to help you build trust back in the most important relationship in your life: the one with yourself.

If you've ever felt as though you aren't worthy or capable of achieving great things, this book is for you. If you need to be reminded not to care so much about what other people think and instead focus on the things you can control, this book is for you. If you want to fill your cup first so you can continue to pour into everyone else's, this book is for you. Its purpose is to be a constant reminder of how great you really are. You are worthy of every success, of love, of fulfilment and finding your purpose. You are worthy and capable of it all.

Steph

I have to be honest: I'm pretty damn content with life right now. I'm an entrepreneur, model, wife and mum – a new one at that. Being happy used to be my goal in life, but my current goal is to continue being content. I'm still driven, I'm still a dreamer, but nothing has grounded me more than getting to a point in life where I feel not only grateful for all of my past experiences but also so grateful for the little things that make me smile each day. I'm that content right now that if this was all there'd ever be, I'd consider myself incredibly lucky and have zero FOMO.

Like Laura, I'm incredibly passionate about healthy living and body confidence. Early in my modelling career, it dawned on me that the industry was fuelling a misconception about what a 'healthy' body looks like. Rather than focusing on weight loss and fad diets, I was determined to create a platform that embraces different body shapes and sizes and promotes body positivity. Alongside my amazing business partner and best friend, Laura, Keep it Cleaner (my first baby) was born. I've established and helped grow a number of businesses since launching KIC and am constantly pinching myself for the incredible experiences and inspirational people I've had the pleasure to meet along the way.

Often, it's the things that make us nervous and the challenges we face that bring about the most discovery and growth.

My proudest achievement thus far, though, has been becoming a mum. It's a dream I've always had and, so far, it's been better than I ever imagined. Motherhood has been a magical roller-coaster ride. Every challenge I face is soon followed by deep belly laughs or tears of joy. The gratitude I feel for this opportunity is indescribable. While I'm grateful, I'm not immune to feeling scared, worried, stressed and lost at times. I take a lot of comfort in knowing I'm not alone in struggling through it, and I often reach out to our beautiful KIC community or my own close friends, who are mothers, for support.

Since becoming a mum, I've realised the insane level of judgement parents face and how unfair that is when there are so many different ways to do things. I'm learning every day, and I'm okay with the imperfectly perfect mum I'm developing into. Becoming a mum has motivated me to do my best, not only as a parent but also as an individual. I have a little being looking up to me and watching my every move, and this is scary and empowering at the same time.

Outside of work and being a mum, I place a lot of value on downtime. One of my favourite ways to unwind and get offline is to read novels that allow me to switch off, or self-help books, like this one, where I can learn something, find motivation and smile (or cry!) as I turn the pages.

I'm incredibly honoured to be writing another book but, if I'm honest, the early stages of writing this book weren't easy! Self-doubt truly got in my way whenever I sat down to write. I spend so much of my life encouraging people to believe in themselves and trust that they have something important to say. I give advice about not comparing yourself to others, yet I fell into the same traps myself. Thankfully, I was able to turn the corner and just do the damn thing. Often, it's the things that make us nervous and the challenges we face that bring about the most discovery and growth. I learned more about myself through writing this book, and reading Laura's words made me so proud – she was so open about her own vulnerabilities and learnings. I hope you finish this book feeling encouraged and motivated to be the version of yourself that you want to be, so you can live the life you deserve.

Make someone smile every day, but never forget that you are someone too.

— Tamara Kulish

HOLD ON TO THAT LITTLE **VOICE** INSIDE YOUR HEAD THAT TELLS YOU TO KEEP GOING. IT'S CALLED **STRENGTH.**

mind

In a survey with over 2500 KIC community members,
61 per cent believed that mental wellness is more important
than physical health, and we couldn't agree more.
It's time we prioritised our mental health.

From reframing shame to combating fear, preventing
burnout and discovering your values, this part of the book
is full of practical tips to help your mind thrive.

Happiness

Happiness is an interesting social construct. One that many (very smart) people have different ideas about.

Laura: There seems to be an expectation that we should all be happy and that if we aren't, it's because we are doing something wrong – that we aren't 'choosing happiness'. But really, happiness is an emotion and, like every emotion, it comes and goes. Chasing a state of constant happiness sets the bar far too high. It's unrealistic, and it sets us up for failure.

I've avoided speaking about happiness in the past because I don't want to push the idea that finding happiness is easy, especially since 'choosing to be happy' is often not possible without privilege. Privilege – particularly racial and socio-economic privilege – can shield a person from some of the challenges that can make moments of happiness hard to find.

Privilege can definitely make happiness easier to come by, but nothing is guaranteed. The old saying, *Money can't buy happiness* is still true. In every life, there will be moments where we simply cannot 'choose happiness'. The challenges will be too great, and some of those times will last longer than others. But, just like happiness, pain is also temporary. If you are reading this while going through a hard time in your life and feel you're doing something wrong because you can't find happiness, I want to reassure you that you aren't. As hard as it might be to imagine, the pain will pass. And if you're reading this and feeling numb of all emotion – not sad but also not happy – that is also okay. That, too, will pass. Perhaps you aren't sure what will make you happy so you don't know how to move towards happiness. If that's the case, then the good news is that you can train your mind to change that and find happiness in small things, right now.

If feelings of numbness or sadness have been going on for a sustained period, and you've been living your life without joy, or finding that in moments where you expected to be happy, you're aspiring to 'the next thing', then I hope the tips I'm about to share will help.

Here are some of the things I remind myself of on days when I need a boost. These help me find moments of happiness.

★ **Take responsibility for your own happiness.** We cannot control how other people react, what they do or if they like us. For these reasons, it doesn't make sense to put our emotional wellbeing and state of mind in the hands of someone else. If you rely on another person to make you happy, you will not be truly happy because you'll never have control of it. Do not 'hope' others will do the job for you. It's too important a job so you must own it yourself.

★ **Let go of the uncontrollables.** Every single day, we have many choices. When we sit in traffic we have two choices: be angry at the world or another driver and let this dictate our mood for the entire day. Or breathe and try to focus on something positive that might come out of this situation. Call a friend, keep listening to a podcast that uplifts you for longer or get through your favourite playlist. In this situation, you can be sure of one thing: the time you get to work will not change whether you are angry or peaceful. Being angry won't clear the road or speed your car up, neither will finding joy in the moment, but how you feel *will* change. You have power over that. You never know what lies in the moments where you did not expect things, and it would be a sad thing to let these pass you by. Let go of the things you cannot control, and focus on those that you can.

★ **Practise gratitude.** Gratitude is the practice of being grateful for what we have in each present moment and not worrying about the next moment or thinking about what we don't have. Most of our daily activities and tasks are heavily moulded into our lives due to constant repetition. Because many of these tasks are monotonous, it's easy to miss the joy that could be found within each of them, and we forget to be grateful for them. How many times have you said to yourself, *I have to go to work* or *I have to do the supermarket shopping*? When we use the term 'have to', things feel like an obligation. That's why I choose to replace that with 'I get to'. E.g. *Today, I get to go to work*, or *I get to do the supermarket shopping*. Admittedly, some days this is hard, but mostly it works. We exist in a world that makes it easy to forget what we actually have. There will always be someone who has more than you and someone with less. Without making peace with this, it is hard to find happiness. We might 'want' something, but that's not the same thing as actually needing it. This is why we must control our minds and find peace and feel comfort in the fact that we have everything we need inside of us to find joy in the moment. There are things to be grateful for all around us. We just need to put on different glasses to see them.

★ **Don't let yesterday define today.** Whether yesterday was the worst day of your life or just a shit one, know that it is okay. It is perfectly normal to have bad days and experience emotions that are unrelated to happiness or joy. Our past experiences do not have to define our future ones. They help to equip us to face tomorrow, but, darling, they do not define you. Not now, and not ever. The sun will rise the next day no matter how bad the day before was. Don't you dare judge yourself or rob yourself of opportunities for joy. We must make peace with our mistakes or things beyond our control and learn to let them go.

Who are you, really?

Are you still looking for your 'true self'? I am, too, and I've realised that that's okay. This question used to bother me. I put so much pressure on myself to work it out, but now, I feel a deep sense of peace knowing that I don't really need to know. To be completely transparent, I have no idea who my 'true self' is. I guess she is still working things out. Through each experience, we grow, we learn, we try new things, and maybe – if we're lucky – we get closer to knowing who this true self is. However, we are humans who are constantly evolving, so we may never know for sure.

Not being able to answer this question doesn't mean I feel lost or that I don't have a purpose in life because I do know what my values are, and they help guide me. I guess the point of including this question in the book is to let you know that it is okay if you do not have a firm grasp on your identity yet. Don't let a series of quotes on social media or an ad make you feel like you are inadequate if you don't know. Trust in your values and your moral compass. That's enough. In fact, if I can ask you to do one thing, it's to complete the exercises on pages 56 and 57.

Be okay with the 'ish'
Deni Todorović

KIC: One of our dear friends, style icon and LGBTQIA+ activist Deni Todorović, spoke about their idea of being okay with the 'ish' on our podcast, the *KICPOD*, and their words have stuck with us ever since. In a world where so many of us feel pressured to be everything to everyone, we expect ourselves to be exceptional in every single way and stand for everything. But by doing this, we are setting ourselves up for failure. Deni spoke about learning to be okay with the 'ish' by acknowledging that you may not be 'perfect' in terms of sustainability or eating vegan, or just generally always getting things 100 per cent right. You're only human.

Instead, they suggest focusing on doing as well as you can in that moment. For example, if you value sustainability but can't afford to spend hundreds of dollars on sustainably made clothing and still pay your rent, you might take a 'sustainability-ish' approach. That might look like using keep cups or water bottles rather than disposable ones, but purchasing cheaper clothing that may not be 100 per cent sustainable. Or, it might mean you shop from op shops most of the time, but sometimes buying an item of clothing you love that isn't recycled. Being sustainable-ish doesn't mean you don't care about sustainability or that you are a bad person, it just means you're allowing yourself space to not be 'perfect' 100 per cent of the time.

Give yourself permission to live in the 'ish'.

Vulnerability

Vulnerability is when we put ourselves out there and take a risk without being sure of or in control of the outcome.

KIC: Being vulnerable can feel like jumping off a cliff without a safety net. We showcase vulnerability when we try something for the first, second or even third time after failing. It can be a very scary feeling, but vulnerability is not a weakness. It takes a lot of courage to put yourself out there when there are no guarantees. It's a lot easier to avoid the unknown and instead exist within a comfort zone. But if we never push ourselves into that unknown space, are we living a life true to who we are?

Research professor, author and speaker Brené Brown has been a true force for championing this emotional state, and she often speaks about the power of vulnerability. She uses the word 'power' with so much conviction and rightly so; there *is* serious power in opening yourself up and living your life in spite of fear. Being vulnerable isn't an easy route to take. In fact, it's almost certainly the hardest one, but on the other side of it lies something very special: your authentic self, deep connection with yourself, love and fulfilment.

Laura: I have experienced so many powerful moments in my life thanks to vulnerability. Allowing myself to be vulnerable and express my true feelings has helped me connect with people on levels I could never have reached otherwise. Most importantly, being vulnerable has allowed me to see that I can be myself – I do not need to change to be someone else to be enough.

One of the biggest misconceptions when it comes to vulnerability is that it involves baring your soul to everyone at all times. That's not what it is. You don't need to run into the middle of a packed stadium and scream your deepest and darkest secret as loudly as you can to qualify as vulnerable. In fact, definitely don't do this as you will most likely get arrested. There are much simpler and more meaningful ways to be #vulnerable.

Vulnerability can look like . . .

★ Telling someone you love them when you don't know if they love you back

★ Telling someone they did something that hurt you

★ Apologising for doing something you know hurt someone

★ Applying for a job you may not get

★ Trying something new (for you), even though you know people may judge you

★ Setting boundaries with people you care about

★ Sharing more of yourself than you usually would with someone

★ Reapplying for a job when you did not succeed the first time.

Being vulnerable
doesn't have to mean
revealing your deepest,
darkest secrets
to the world.

Mum guilt

Steph: Quite possibly one of the most vulnerable times in a woman's life is when she becomes a mother. Talk about jumping into something with no experience and no guarantee of the outcome. It's not like parenthood comes with a guidebook. The advice is constantly changing, and there's no one magic set of directions to follow and no way of knowing if you're doing things right. You just make it up as you go, try your best every day, and hope it all works out.

The hardest judgement to swallow can sometimes be the judgement we serve ourselves. I heard about 'mum guilt' before becoming a mum but naively thought that it wasn't going to be something I'd have to deal with. I figured I'd be able to just go with the flow, go easy on myself and enjoy the juggle of life as a mum. But wow! Now that I'm a mum, I can't get to the end of the day without questioning myself. Have I fed my son enough? Have I spent enough time playing with him? Did he sleep enough? Could I have read more to him? Did he spend too much time in front of the telly? And that's on the days that I'm home. On days that I'm in the office or out of the house due to other commitments, mum guilt hits even harder.

We HAVE TO go easier on ourselves and give ourselves more credit. Keeping a little human alive is not an easy task, and even if you're a full-time stay-at-home mum, there simply aren't enough hours to get absolutely everything in their life (and yours) right. Celebrate the little wins in your day and put your head on the pillow every night knowing you did your best.

We are our own worst critics.

Little wins I like to acknowledge when mum guilt hits

★   We practised tummy time

★   We went for a walk and got outside

★   I squeezed in a workout during one of his naps

★   I got to that appointment on time

★   I got dressed and looked after my skin

★   I nailed my presentation at work

★   I made a fresh, healthy dinner from scratch

◆ WISE WORDS

There's beauty in this chaos
Emma Heaphy

Steph: There's a poem I love by Emma Heaphy called *Know this*. I revisit it at times when I feel hopeless (which can be quite often).

Dear Mama,

I see you.

Underneath the dark bags that hang from your eyes, the deep wrinkles in your forehead and the untidy messy bun that sits on the top of your head, you are plagued with self-consciousness.

Between the messy unvacuumed floor, the unmade beds and the basket full of washing, you feel like you are in a constant state of overwhelm.

Amidst the endless painful cries, the public tantrums and the unruly broken sleep, you pray for things to get easier.

Amongst the constant external pressure, the unhelpful opinions and the personal challenges, you crave approval and validation.

But know this.

To your child, you are the most beautiful thing they have ever laid eyes on, and to everyone else, you are a natural reminder of the amazing sacrifices you make.

The state of your house does not define you. It is just a stage that will pass, and before long you will desperately pine for this time back again.

You are currently doing the hardest job you will ever do. Vocalising the struggles is healthy and should not be discouraged.

Doubt is unfair and unkind. It doesn't matter the source from which it derives, you must not let it win. Trust your decisions and believe in yourself always.

There's no such thing as the 'perfect mum'. The 'imperfectly perfect' mum for your little one, is you. You've got this, Mumma.

Shame

When I'm working through feelings of shame, the thing that helps me the most is to say that thing I'm ashamed of out loud.

Laura: I have read many definitions of shame from the dictionary and from different researchers, but the one that speaks to me the most is from Brené's book *Atlas of the Heart*. She defines shame as 'the intensely painful feeling or experience of believing that we are flawed and therefore unworthy of love, belonging and connection'. What resonates with me the most is the feeling of being flawed. It's a devastating feeling to experience within ourselves and also see in others. Knowing that someone is going through life without realising how incredible they are and what they are truly capable of is heartbreaking, yet it is something so many of us live with deep inside. If allowed, this shame will take over a person's perception of ability in all that they do.

Shame, for me, is one of the core negative emotions that impacts our belief in ourselves and whether or not we believe we are worthy of love, connection and success in our lives. We all deserve to feel worthy of all of these things, but we need to make sure we break down any of the barriers we have to receiving them, and shame can be one of them. This is another part of Brené Brown's work that I am so grateful to have absorbed. Brené has led the way with her groundbreaking research and work and has made it a mainstream conversation. Before reading and listening to Brené, I had never spoken about shame with anyone. I'd felt it, of course, but I'd always kept that to myself. But by keeping it inside, I was giving power to my shame, and none to myself to help me release it. If I think deeply about my relationship with shame, the place it rears its head the most is in my work life.

My work is something I care deeply about, and it's precisely because I care so much that shame cuts deep when I have fallen short in some way. When I know I have missed a target or not presented well with my work, my first go-to emotion is shame. In the moment I knew I should have done better or given more, I think of that failure or miss as something that happened because of who I am. I might listen to a podcast interview I've done where I stumbled over an answer. Instead of showing myself compassion, my first thought is, *I'm stupid. I should be able to articulate myself better by now. Next time, I'd better prepare five times as long since I clearly can't get it right on the spot.* It makes me feel sad to type those words out, but if I'm honest with myself, I know they are true.

When shame thrives inside us, it becomes impossible to decipher the difference between a bad thing that happens because of us and a bad thing that happens because of an uncontrollable external factor. Shame leads us to believe that *we* caused that bad thing to happen because *we* are flawed, and that is what *we* do. It's like doing multiple equations with many different variables, but no matter how many variables or equations you use, the answer is always the same. No matter what, we find a way to blame ourselves for the problem, even when it was caused by something outside our control.

When I'm working through feelings of shame, the thing that helps me the most is to say the thing that I'm ashamed of out loud. I write out whatever is causing the feeling in me and then list the factors that contributed to the outcome. I list myself as one of the factors since that is true to how I am feeling at the time, but I also write down any other factors that I can identify. For example, if I present a piece of work and someone shuts my idea down, pulls it apart or says it was wrong, I immediately think *They are right. My work sucks because I suck, and I'm not smart enough to attempt what I tried to do.* In that moment, my thoughts have nothing to do with my behaviour or the other person; all I can think of is how the problem is inherently inside of me. *I'm the issue.* Not my behaviour. Not other factors. Me.

By working through that activity and writing down what could have gone wrong or been a contributing factor (whether I believe it or not when writing it down), I am able to pull myself out of those thoughts that led to me being the cause – that who I am is the reason I failed.

TRY THIS

Zoom out and see the big picture

Before blaming yourself for a failure, go searching for the bigger picture. Write down any factors you can think of that could have contributed to the negative outcome. Let's use my experience of having my work shut down as an example. Here are some contributing factors that *may* have played a role in me not smashing this one out of the park.

★ I had a big week the week before and wasn't able to put enough hours into the task.

★ I rushed through the presentation because I had a meeting straight afterwards, so I didn't provide enough context to the idea.

★ The person I was presenting to was having a bad day and didn't actually listen to my idea, nor were they open to it in the first place.

★ The person I was presenting to had already heard another idea and they favoured that idea over mine, so they weren't in a place to take mine on.

★ The idea wasn't the best, but I am not the idea.

These reasons have nothing to do with me not being worthy or sucking or not being smart enough. It's only when I pull myself out of my shame spiral and zoom out on the situation that the points above start to make sense – certainly a lot more sense than simply concluding 'I suck'.

you take care

Four major shame triggers

KIC: While writing this book, we surveyed our KIC community to ask them how they experience shame and where it shows up in their lives. The respondents, predominantly women, highlighted a few key areas for us. The most common areas are below. It is important to remind ourselves that shame will creep into our lives because it is a human emotion. We can't stop it, but we can make sure we have the tools to push it away and remind ourselves how worthy we are.

1 Break-up shame

Being broken-up with came up a lot in our survey. Many people spoke of feeling shame after a break-up and said they worried that it had happened because they are unworthy of love. The truth is much more complicated. Relationships are hard. People grow and change in so many ways, and there are hundreds (maybe thousands) of reasons why people break up. Someone may decide they want different things for their future; one person's interests might change; one person may want to pursue life in a different city while their partner wants to stay put; a passionate relationship might mellow to friendship; other times, people just aren't right for each other . . . the list goes on. These reasons have nothing to do with how worthy someone is of being loved.

The break-up or fading away of a platonic relationship can also cause us to feel shame. We might feel there is something wrong with us when our friends leave us out and don't invite us places, or if they make comments that make us feel small in front of others. Remember that someone else's cruelty is not a reflection of your worth. It says much more about their own situation and state of mind. How a person treats you doesn't mean you aren't worthy of connections or friendships.

It is, of course, always important that we check ourselves to make sure that we are being a good friend and person, too. Taking accountability for our actions and behaviour is important. Control how you are in the world while also reminding yourself that you can't control others. Often, growing apart is a way of evolving in life. Things outside our control cannot dictate how we feel about ourselves or, in turn, affect every relationship we have going forward.

We've all been there

Steph: The breakdown of a romantic relationship can be the absolute worst. I only had a few serious relationships prior to dating my now-husband, but boy, oh boy, they were exhausting. In my personal experiences, the break-ups were anticipated, but that didn't make them easy. When you're ending a long-term relationship, IT SUCKS whether you're the one initiating it or it's coming from your partner. The hardest thing besides the loneliness that can follow a break-up is the journey to form new habits. Because, really, when you're in a relationship, you form a whole lot of habits that you now have to break – starting with not seeing or speaking to that other person every day.

When I reflect on my most recent break-up, which was ten years ago now (wow, feels like yesterday), I certainly saw it coming. We dated for about two-and-a-half years, and for the last six to 12 months we were really on the rocks. We went on breaks and came back together so many times in that period. Even when it finally ended, we were going to get back together again until I heard that he had cheated on me multiple times over the last year. I was incredibly hurt and blindsided. I felt sick. I want to say that having that new information at least made the break-up easier because I could be angry with him, but it didn't. There was still that short period after I found out when I contemplated forgiving him and getting back with him because being together was a habit.

As hard as it may sound, more often than not, the only way to get over them is to completely remove them from your life. Sure, there are people who end up rekindling a friendship after some time, but that's a rarity, and it takes a unique relationship to be able to break-up and head straight to being friends.

The hardest thing besides the loneliness that can follow a breakup is the journey to form new habits.

Our romantic partner is there to support us, love us, encourage us, and bring us a sense of security. When we lose that person, it can be hard to remember or to recognise that many of our platonic relationships can support us in the same way.

When it comes to getting through a break-up and coming out the other end, that journey may be long or it may be short, but it certainly looks different for everyone.

It's been a while since Laura or I have been through a break-up, but someone who has been incredibly raw, open and honest about a recent experience is Kath Ebbs. Kath is the kind of person that you meet once and find yourself drawn to following on every platform because of their incredible energy and creativity. They have many talents and are an amazing champion for the LGBTQIA+ community. On their podcast (*Conversations with Kath*), they discussed a recent break-up they went through and shared some really valuable tips that I thought would be helpful for anyone going through a totally unexpected break-up. ≫

 TRY THIS

Reframe the shame

Once you've accepted the break-up and feel ready to move on, get out there and remember you're a desirable human being. You don't need that past love in order to feel desirable. Flirt, go have a boogie and meet some new people. You don't have to jump into another relationship; it's not about that. Thrive in this time where you're unattached and focus on rediscovering yourself.

Great post-break-up tips
Kath Ebbs

★ **Go for therapy if you can.** Life is wild, and having a therapist you can reach out to when the rug is pulled out from underneath you can be so comforting. A therapist is an anchor, a rock. They're a professional there to help you get clarity on the situation and also allow you to just express your emotions in a safe and open space where it's all about you. It's important to heal the actual problem rather than just putting a bandaid over it.

★ **Find joy in the small things.** Appreciate little moments like sitting in the sun and being present in the midst of a busy day. Go for a walk, stretch your body and just take time to be present and grateful.

★ **Surround yourself with people who love you.** Lean on them for support, for company and for a bit of an escape when you need it.

★ **Slow down and look after your body.** Listen to it. If you're someone who loves moving their body, you can still move but be open to changing up what that looks like. Yoga is a fantastic way to move your body while focusing on your breath, which can get you into a meditative state. It's super grounding and good for both your mind and body.

★ **Change up your routine.** Try something new. Start new rituals to break the old habits you had in your last relationship. Find your new normal.

★ **Set boundaries and remove triggers.** If it hurts every time you see or hear about your ex, mute the friends you have in common on social media for a while and hide or completely remove photos/jewellery/memories you have of them around your house. You might even have certain songs in your playlist that you can't bear to hear right now, and that's okay. Remove them. These are all things you can just do temporarily. Triggers are sometimes unavoidable in the long run, but when you're in the thick of it all, know that you can do these small things to keep your mind off them.

★ **Journal. Reflect and gather your thoughts.** But also, think ahead. Set goals, write out intentions and practise gratitude by writing out what you're grateful for each day.

★ **Allow yourself to be a sloth for a while.** Give yourself time to work through your grief without trying to conquer the world at the same time. Look at this time as a free pass to be a sloth and do nothing at all if that's what you want to do.

The most important thing to remember when going through a break-up is that you are not alone, and you will not feel like this forever.

Choc Popcorn

Steph: My favourite way to give myself a hug from the inside is to pop on *Bridget Jones's Diary* and make a bowl of this popcorn.

½ teaspoon
  coconut oil
¼ cup (60 g)
  popcorn kernels
20 g (¾ oz) dark
  chocolate
Salt

1 Melt the coconut oil. Place the popcorn kernels in a bowl and cover evenly with oil. Transfer the kernels to a paper bag. Fold the top of the bag over twice to prevent the kernels from coming out while popping.

2 Place the bag in the microwave (folded-side down) for 2–3 minutes. Finely chop up the dark chocolate and sprinkle over the warm popcorn in a serving bowl and stir through. Add salt to taste.

2 Work shame

This is another area where so many people feel shame. Shame about losing a job, making a mistake at work, not being paid enough, being paid too much, missing out on a promotion or getting a promotion and then finding out that colleagues don't think it's deserved. When shame creeps into our mindset at work it is almost impossible to do our jobs well. If we continually tell ourselves that we are not smart/experienced/good enough, we will start to believe these thoughts, and they will consume us. If this type of shame is something you experience often, take time regularly to focus on your strengths instead of allowing yourself to be defined by your weaknesses.

 TRY THIS

Reframe the shame

When your mind goes there, try reminding yourself of this tool that we read online that has stuck with us ever since. Think of someone you admire or aspire to be like, and then think about something they are good at. For example, Beyoncé is a great singer/dancer. Now, think of something that she doesn't often do and might not be great at – physically building a house, for example. Now, imagine if Beyoncé defined her worth based on her carpentry abilities. Imagine if she focused all her time worrying about how few walls she built in a house that month instead of her singing. Seems ridiculous, right?

When and if you do face rejection of your *strengths*, it can hit harder, but remember that another door will open for you. We like to view rejection as life's way of redirecting you to something better.

3 Body shame

Devastatingly, body shame was one of the top responses in our survey. When we believe that the way our body looks matters, it can affect so many areas of our life. Our body helps us move around, do things and stay alive. The way it looks has absolutely nothing to do with our worth or our capabilities. For many of us, the way we feel about our bodies is often shaped when we are younger. We've spoken to many women who really struggle with letting go of the shame around their body because of experiences in their early childhood. One woman shared how her mother would weigh and measure her and her sister when she was younger. Being compared to her sister in that way took this woman years to work through – it was devastating to read. In all that we do, it is so important to be conscious of how we speak about our bodies around others, and to never compare other people's bodies with our own. We are *so* much more.

 **TRY THIS**

Reframe the shame

If body shame is something you struggle with, try spending time each day thinking about one or two things your body does for you without you even asking it to, no matter how small. For example, if you are physically able to walk and run, thank your legs for taking you places and carrying you. Thank your heart for allowing you to love (and to stay alive), thank your brain for letting you think, process and learn things, thank your nose for letting you smell your coffee in the morning, your hands for holding on to your coffee and absorbing the warmth from the cup into your body. You get the idea.

4   Fertility shame

This one breaks our heart, as fertility is one of those things that is almost always out of our control. Based on the responses we had, in heterosexual relationships, nine times out of ten, shame over not being able to conceive falls on the woman – not the man, even though sperm problems are the cause for two out of every five couples facing infertility.

One of the main reasons fertility shame falls on women is that we grow up being taught that pregnancy can happen just like that. Throughout school, sex education classes drill into us that we're likely to fall pregnant if we so much as look at the opposite sex. And if we don't use a condom, well, then we're *definitely* falling pregnant. And there's always that one teacher who knows someone who conceived despite being on the pill *and* using a condom.

The reality of conception is very different. When the type of idea of false fertility is drilled into us from a young age, once we start trying to conceive (if we decide to), and we cannot fall pregnant, it is almost impossible to not blame ourselves. If it's so easy to get pregnant, then there must be something *wrong* with us. But when it comes down to it, most of the time we cannot control if or when we get pregnant, and this can be really hard to swallow.

KIC's qualified obstetrician, gynaecologist and passionate women's health expert, Dr Bronwyn Hamilton, explains that infertility is defined as the inability to conceive a pregnancy after 12 months of unprotected sexual intercourse. Infertility, unfortunately, affects one in six Australian couples of reproductive age. It's extremely common and definitely not something to feel ashamed about. However, if you are experiencing feelings of shame, you are not alone.

As women, we place so much pressure and judgement on our bodies when we're trying to conceive. We often jump to conclusions that there 'must' be something 'wrong' with our reproductive system when, in fact, only 40 per cent of infertility is caused solely by factors relating to the female. In 40 per cent of couples, the cause of infertility is attributed to the sperm, while other causes occur due to a combination of both male and female factors.

A myriad of factors can cause infertility, from problems with sperm production or egg viability to the structure or function of the reproductive systems and/or immune or hormonal conditions. If you believe you're experiencing infertility, don't be afraid to be proactive and reach out to your GP. They'll be able to refer you to a fertility specialist who can help you on your personal journey.

 TRY THIS

Reframe the shame

1   Firstly, it's important to acknowledge that being held back from your dream to start a family is incredibly unfair. This is no doubt an emotional time, and your feelings are valid.

2   Speaking with a psychologist can be REALLY helpful, especially one that specialises in infertility. They can help you understand that this is out of your control and provide you with practical tools to switch your mindset and help you through these hard times.

3   Set boundaries and be selective about when you spend time with your friends and family that do have children. It's completely normal if you find these situations triggering. Be open with them about how you feel – they will understand.

4   Listen to your body and your mind, and set aside time for things that make you happy. Be kind to yourself. This is a very tough and emotionally draining time, so it's important to pause and fill your cup along the way.

Invest in yourself

Self-development, self-improvement, personal growth . . . Whatever you call it, it's about levelling up, and – like anything in life you want to get better at – it takes work.

KIC: If you wanted to learn a new language, you wouldn't expect to be fluent without practising or putting time into learning that language, would you? Well, think about improving yourself the same way. Investing in yourself is one of the most important investments you ever make, and it can take many different forms. It can be taking time to heal and reconnect with your identity after a heartbreak. It may be learning to meditate so you can be more mindful and present. It may be reflecting deeply to figure out what really matters to you. There are a million ways you can grow and improve as a person: read books that challenge the way you think and open your mind, talk to interesting people or switch off your phone and dedicate time to being in nature. Self-development looks different for everyone, and it is an ongoing lifelong process. There's nothing more empowering than learning. How lucky we are to live a life where we have countless opportunities to learn and challenge the way we think. It doesn't matter what you choose to learn about – just make sure it is something that enriches your life in some way.

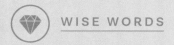

The power of self-development
Danny Kennedy

KIC: Our good friend and master trainer at KIC, Danny Kennedy, often speaks about the power of self-development. As a personal trainer for the past nine years, he has empowered thousands of people by giving them the tools to change their mindset. Danny is kindly sharing some of this wisdom with us here.

Danny: If you're reading this book, at some point in your life you've most likely learned how important it is to move your body regularly and eat well, and how much these two habits can affect your physical and mental health. They work hand-in-hand to improve your life so why not apply the same effort and principles – that daily effort, the training and habit forming – to the quest to learn more about your own self?

Self-improvement and personal development are a never-ending journey, but with just a small amount of daily effort, you'll be able to take your life to the next level across all areas.

What does self-improvement look like?

To put it plainly, any effort/task completed with the intention of finding out more about yourself, levelling up either mentally or physically (or both), can be seen as a form of personal development.

For some, the journey may begin with a guided meditation. For others, it may be journalling, deep conversations, education, reading or learning from others' experiences or philosophies.

The goal of personal development is just as the name suggests: to develop yourself as an individual by learning more about how you operate (the good and the bad) and use tools that stretch you in as many ways as possible so you can ultimately live true to your values, exist as a decent human being and improve the lives of those around you.

Where to start?

★ **Meditate or explore mindfulness techniques** so you can become more present in your life.

★ **Educate yourself.** Think podcasts, books/audiobooks, school/university, seminars, courses, etc.

★ **Journal regularly.** Laying your thoughts out on paper, which may involve answering prompts or questions, can help you gain clarity on what it is you want out of life and how you can improve.

★ **Have deep conversations** with people close to you.

One thing about personal development that's non-negotiable is honesty – more specifically, honesty with yourself. If you cannot be honest with yourself about where you're currently at in your life, what your strengths and weaknesses are, and everything in-between, your journey will lack authenticity.

Just like compounding interest in finance, small efforts implemented on a daily basis, working on the most important asset you have – your mental and physical health – will compound over time to help make you the very best version of yourself.

Teachers are everywhere

Laura: As co-founder and CEO of KIC, I am very aware of how much I still have to learn. But rather than see this as something that holds me back, I try to look at it as an opportunity to learn. Recently, I had one of the biggest years of growth, both personally and professionally, and I owe that to the wonderful teachers who turned up in my life unexpectedly.

Knowing that I was ready to learn, I put myself out there by reaching out to the people around me and asking for help. Through this process of opening up and showcasing vulnerability about how I was feeling, people began connecting me with others who could help and offered resources that had helped them through similar challenges. I went on blind coffee dates with potential mentors and advisors (despite wanting to pull out at least ten times before every meeting), and even though I was nervous about meeting certain people or not 100 per cent sure of what I would say or ask at those meetings (despite putting hours of preparation in every time), I went to each one. I was pleasantly surprised when my biggest fear – that there would be lots of silence and the person on the other side of the table would be thinking they had wasted an hour of their day – did not play out.

I learned that humans have an innate desire to help others. If people accept a catch-up with you, it's very likely they're doing so because they want to help. No one accepts a blind coffee date so they can sit there and judge the person sitting across from them.

I became a sponge for the whole year. I listened to more podcasts, read more books and carried a notepad with me everywhere I went. If I had a phone call or a meeting with someone who was sharing their knowledge, I scribbled down everything I learned and typed up those notes once I got home so I could reflect on the learnings later. Having access to incredible minds through books, audiobooks, podcasts, etc., is one of the best things about our modern world. If you are lucky enough to have access to the internet and a phone, you have so many incredible resources available to you right now.

Whatever you do, never stop learning.

Why you are never 'too much' of anything

Do not fear to walk on a path that society makes you believe was not made for your feet.

KIC: YOU decide the route that you take. We live in a world where we are constantly brought down to the level that other people feel comfortable with us being on. Being different or wanting more for ourselves than others believe we are capable of is uncomfortable – for them. But the only person who should decide what you are capable of is you.

Women, especially, are often told that they are 'too much'. Too loud, too talkative, too opinionated, too driven, too ambitious, too arrogant . . . The truth is no one is ever too much of anything. The people who make this judgement are small. They feel intimidated by you because you do not fit into the box they created for you in their heads, and therefore they need to try and squish you back into their mould. You, darling, should never, ever be forced into a mould you did not create for yourself or let someone else decide who and what you should be.

Use comparison to your advantage

One of our favourite Oprah quotes is, 'Be thankful for what you have; you'll end up having more. If you concentrate on what you don't have, you will never, ever have enough.' This quote rings so true for us. So many of us have been tricked into living our lives and searching for happiness. We live in a state of always wanting more, and then when we get it, our goal changes again. Having more will (most likely) not make you happier. In many cases, it might even make things worse as we search to fill a void that cannot be filled by things.

If you feel this way, know you are not alone. Comparing ourselves to others is an innately human trait. In fact, social comparison theory is a scientific concept used by psychologists to explain why we compare ourselves to others in the way that we do. It's one of the ways that we judge ourselves and a tool we use to assess how we are going or doing at a particular thing. This leads to both upwards and downwards comparison, and both can affect how we feel about ourselves now and what we are capable of in the future. But in some instances, comparing ourselves can actually be a good motivator.

For example, if your friend is a good runner, that might inspire you to start running consistently. However, where comparison can become really damaging is when we expect too much of ourselves and don't accurately evaluate where we are at a certain point in time. Take the running example above: if your friend regularly runs 10 km because they have been running regularly for years, but you are just beginning, it's very likely you'll fail if you try and run 10 km. And then you'll feel inadequate. Comparison can become dangerous when we compare our day one to someone else's day 100.

Try not to chase happiness or success as if they are final destinations. Take in the journey. Balance striving with finding gratitude for all the things you *do* have in your life at this moment.

You can't stand out if you're trying to fit in

Laura: Reframing how I think about comparison has helped me so much. Let certain people inspire you and admire them, but never, ever cross the line and compare your life to theirs. Brené Brown's definition of comparison in *Atlas of the Heart* is one I initially found very confronting: 'It's the crush of conformity from one side and competition from the other – it's trying to simultaneously fit in and stand out'. With time, though, this definition became extremely freeing and actually changed my mindset around comparison. To me, these words are a perfect summary of why comparison can be so dangerous and why, when we compare, we will never win or feel good inside.

Validate yourself

Laura: In the world of social media, we get validation when people tap a photo (to like it), make positive comments about the outfits we wear or our dramatic hair changes, or swoon over a luxurious holiday (often paid for by a credit card). But none of these likes or comments really matter, nor are they within our control. If we only allow ourselves to feel good and worthy when others validate us, we might be waiting our whole lives for a feeling we can give ourselves from within.

There is an amazing interview Oprah did for the podcast *We are supported by . . .*, where she touches on how universal the need for validation is. When I listened, I had a big 'aah' moment while Oprah was talking about her show, which she'd done for decades and interviewed thousands of people for. She said, 'Every single human being, no matter the subject, wants to know that they were seen, heard or that they mattered'. She went on to say that at the end of the interview, every guest – from movie stars and politicians to iconic performers and everyday people – always asks if they were alright, if they were good and if they said the right things, etc. To me, this is a reminder that validation is something *everyone* is seeking. Even the most successful people in the world question themselves, so you are definitely not alone in feeling you need it. Our need for external validation doesn't stop unless we take that control back.

If you are living a life true to your values and doing what feels right to you, then that's all the validation you need. You don't need to do 'big' things in order to achieve that validation, and you don't need likes or followers or anything of the sort. We can't leave it up to others to be our biggest cheerleaders or supporters. We must take this on first, ourselves.

Validation is something *everyone* is seeking. Even the most successful people in the world question themselves, so you are definitely not alone in feeling you need it.

Settling vs. chasing someone else's version of ideal

Laura: I hope that while reading this book, one of the biggest messages coming across is that you are so incredibly worthy of love, happiness and success just as you are right now. It's important not to forget this. You don't need to settle for a relationship that does not serve you or where your actions and life are controlled, or where you cannot be yourself or where you are made to feel like you are not worthy of love and affection. At work, if you are not valued, or if you are made to feel inadequate or that you cannot contribute to your company or organisation, then you shouldn't settle. In friendships, you shouldn't feel that you need to be a 'better' version of yourself (by their standards, not yours).

There is a very big gap between settling for less than you deserve and chasing someone else's version of ideal. In order to find joy in our lives and feel content, we have to understand this. One of the major downfalls of social media is that it magnifies our natural tendency to compare ourselves, robbing us of appreciation for what we do have and making us believe that we need to be happy all the time. If you search 'dream job' or even 'dream life' online, many options pop up instructing us how we can change the life we have for a 'better' one. This is very dangerous.

Take a moment to step back and be an observer of your life from the outside. Chances are, your life *does* have purpose and value, and there are things in it that bring you joy. You might just be looking at it from the wrong angle, or you may be caught up chasing a version of life you have seen online – one that's made you feel like your job/life/car/partner/ friend is inadequate, when in reality they are the opposite. We live in a world of more, more, more, and we are programmed to always be looking for the next big thing.

Set realistic expectations for yourself

It is important to remember that even a dream job has its challenges, and there will be aspects of it that you may not enjoy. In my career, I haven't met anyone who has a job where they feel 100 per cent passionate about every single task they do. Heck, even in my role at KIC – a job I love so much – there are things I have to do that make me want to pull my hair out. I have days and weeks that I find really hard. Hard enough that I question if the job is right for me, if I am good enough for the job or if it's even what I want. I get through these tough times by trusting the process and persevering, and I'm grateful that I can do that. Nothing is ever perfect, and if we only strive for this ideal only, then we will always struggle to feel like we have enough.

Romantic relationships also suffer from 'perfection pressure', but no relationship is going to be free from arguments and issues, but good relationships will overcome these challenges. Even great relationships require work. Some of the most beautiful relationships I've witnessed between people in my life are ones where the couple have gone through hardships they did not think they would get through. But they have, and when they reflect on those times, they are so grateful they put the work in and that they still have that special person filling their life with love to this day.

It is not possible to avoid pain and sadness or live a life free of ever feeling angry or disappointed, but these feelings are temporary. You won't always know the right decision to make, but each one you do make will help to shape your unique story.

Don't miss those special small moments in between big life events or lose sight of yourself by comparing your situation with someone who appears to be living your dream life.

You will not be happy every single second for the rest of your life, but you will find happiness in many moments for the rest of your life.

You've survived 100 per cent of your bad days

KIC: This is something we remind ourselves of often. We repeat it as much as we can so that in harder times (which are inevitable) we can feel reassured that we *will* get through it. Can you think back to a time that you truly didn't think you would ever get through? Some pain or emotion that was so intense and constant you thought it had become part of your being? Something you went through that you thought may ruin your life or prevent you from feeling happiness again? Now that you are on the other side of that experience, how do you feel? What did living through that pain or trauma teach you about yourself? Have you found happiness since? As human beings, we are incredibly strong. We can do hard things and we can get through hard times. Next time you face a difficult situation, remind yourself that you have done this before, and you will do it again and again. Don't forget your power and inner strength – strength you didn't know was there until you needed it. This type of strength will be there for you no matter how many times you need it.

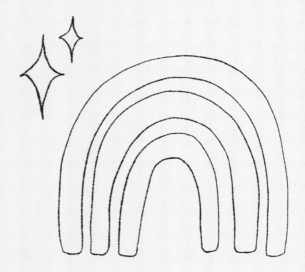

Values

A value system is like an internal moral compass. It is a set of behaviours and traits that we value in ourselves and in others.

KIC: When we have a strong value system, we live our lives through our choices and behaviour in alignment with these values. Among many things, a value system helps us determine which decisions and choices to make, how to spend our time, why we need or don't need certain things, how we should behave and what is important to us, among many other things.

Mark Manson, the best-selling author of many books, including *The Subtle Art of Not Giving a F*ck*, makes a great distinction between what constitutes a good and a bad personal value. He says that good values are 'evidence-based, constructive and controllable' while bad values are 'emotion-based, destructive and uncontrollable'.

So, how can we tell if the values we hold are actually good or bad? If we take two examples from Mark's book, where a good value is creativity and a bad value is being rich for the sake of being rich, we can apply his description and see clearly why the first example is a good, healthy value and the latter is not. Creativity is something that you can control, and the things you create can bring positivity to others, while fulfilling you and connecting you with your purpose. On the contrary, money is something that you have *some*, but not full, control over. For example, if you're an artist selling your art through your online shop, you can control how many pieces you produce and how you promote them, but not how many people will buy them. And if you cannot fully control one of your values, you're setting yourself up to fail. This is why the values you choose should be things that are entirely within your control.

If the reason behind choosing money as a core value is 'for the sake of it', there is going to be nothing stopping you from wanting more, and chasing an unquantifiable amount is impossible to sustain long term. This value can also be extremely destructive because if your life is centred around making money no matter what the collateral damage is, you could end up hurting the people around you and losing deep and meaningful connections as a result.

Choose your values wisely according to things that are within your control. Remember, too, that it is absolutely fine if your values change over time. We evolve and grow as humans, and our values can, too.

Write down your values

When you have some free time, sit down with a cup of tea and a pen and paper, and think about your values. While taking the information on the previous pages into account, ask yourself, *What is truly important to me and why?* The why is especially helpful, as it helps you to really identify if the value is meaningful to you and worthy of making your list.

Some things that may be in your value system

★ How you make people feel

★ Feeling mindful and truly embracing the present

★ Creating moments and experiences with loved ones

★ Making the people you love feel loved

★ Helping others

★ Feeling fulfilled

★ Making a difference with the work you do (doesn't matter how big or small)

★ Having a purpose

★ Having financial security

★ Always learning and growing

★ Having meaningful conversations

★ Meaningful connections with others

★ Respecting your body

Being clear on your values can make life so much easier to navigate. When you understand what truly matters to you, it's easy to know when to put more time or love into something that is truly important, and when to let go of things that don't actually matter. Things that fall outside your value system become less important and don't warrant worrying about.

Some things that shouldn't be included in your value system

- ★ What others think of you (we *cannot* control this)

- ★ How your body looks

- ★ Dress size

- ★ Your weight (the best way to forget about this one is to throw out the scales)

- ★ How many things you own

- ★ How many followers/likes you have on social media

- ★ Which brands of clothing you wear

 **TRY THIS**

Does the life you're living reflect your values?

Once you've written down your core values, another great exercise to do is to check how your values match up with how you are spending your time. Try keeping track of everything you do over the course of a few days, and then check this log against your list of core values. Are your daily actions aligned with the life you want to live or the values you've written down? If not, what can you do to make your life a better reflection of your values? This is such an important exercise. Check in with yourself often, and make changes wherever needed. Reminding yourself of your values makes saying no (and yes) so much easier. If something doesn't align with your values, there's no need to feel guilty about saying no.

Anxiety

Anxiety, for me, is like throwing all logical probability out of the window and multiplying something with a 0.0001 chance of occurring by 1,000,000, and then acting like *that* is the actual risk of each situation.

Laura: When we feel anxious, we can't tell the difference between perceived and *actual* risk. We convince ourselves that what we perceive is true, and then we spiral from there. And once the perceived threat/ stressor is gone, the anxiety can still be persistent and ongoing. For example, I have a friend who gets anxious every month that she might be pregnant, even though she uses condoms and is also on the pill. Even so, she worries and worries even before her period is due. I tell her she shouldn't worry because, as an anxious person myself, this is something that *I* have never worried about – at least not since I found out that the percentage of this happening when two forms of protection are used is very low. When I consider the actual risk, I don't see the point in her worrying. But man, oh man, if I'm home alone, I am 100 per cent convinced that I will be robbed, tied up and hurt. It doesn't matter that the chances of this actually happening to me are very low. She is worried that the life she loves might change forever while I fear losing my autonomy and safety. Anxiety shows up very differently in people.

Beyond Blue reports that one in four people in Australia will experience anxiety in their lifetime. That is a 25 per cent chance, and if you identify as a woman, that increases to 33 per cent. Anxiety is the most common mental health condition in Australia, and Dr Jodie Lowinger is an amazing expert working in the anxiety arena. She runs an anxiety clinic in Sydney and has written a fantastic book about anxiety, *The Mind Strength Method*. Dr Jodie has a beautiful view on anxiety: *You care because you care*. I remind myself of her words and use her strategies (pages 66–69) whenever I feel limited by my anxious thoughts. Experiencing anxiety doesn't make someone flawed or 'less worthy'; it simply means they really care. This thinking provides me with calm in times of worry, and I hope it does for you, too.

Social anxiety

This is one of my least favourite types of anxiety (not that any are winners). It comes up for me when I'm in social situations. I find myself worrying about everything I say and do. There's so much fear: fear that people will not like me, that I will be too loud, talk too much or just be 'too much' in general. There's fear people will not like the way I've dressed and will judge my style. I worry that my jokes won't be funny or that I'll say the wrong things. I fear that people will not find me interesting and won't want to invite me back. And, if I'm exhausted and want to leave early, I worry that everyone will be mad at me for leaving.

If any of this resonates with you, you are not alone. I've had conversations with many young women and learned that fear of rejection within social situations is incredibly common. One woman told me that she only books things with her friends when she knows they definitely don't have anything better to do because she has such a big fear of rejection. Another woman recalled constantly reminding everyone at her birthday party that they could leave whenever they wanted and that they shouldn't feel like they had to stay because she was so worried they all wanted to leave. Another woman's fear of abandonment stopped her from ever speaking up in relationships for what she needed. If her feelings were hurt, she would be so scared of losing the person that she'd say nothing. Another felt she could never speak her true opinion unless it was one shared by everyone around her as she never wanted to make anyone feel uncomfortable.

Health anxiety

Laura: This type of anxiety has been the most debilitating for me. It's why I get two skin checks a year, at different clinics, just in case one misses something. It's why I spend nights lying wide awake wondering how I will tell my partner I have cancer (diagnosed by Dr Google). It's the reason I spent years not eating on planes because of my nut allergy. In the case of nuts, my anxiety wasn't unwarranted; I'm anaphylactic, which means nuts can be life-threatening for me if I don't get adrenaline/treatment quick enough.

It's true that a serious allergy like mine absolutely warrants a level of worry, and risk mitigation is important, but in my mid-twenties, my worrying became all-consuming. Flying became overwhelming because I was unable to eat anything on the plane except fruit (and only when I could be completely sure it hadn't touched nuts).

It got to the point where I stopped eating things I'd eaten my whole life that I *knew* didn't contain nuts. If someone was eating nuts around me, I'd convince myself I was going to have an anaphylactic reaction, and I'd escape to a bathroom for an awfully long time to breathe through it and get away from the risk. In those situations, the risk to my health probably wasn't that great, but the risk I perceived was 99.9 per cent.

Cancer, unlike my allergy worries, was something I had anxiety about but no history of. I used to think my worries about having cancer came from previously working as a ward clerk in a hospital oncology ward. In that job, I saw people with cancer every day, and because of that, I perceived that my risk of having it was higher. In 2004, the year I learned about meningococcal disease, I thought it was pretty normal to wake up daily and check myself for it. Was my neck sore? To this day, I press down on any rash I have with the side of a glass to check if my spots stay visible when pressed (this was the test we learned at school to check for meningococcal).

What I try to do in these situations that can help (sometimes) is saying the worst possible thing that could happen out loud. Then I say out loud what I think the chances are of that actually happening, then I google to find the actual chances and then I say that out loud too. If I can't say it out loud (because of where I am), I will write it out in a text to someone close to me (usually Dalton or Steph) and they will often call or send me back a text confirming for me how small the actual risk is, which helps confirm the fear is just in my head.

Procrastination anxiety

KIC: Procrastination can be one of the biggest causes of anxiety. The anxiety about failing or that a task will be hard or boring prevents us from doing the thing in the first place, which in turn causes us more anxiety because the thing is not done. It's a trap that many of us fall into, but don't get it mixed up with being lazy. Procrastination is an active process where you simply choose to complete a more enjoyable task over the one you've been dreading. Sound familiar? The thing is, more often than not, when we procrastinate the task is actually taking up a higher mental load than it would if we simply got the job done. Whether it's life admin or a task at work, think about the niggly things that get transferred from one to-do list to another, you know it needs to be done, but you keep putting it off. Those tasks will literally linger in the back of your mind until you physically complete them.

In order to manage your procrastination, you need to understand *why* you're procrastinating. It could be down to avoiding anxiety, craving perfectionism, fear of failure or simply poor time management. We spoke about shame earlier, and now it's time to let go of any shame you have around procrastination. You're only human, and everyone procrastinates to some extent. Whatever task you're putting off, try breaking that larger task into smaller ones. For example, instead of writing 'marketing strategy' on your to-do list, break it down into specifics: marketing objectives, marketing channels, marketing tactics, etc. Then focus on completing one small step at a time.

Try setting yourself rewards as you complete each smaller task. The reward might be 15 minutes on your phone, a hot cup of coffee or a walk around the block. Find something that motivates you to get stuck in. And remind yourself how amazing it feels to cross something off your list. Once it's done and dusted, you can forget about it and move on. If you've been putting something off, use this as your reminder to chunk it up into smaller tasks, take a breath and GET IT DONE.

Pregnancy anxiety

KIC: While wonderfully exciting, pregnancy can also be a time when we experience a lot of anxiety. Overnight, we are responsible for the health of a baby, too, and it can suddenly feel as though there are hundreds of rules and guidelines about what we should and shouldn't eat and drink, how much we should exercise, what we should wear, when we should travel. Things that didn't require a second thought before, now require careful consideration. It's a lot! And if that mother-to-be isn't in an ideal situation – perhaps financially or romantically – then life can be even more complicated. Another area of fear and anxiety for so many women can be related to a prior miscarriage or stillbirth. A pregnancy following that type of trauma and loss presents a lot of emotional challenges, and that can be a hard path to navigate.

Sadly, around one in four pregnancies ends in miscarriage or pregnancy loss. We asked Dr Bronwyn to write a blog for our KIC website to help our community better understand what a miscarriage actually is and she defines miscarriage as any pregnancy that is lost before 20 weeks' gestation. The majority of miscarriages occur before the ten-week mark. A pregnancy loss after 20 weeks of gestation is considered a stillbirth. Devastatingly this happens to around six babies a day here in Australia.

If you think about it, it's a miracle that an egg and a sperm can find each other, become one cell and then divide again and again to make a healthy baby. Occasionally, things go wrong along the way for myriad reasons. Maybe the individual egg or sperm hasn't developed properly. Perhaps something goes wrong when the cells divide or when the embryo tries to attach to the lining of the uterus. When things don't go well for whatever reason, the result is that the pregnancy fails.

The female body is designed to ensure that only healthy pregnancies progress. This is why embryos that aren't healthy stop growing and miscarriage occurs. Your body is incredibly clever to recognise that things aren't quite right, but that doesn't take away the pain and heartbreak of losing a baby.

Managing anxiety during pregnancy

Anxiety during the first trimester is extremely common and normal, even if you haven't experienced a miscarriage. We spoke to Dr Bronwyn about how to manage anxiety during early pregnancy.

★ **Avoid Google/the internet.** There is so much misinformation out there that is going to lead you to believe that something is wrong even if things are fine.

★ **Focus on your pregnancy symptoms.** Tiredness, fatigue, nausea, shortness of breath, and many more symptoms are all reassuring signs that your pregnancy is progressing.

★ **Talk it out.** Tell your partner or a friend who has been by your side during your pregnancy about your concerns so they can reassure you.

★ **Work with a health professional.** They can reassure you when you are not sure how things are going. You can always book in for extra scans if you are worried things aren't going well.

★ **Focus on the positive statistics.** Even though one in every four pregnancies ends in miscarriage, the majority of pregnancies progress normally. Once past the 13-week scan, 99 per cent of pregnancies will go on to be fine.

★ **Take reassurance in each major milestone.** Get through the first few weeks with some blood work to confirm that your pregnancy hormone (BHCG) is rising. Then there's the dating scan to see the heartbeat at six or seven weeks. At ten weeks, there's the non-invasive prenatal test (NIPT) for chromosome number and to screen for chromosomal abnormalities. The first early anatomy scan happens at 12 or 13 weeks. And once you get through 24 weeks, you have a viable baby on board.

★ **Find a release.** Try exercise or mindfulness.

★ **Seek professional help.** See a perinatal psychologist if things are getting too hard to manage by yourself.

WISE WORDS

Pregnancy after loss
Nicole Maycroft

KIC: Nicole is many things, including a writer, marketing whiz, and mumma to be, and she heads up our PR and Comms at KIC. She's selfless, sweet and unapologetically herself and we're lucky to have her in our team.

Nicole: Pregnancy after loss is a wild experience that's not often spoken about. The moment I saw those positive lines on the pregnancy test, I was flooded with mixed emotions. On one hand, I was insanely excited that my husband and I were one step closer to holding our baby in our arms, but on the flip side, I was shit-scared that our dream could, and would, be taken away from us again. If you've experienced pregnancy after loss, you may relate to the feeling of being 'robbed' of the blissful excitement that comes with early pregnancy, you're nervous about going to the bathroom as you're terrified of seeing blood, you over-analyse every cramp and ache in your body, or you put up a barrier to protect yourself 'just in case'. I've been there.

Whatever you're feeling, know that this is completely normal. You've gone through a traumatising, heartbreaking experience, and it's only natural to feel these concerns. It might be easier said than done, but hold on to those feelings of nausea, the tenderness of your boobs, and the exhaustion because these are all positive signs that your pregnancy is progressing as planned. Hold on to the fact that the majority of people who experience a miscarriage will go on to have a healthy pregnancy. Just because you've lost one doesn't mean you will lose another. Hang in there, sunshine. It will all be worth it when you're holding your rainbow baby in your arms. Sending you so much love, strength and positive fertility vibes.

YOU'VE **OVERCOME** MANY **OBSTACLES** IN YOUR LIFE. YOU'RE MUCH **STRONGER** THAN YOU KNOW.

Feeling overwhelmed with worry?
Dr Jodie Lowinger

Laura: In her mission to help people living with anxiety manage its symptoms, Dr Jodie Lowinger has kindly shared some of the tools and powerful words from her wonderful book, *The Mind Strength Method: Four steps to curb anxiety, conquer worry and build resilience*. These tools have really helped me, and I hope if anxiety is a part of your life, too, Dr Jodie's words will also help you.

Here's how Dr Jodie described anxiety when we spoke to her:

'Anxiety is the protective instinct at play – a struggle with uncertainty to make sure everyone and everything is safe and well. You truly do care because you care. This underpinning of a caring heart and deep-thinking mind is core to the superpower of anxiety. It is, however, a double-edged sword, filled with challenging thoughts, feelings and behaviours that can take you out of line with your values and get in the way of your ability to flourish and thrive – it tips you into fight-or-flight where adrenaline and cortisol take over.'

Tool 1: Name your worry story

Naming your worry story is a practical tool that really resonates with me. It involves thinking of your worry as a story and then giving this 'worry story' a name – perhaps the 'You're Not Good Enough' story or the 'You Will Fail' story. Picture it as a book. Dr Jodie explains that this exercise is not about hating or challenging the story or arguing with the content. In fact, doing this will only fuel your worry because when you hate your worry or get angry with it, it takes you on an anger and aggression pathway that keeps the amygdala firing. That's the part of your brain that revs you up for fight or flight. This, in turn, will activate hypervigilance to threats and keep you focused on your worries.

Instead, Dr Jodie suggests that all you want to do is notice worry as the bully it is. Don't give in to the attention it's demanding. How? By employing these steps.

1   Notice when your worry book has come off the bookshelf.

2   Label it as the worry story: 'I know you, you're the "I'm Not Good Enough" story' (or whatever title is relevant to you).

3   Gently and compassionately imagine closing that book and putting it back on the shelf.

4   Take a long, slow breath out to create the space to choose a values-driven action as an alternative.

5   Continue on with your day (or night) and do something that is values-driven, not fear-driven.

The steps Dr Jodie lays out have helped me acknowledge my thoughts, realign my mind and turn my attention back to what I want to do. Sure, my worry stories pop back into my mind every now and then, but now I'm armed with tools to put them back on the bookshelf, where they belong.

Tool 2: Problem-solving and taking back control

As we mentioned at the start of this book, not every piece of advice we share in these pages is going to resonate with you. If the worry story tool didn't quite hit the mark, here's another strategy from Dr Jodie that I really want to pass on to you. This four-step strategy has helped me break down my worries and use problem-solving to take back control of my mindset. If you're feeling overwhelmed with worry, let's give this a go together. ≫

Troubleshoot your worries

Step 1: Grab yourself a pen and paper or open the Notes app on your phone. Go on, trust me. Next, write down any worrying thoughts that pop up. By doing this, you'll be able to get some distance from those thoughts and stop them from spiralling out of control.

Step 2: Differentiate between the four types of worries below. Dr Jodie recommends setting aside 15 minutes at whatever time of the day suits for you to work your way through your list.

★ **Worry type 1:** The ones that are no longer relevant. Cross them out. An example for me would be about one of my golden retrievers, Ben. I fretted over his trip to the vet, but now he's safe at home, so I no longer have to worry about this little devil (for now – ha!).

★ **Worry type 2:** The ones that are out of your control – like the results you're going to get on a uni assignment you've already submitted. We spend so much of our time dwelling on things that we are simply unable to do anything about.

★ **Worry type 3:** The ones that are in your control, such as the fight I had with Dalt last night.

★ **Worry type 4:** The ones where you are focusing on the outcome – I don't know about you, but these are the worries that can trigger my stress and anxiety. Dr Jodie explains that when outcomes are out of our control, focusing on effort brings you one step closer to engaging in problem-solving and action-planning around the elements that are in your control.

Step 3: Practise mindfulness strategies to let go of the worries that are out of your control. One that really works for me is to visualise a leaf floating down a river, wrap up the worry in a bundle, place it on the leaf, and then let it float away.

Step 4: With the worries that are in your control, instead of focusing on the problem, it's time to problem-solve and focus on a solution. Where worry leads to more worry, problem-solving leads to solutions. Try following Dr Jodie's problem-solving process.

1   Specify the problem. Tick! You've already done this.

2   Brainstorm solutions.

3   Develop an action plan.

4   Implement the plan.

5   Review and revise the plan as required.

Next time you find yourself feeling overwhelmed with worry, I highly recommend giving some of Dr Jodie's strategies a go. They're such powerful tools to keep in your back pocket or simply bookmark this page to come back to in the future.

Where worry leads to more worry, problem-solving leads to solutions.

Fear

Overcoming fear, I believe, is one of the main differences between people who live their lives for themselves and find fulfilment and those who struggle to find it. Fear not only holds us back; it can take things from us.

Laura: One of the biggest fears of all (and yes, there are *many* types of fear) is fear of judgement. Being trapped in a constant state of worrying about what someone else is thinking of us. Hoping they like us. Hoping they agree with us. Hoping they'll take us seriously. Wondering if they're plotting their escape route from this conversation.

Another common fear is of trying your best in case you fail when you do. When things don't go your way, it's easier if you can tell people (and yourself) that you didn't 'really try' anyway. I remember being 18 and getting my final year score so clearly. I was really proud of it, but I had a friend who made the same comment every time someone asked me how I'd done. (It's probably important to mention that I know that grades do not define who we are, nor do they matter in the grand scheme of things, but at this time in my life, they were something I was very proud of.) This friend was much smarter than I was but she didn't get the score she'd hoped for. When someone would congratulate me on my score, she would always say, 'Well, Laura didn't have a life in year 12, so you'd hope she'd get that score'. Perhaps she didn't feel she'd done her best or put in enough effort, but she felt the need to remind me of the effort I'd put in.

On reflection, I knew the moment I put my pen down in my last exam that I had given it my all. I couldn't have done more or studied harder, and for me, that feeling was much more fulfilling than actually getting a good grade. Every time I'm scared to fail, I remember this feeling and give it my all. The journey gave me more purpose than any result could or would.

Don't let fear of failure stop you from experiencing the amazing high of giving everything to a journey. If you do, then you, darling, are selling yourself so short. You deserve to give your all when you want to, and to release that fear. Take a breath in and out, and let the fear go. You are so worthy of it all.

I chatted to about 150 incredibly generous people who shared their fears with me. The fears listed on the next page came up multiple times. Some were in almost 50 per cent of the answers. I hope if you read this, you feel less alone and also realise that fear is so normal and that everyone experiences it. You mustn't let it hold you back from all the wonderful things waiting for you on the other side.

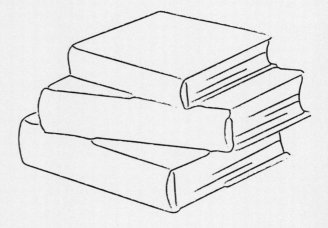

Common fears

- ⭐ People not liking us
- ⭐ Rejection
- ⭐ Abandonment
- ⭐ Being judged
- ⭐ Regret
- ⭐ Not having enough money
- ⭐ Losing all of our money
- ⭐ Being alone
- ⭐ Being too old or too young
- ⭐ Being 'too much' or not enough
- ⭐ Being boring

- ⭐ Not being good enough
- ⭐ Being vulnerable
- ⭐ Being truly honest with ourselves
- ⭐ Loving someone or being loved
- ⭐ Perfectionism
- ⭐ Not being taken seriously
- ⭐ Making the wrong decision
- ⭐ Letting a loved one down
- ⭐ Letting anyone we know down
- ⭐ Our appearance
- ⭐ Not being in control

Fear can hold us back from . . .

- ★ Feeling capable of achieving things
- ★ Wearing bathers at the beach
- ★ Leaving a relationship that doesn't serve you
- ★ Leaving an unhealthy marriage
- ★ Staying single
- ★ Wearing shorts
- ★ Applying for a new job
- ★ Going on a date
- ★ Having meaningful friendships
- ★ Taking a promotion at work
- ★ Starting a degree past the age of 25
- ★ Being confident

- ★ Experiencing new things
- ★ Deep connection
- ★ Being open to love
- ★ Looking after yourself
- ★ Slowing down when you really need it
- ★ Pushing yourself out of your comfort zone when you need it
- ★ Exploring new opportunities
- ★ Letting go of people who bring you down
- ★ Changing careers
- ★ Starting a podcast, a blog or a YouTube channel
- ★ Talking to a counsellor

This list was really sad to compile. There are so many things that we are missing out on because of fear. The experiences on this list are things we deserve to be able to do without worry - things we need to take back control of.

Break the fear cycle

If there is something you want to do, but fear has kept you from doing it, write it down, and then write down how you are going to do it and why. If it helps, try writing out *what* you are actually afraid of. Sometimes, facing the worst possible scenario and being okay with it takes power away from the fear and gives you that power back. Hold on tight and live your life the way you want to.

When fear consumes you, remember that

★ It most likely only exists in your head

★ You are so wildly capable

★ You are most likely (almost always) underestimating your strength

★ You have everything you need right now

★ You are enough, just as you are

★ Protecting ourselves is not a good thing if it is holding us back

★ You are *never* alone

★ Many things in your life ARE within your control.

Some not-so-obvious (but actually really obvious) things you have control over

★ Your social media feed. Choose who you follow wisely and take control of what you see and who you are influenced by

★ How you react to situations

★ Who you spend (most) of your time with

★ How much time you allow yourself to worry about what others think of us (or if you care at all)

★ The lens through which you look at the world

★ The choices you make each day. Make choices that will set you up for your future.

Don't tick off any 'boxes' unless they are yours

Laura: Have you ever done anything in your life that wasn't for you? (If not, I would love to know your secret!) Every now and then, we may get dragged to an event or into a situation that we *really* don't want to participate in. For example, we may not really want to attend a distant friend's baby shower on a Sunday morning after a night out. Other times, there will be things outside of our comfort zone that will challenge us and make us uncomfortable even though that's where we are likely to find the most fulfilment. What I'm talking about here, though, are big things like, doing a law degree just because your parents want you to even though you hate every second of it. (I should confess that I chose my degree because I thought it would make my parents proud, but I did love it in the end, so I don't regret it.) Another example of ticking off someone else's box would be getting married when you know deep down your partner isn't your person. You might say yes because they proposed and you feel you *should*, but know that it is okay to make big decisions and changes in order to move away from situations that make you unhappy. Write your own checklist for your life, change it as you grow, cross things out, tick things off (if you want) but whatever you do, choose yourself.

You are exactly where you need to be

The idea that you are exactly where you need to be is very simple, but it is something I have to remind myself of daily – sometimes even several times a day. I kept forgetting, so I bought a phone case with this exact quote on it. Every time I pick my phone up and notice that I've fallen into the endless social media hole, I'm reminded that I should stop scrolling and return to the moment in front of me. As you are reading this note right now, you must know that right now, darling, you are exactly where you need to be. You and I both.

Quit perfectionism and embrace your best

KIC: We expect more of ourselves than we do of anyone else. We hyperfocus on our flaws, yet we ignore our strengths. We expect ourselves to be better, do more and try harder instead of realising that these expectations are based on unrealistic expectations and are not really for us. We don't set these expectations because we want the best for ourselves; we set them because we think we aren't good enough as we are.

The standards and expectations set by society are usually biased and unbalanced, so what sense does it make to chase them? Perfectionism – especially when the 'ideal' being chased doesn't actually exist – is toxic and does us no favours. Letting go of the idea that we should do things 'perfectly' is liberating. Being satisfied with what we *can* do is a much healthier approach to life. All we can ask of ourselves is that we do our best – and that 'best' does not need to be better every day. It simply needs to be whatever we are capable of at that time based on what is available to us.

The things we are capable of will change from day to day. Energy and motivation ebbs and flows. We will go through hard times and happy times, and we will adapt accordingly. Some days, doing our best will mean achieving great things. Some days it will mean just getting out of bed. Both are valid and 'enough'. One is not better than the other. Be equally proud of yourself for simply turning up as you are for achieving extraordinary things. Both make you worthy.

 **TRY THIS**

Compare yourself to yourself

Next time you are struggling, try reflecting on where you are now versus where you were three, four or five years ago. Instead of thinking about what we are not or who we 'should' be, there is so much more to be gained by focusing on where we have come from, what we have overcome and then leveraging that power to go where we want to go next.

Imposter syndrome

Laura: I like to describe imposter syndrome as a villain in my head who likes to remind me (often) that I am not good enough or worthy of what I have. That voice tells me that, any day now, someone will tap me on the back and tell me that this dream I've been living is now over. As our business has grown beyond our wildest dreams, I've been hoping that this imposter syndrome would go away. I truly believed it was linked directly with success and that the more successful we became, the less imposter syndrome I would experience. I used to think, *If we get to 'X', then I'll be more deserving of any success we achieve.*

What I've actually discovered is that imposter syndrome works in the opposite way. The more successful our business has become, the more this feeling has grown. In an effort to understand it better (I find learning a great coping mechanism – it's often the way I combat self-doubt) I researched imposter syndrome and learned that many of the world's most successful people also feel this way. Mike Cannon-Brookes, founder and co-CEO of Atlassian, is one of Australia's most successful tech entrepreneurs of all time. He has spoken openly about his experience with imposter syndrome and how it has affected him despite his tremendous success. In his Ted Talk, 'Imposter Syndrome', he tells of how – despite having thousands of employees and 15 years of experience under his belt – he often feels out of his depth at work or like he doesn't know what he's doing. He talks about how this isn't the same as fear of failure, but rather the sensation of 'getting away with something' and a fear of being 'discovered'. Research has found that there are some personality traits that can contribute to a higher risk of contributing to imposter syndrome, including low self-efficacy, perfectionism and neuroticism, and 70 per cent of us will experience it in at least one stage of our lives. So, I guess it just makes us . . . human?

If you are reading this and nodding your head in recognition, please do one thing for me: You must ensure that you work out ways to quieten that voice in your head telling you that you can't because you *can*. You have come so far. You are where you are because you got yourself there. Far from being an imposter, you are worthy of every single success. Don't let a voice inside your head tell you lies that stop you from feeling the pride you deserve to feel. Do whatever it takes to squish this voice and lower the volume on it as much as possible.

I know this is easier said than done. Sometimes, the voice is very loud, so on those days when it is hard not to listen to it, cut yourself some slack. Recently, I finished up a very important meeting, and the moment I pressed exit on my Zoom screen, I was filled with disappointment in myself. Right on cue, my imposter syndrome triggered negative thoughts: *I should have done so much better. I should have used bigger words. I should have been clearer in my delivery. I should have been more impactful.* In the weeks following this meeting, that voice became louder. Usually, it's a background noise that I can turn down, but it moved to the front of my mind and affected a lot of my work for a few weeks. Everything I did took twice as long because I was second-guessing myself so much. This was exhausting and draining.

About three weeks later, I got a call from someone who had been on that Zoom meeting. They had feedback for me about how it had gone and it was wonderful! As I hung up the phone, all I could do was laugh. By leaning into the voice telling me that I was not good enough, I'd made up a terrible story in my head and spent weeks in a state of anxiousness and self-doubt because of it. Our mind is extremely powerful. But in the same way that we can convince ourselves that we *can't*, we can also convince ourselves that we *can*. We have that power. ≫

Don't let a voice inside your head tell you lies that stop you from feeling the pride you deserve to feel.

One thing that does (mostly) help me in times of self-doubt is reminding myself of how far I have come. In the process of researching and writing this book, I relistened to some of the KICPOD episodes we've recorded. We've been so lucky to have conversations with many incredible guests who've shared brilliant insights with us. One of the episodes I listened to was with Dr Jodie Lowinger. This interview, which was recorded two years previously, was a big reminder to me in two key ways: firstly, how much my interviewing skills have improved. When Steph and I started our podcast, we had minimal experience in interviewing people, but we gave it a go. I was not great at it, and while I may not be a world-class journalist, I am so much better. We could have let the fact that we weren't experienced podcasters/interviewers stop us from starting the podcast and giving it a go, but then we would never have had the chance to learn and grow along the way.

Secondly, I was reminded how much my mental health and mindset have improved in the past two years. When I listened to those earlier episodes, I could hear the lack of confidence in my voice and in the way I spoke about myself – to the point I almost couldn't recognise the voice playing through my speaker. I felt sad as I listened to myself at such a low point, but proud, too, for where I am today. I know that confidence is not a forever state of being or a sure thing – it ebbs and flows, and that's why it's so important to constantly remind yourself that you can always build it back up when it gets low. If you have done that or are in the process of building it back up right now, be proud of how far you have come.

How to kick imposter syndrome in the butt

★ Remind yourself of all the other awesome people (just like you) who also experience these feelings. If it helps, google 'successful celebrities with imposter syndrome'. I literally do this because it makes me think, *Wow, if Lady Gaga doesn't think she is worthy of her success* (and we can agree that she definitely is), *then maybe I'm making this up in my head, too.*

★ Write down the name of a person you look up to – someone whose success or life is the most inspiring. Then, ask yourself if they would be where they are today if they had stayed stuck believing they weren't good enough and hadn't been able to overcome their feelings of self-doubt.

you take care

* Write a list of things YOU have achieved and done when you've pushed yourself out of your comfort zone and squished that negative voice in your head. Remind yourself that the person who achieved every one of those things was *you*. Next, write down all the things you haven't done because of imposter syndrome. Remind yourself that the person responsible for those was also (unfortunately) all *you*, too. The only difference between what you did and didn't do is that you either ignored or listened to that pest of a voice in your head. Don't let it rob you of any more good things.

* Bring awareness to the fact that - when it all comes down to it (in science and everyday life) - we are each just billions of atoms bonded together walking around and living life. No one collection of atoms is better or more worthy than another.

* Give your imposter syndrome a really *ugly* name (maybe after someone you don't like or respect). Next time it pops up, respond with, *Well, X, it's nice that you have an opinion, but I don't really care what you think, so I'm not going to listen to you. I'm going to live my life now.*

Recognising and preventing burnout

Ahh, burnout. Anyone who has experienced any level of burnout will know how absolutely debilitating it can be.

Steph: Every aspect of your life suddenly feels weighed down by huge boulders or like there are hurdles in the way at every turn. Even simple tasks feel impossible, and all emotions (good or bad) are heightened and uncontrollable. I have been burnt out on a couple of occasions over the last few years, so I have personal experience with these feelings. Not acknowledging it at the time and not knowing what to do about it left me feeling incredibly lost, hopeless and exhausted, and it felt like there was no end to it. So I'm really hoping that sharing tips and tricks and ways to identify burnout will help you avoid it, or at least move through it quicker than I did. Let's become aware of what it is, why it comes about and what you can do to manage it.

What is it?

Burnout can happen to anyone, but it does tend to come knocking more often on the doors of those working in high-stress environments, those with A-type personalities or those juggling too many things at once. Basically, anyone who's continuously stressed out.

Signs of burnout

* **Exhaustion:** Burnout can lead to forgetfulness and difficulty concentrating.

* **Isolation:** When someone is struggling with burnout, they're likely to feel overwhelmed. And when someone's overwhelmed, they are likely to retreat and avoid social occasions with loved ones or co-workers.

* **Loss of motivation:** Some people find they lose sight of their own career goals and ambitions, and even lose pride in their own work.

* **Irritability:** All emotions are heightened, and some people find they are short-tempered or easily irritated by things that wouldn't usually make them feel this way.

* **Frequent illness:** Burnout can affect an individual's physical and mental health. Long periods of stress can equate to a lower immune system.

After reading through the signs, do you think you've experienced burnout? Let's discuss the ways in which we can avoid that ever happening again. If you've never experienced it, let's keep it that way.

How can we prevent it?

If being overly stressed for a long period of time is one of the main factors leading to burnout, then managing stress is one of the best ways we can avoid it. So, how do we manage stress? Here are some ideas.

* **Look after your physical self.** We all know that when we're eating well, fuelling ourselves with the right nutrients, moving our body regularly and finding exercise that we enjoy, we feel better from the inside out. Exercise can have a huge impact on not only your physical health but your mental health, too.

- ★ **Set boundaries.** This is a big one. A lot of the time, a busy schedule can tip us over the edge when we're overwhelmed. Whether you have a lot on your plate as a full-time mum or a full-time lawyer, everyone in the world needs time to recharge. What you do with your free time is up to you, but work through your priorities and start becoming comfortable with using the word 'no'.

- ★ **Reach out.** If you're struggling, don't be afraid to ask for help. Whether it's friends and family helping with things around the house or a colleague taking a task at work off your hands, be okay with not doing it all on your own.

- ★ **Get some sleep.** I never struggled with sleep until becoming a mum. And I can confirm that being sleep deprived is honestly one of the most challenging things ever. It makes everything that much harder. Find a reasonable bedtime that suits you and your lifestyle and try to stick to it. Sleep is so important, so think of yourself as a piece of technology – you need time to recharge in order to work.

Think a friend might be struggling with burnout? The best way you can help is by letting them know you're there for them. Offer to help out where you can and if you know they're the type to always refuse help, jump in with a kind gesture that you know will take something off of their plate.

Fill your own cup first

KIC: From a young age, children (especially female children) are taught certain social conventions to help them 'fit in' and be seen as polite. These conventions include never pouring a drink into their own glass before filling the glasses of those around them. Waiting for everyone to be served before they start eating. Never getting anything for themselves in a group scenario without first asking others if they would like something. These behaviours are polite and intended to make the people around you feel good. And it's true that when we are literally filling up our cup, it is kind to fill others', but when we are talking about figuratively 'filling our cup', it can be damaging to think this way. In fact, we need to think the opposite way.

Try thinking about it like this: you know the feeling you get when your car is down to the last ten kilometres of fuel, and your petrol light starts flashing? Mild panic, right? You recognise that you are nearly on empty, so you rush to the closest petrol station because you know that if you don't fill up, your car will stop dead in the middle of the road until it's refuelled. Once that tank is empty, you cannot scream at your car and ask it to practise manifestation and magically start again. Unless it has fuel in it, it simply will not run. (If your tank never runs low because you are a very organised person, then kudos to you!)

Now, think about your body and mind the same way. The body's warning systems are not quite as straightforward as a flashing light on a dashboard, but the mind is very smart, and it sends warning signs when you need to slow down. The more these are ignored, the louder they get, and the bigger the risk they are to your overall health. In our busy world, it can be hard to recognise these warning signs amongst all the noise, but you must try. It is vital to your wellbeing. When we are overworked and our tank has been running on empty for too long, we can arrive at burnout, and that's a place we really want to avoid.

Easy ways to fill your cup

- ★ Read a book in the sunshine

- ★ Walk in nature

- ★ Swim in the sea

- ★ Meditate

- ★ Have dinner with someone who makes you smile

- ★ Dance to your favourite music

- ★ Take yourself out for breakfast

- ★ Bake a cake (only if you find baking therapeutic)

- ★ Take a nap

- ★ Listen to a podcast in your favourite park

Me-time

Steph: I'm a huuuge fan of me-time. Without it, I am far from my best self. I've worked hard throughout my twenties and have really thrived on the hustle and bustle life for most of it. But when COVID hit (of course, the global pandemic would make an appearance at some point in this book), most of us were forced to slow down. Over a two-year period, I, like a lot of people all over the world, spent most of my time in lockdown. Suddenly, all modelling gigs went out the window, travel opportunities faded away, and events for our company kept getting pushed back. Weekends that used to be filled with catching up with friends and family were now filled with bingeing a new TV series and, even though everyone hates traffic, I found myself dreaming of getting to go somewhere in my car that wasn't the supermarket. Anyway, the point is that life changed dramatically. I was extremely fortunate to still be able to work from home on our business, but outside of that, there really wasn't much to do. I started to take my time in the morning and would go for a walk with my husband, Josh, and spend some quality time with him before logging on to work that day. At lunchtime, I would have enough time to fit in a workout, or I'd take time to create a delicious meal and actually sit down for lunch with Josh rather than at my desk. In the evenings, I had so much time to wind down however I wanted as we had no plans. I found that when I slowed down, I was *way* more productive with my work and a much happier, less stressed version of myself.

'Me-time' can be for anything you want it to be – it's a time for self-love. It should bring you peace, bring you joy, allow you to lose track of time and connect with yourself.

Things I do during my me-time

★ **Move my body.** I love going for long walks by myself or following a KIC workout at home.

★ **Take a bath.** A bath bomb or bubbles are an absolute necessity. I grew up watching my mum draw herself a bath at least once a week, and it was her 'alone time'. She always lit a candle and read a book in there. Now that I'm an adult, I can see why she found this so relaxing.

★ **Watch a movie.** I absolutely love watching movies, new or old, funny or sad. I just love getting lost in another world and another story that isn't mine.

★ **Draw.** Drawing cartoons has been something that has brought me a lot of joy since I was a kid. The thing I love about it the most is how I always lose track of time once I start. Plus, it takes me away from my phone.

★ **Paint my nails.** I don't know why, but I find it so therapeutic.

★ **Bake a yummy sweet KIC recipe**. One of my favourites is on page 89.

Making time for yourself should be non-negotiable. As we've already mentioned, you cannot pour from an empty cup, so make sure you're making time for the things that fill that cup back up.

You wouldn't leave a friend hanging, so don't forget to show up for yourself.

Chunky Chocolate Chip and Peanut Butter Cookies

Two of my favourite things in life: peanut butter and chocolate. If you're the same then you have to try this recipe. They are moreish, and the best part is you probably have everything you need for them in your pantry.

125 g (4½ oz) peanut butter

30 ml (1 fl oz) coconut oil, melted

85 ml (2¾ fl oz) maple syrup

1 teaspoon vanilla extract

90 g (3¼ oz) rolled oats

20 g (¾ oz) almond meal (ground almonds)

½ teaspoon salt

100 g (3½ oz) dark chocolate chips

1 Preheat your oven to 175°C (345°F) and line a baking tray with baking paper. Place the peanut butter, coconut oil, maple syrup and vanilla extract in a large bowl and whisk to combine.

2 Add the oats, almond meal, salt and chocolate chips to the bowl and mix until everything is combined. Set the batter aside for 10 minutes to thicken.

3 Roll the batter into balls (approximately 1–1½ tablespoons per cookie), place on the baking tray (leaving a little room between them so they can spread as they cook) and flatten slightly with your palm.

4 Bake for 10–12 minutes, or until the edges are golden. They might seem quite soft so try not to touch them or move them – they will harden over time once cooled. Once cooled completely, store cookies that you're not eating straight away in an airtight container and enjoy.

Meditation

Before you skip this chapter and think, *Meditation just isn't for me*, I urge you to read on. I promise you that I had the exact same thought a few years back before learning more about it, but I'd love for you to give meditation a crack.

Steph: First, what is meditation? It's is a mindfulness technique that involves relaxation, focus and awareness. It involves bringing your attention inwards, being present with your thoughts and focusing on your breath.

Now let's think about *why* we would meditate. Would you try meditating so that you can feel calmer? Maybe you'd be willing to meditate to help you switch off, or to ground yourself or help you slow down just for a moment. If you aren't familiar with the many benefits regular meditation can have on your life, here are three of the best.

1   Reduces the fight-or-flight stress response

2   Clears (and calms) the mind

3   Brings awareness to the present moment

Even if you have heard of the benefits, you may not know of the many different ways you can go about meditating. When we think of what meditating looks like, we often think of someone sitting in a dimly-lit room or, better yet, a candlelit room, cross-legged with their palms on their knees and eyes closed. While that is a beautiful setting and way to meditate, it doesn't have to be the way you meditate. Much like exercise, you're more likely to stick to a regular meditation practice if you find a way to drift into a meditative state that you enjoy. For some people, that's via guided meditation. For others, it's sitting outside in nature and listening to the noises around them or simply focusing on their breath. These are just a few examples of 'still' ways of practising, but if those aren't for you, you can also fall into a meditative state when walking or even running. This is known as 'moving meditation'.

Here are some of our favourite ways to meditate. These are especially good right before bedtime.

Our favourite ways to meditate

★ **Body scan meditation:** Similar to Yoga Nidra and progressive muscle relaxation, body scan meditations guide your awareness through different parts of your body with the intention of releasing stress, tension or pain.

★ **Mindfulness meditation:** These practices are centred around focusing the awareness on the present moment by connecting with your sensory experience of sounds, the breath, the body and so forth, while also welcoming all thoughts, emotions and sensations with openness, kindness and curiosity.

★ **Visualisation meditation:** Guided visualisations help you to relax by instructing you to imagine yourself in a calming place, such as a beach or forest, drawing you into a state that is similar to hypnosis.

★ **Deep breathing:** One of our personal faves, also known as Pranayama, these breath-related practices involve regulating your breath by engaging the diaphragm, which helps to engage the parasympathetic nervous system (which comes into use when we are at rest).

Top-5 tips for newbie meditators
Meg James

KIC: Meg James is our inspirational go-to expert for all things relating to meditation and mindfulness. She has a background in psychology, and you'll notice her name pop up throughout this book. Meg has developed countless meditations for the KIC app to help us feel our feelings, listen to our intuition, develop our sense of self and manage the unhelpful thought patterns that keep us awake at night. If you've tuned in, you know her voice is unbelievably soothing. Here are five tips from Meg that we found really helpful when we started practising.

1 **Start small.** The most effective meditation practice is one that's done consistently, so start with short sessions between 2 and 5 minutes long and work your way up as it becomes easier and more enjoyable.

2 **Expect your mind to wander.** Meditation isn't actually about emptying your mind of thoughts but rather changing your relationship with them. Each time your mind wanders off, simply notice yourself thinking and return your awareness to your practice.

3 **Meditate at whatever time of day works for you.** Whether that's morning or night, you'll find it easiest to stick with your meditation if you commit to practising at the same time each day.

4 **Listen to a guided meditation.** Meditating without guidance is incredibly challenging, particularly for beginners. There are many guided meditations available on the KIC app, so you can start by listening to one of those and following the guidance of an instructor.

5 **Be gentle with yourself.** Starting something new isn't easy, so be sure to exercise compassion, kindness and patience with yourself as you learn to meditate.

One of the simplest and most effective ways to combat the mind's tendency to focus on negative thoughts is to practise a gratitude meditation, as your mind doesn't have the ability to feel anxious and appreciative at the same time.

Steph: Another expert we are so fortunate to work with through KIC is one of our yoga instructors, Jamie Strathairn. Jamie, along with his wife, Karen, is a good friend and one of my biggest inspirations and motivators for all things mindfulness, but particularly for practising yoga. His general energy is incredibly soothing, which makes his yoga flows and meditations a joy to practise. I couldn't finish this chapter with 'give it a go and let go of expectations' without giving you something specific to try. Outside of guided meditations, practising this particular breathing technique that Jamie has kindly shared with us is one of my favourite ways to stop, breathe, reset and find clarity.

I know this technique as '4/4 breath', but it is actually called *samavṛtti* in Sanskrit, which is the language of yoga. Samavṛtti (pronounced 'summa vrittee' but rolling the 'r') translates as 'equal turning', and it's a breath practice that leads to quieting the mind. Our mind is good at being noisy and turning things over and over – after all, it's a processing organ for our sensory experiences, and it craves activity. This breathing technique helps the mind stop for a moment and allows you to gain control and start living in the present moment.

Let's slow things down and try this 4/4 breath exercise with Jamie.

4/4 breath
Jamie Strathairn

The lovely thing about this technique is that we always have our breath with us, so we can do it at any time. We can do it sitting in a park, in our car, on the couch, at work, anywhere. Better still, just a few minutes of this each day quickly trains the mind to be less concerned with things that don't matter. We start creating a new groove where the mind can practise being more still and less worried. Brilliant!

My suggestion for this breath practice is to do it at least once every day for between 5 and 10 minutes (though you can do it even longer, up to 20–30 minutes if you like). To begin with, do it with your eyes closed and in a quiet place so that you limit outside distractions. If, during the practice, you notice your mind wandering off to other thoughts, just remind yourself that you are paying attention to the breath and come back to it.

Most of the time, we don't think about our breathing at all. The only time we really pay attention to our breath is when we've been working out and are puffed or when we have a blocked nose or something. But this practice is all about paying attention to the breath.

Step 1: Take a moment to notice your breath. Breathe in. Breathe out. Do a few rounds slowly, belly relaxed, breathing in and out through your nose, noticing the air flowing in and out. If you pay attention, you will notice the constant movement of the breath. It cycles or turns like a wheel. But if you pay even more attention, you might be able to notice the exact point where the breath changes from in to out and from out to in. Normally, we don't notice these pauses.

Step 2: Come back to noticing the turning of the breath. Breathe in and out for a few rounds. Then, start to notice the exact points where the breath changes from in to out and from out to in. Now, start to lengthen those points where the breath changes direction. Create longer pauses – a pause at the top of the breath when the lungs and belly are full; and a pause at the bottom of the breath when the lungs and belly are empty.

See how there are actually four parts to the breath?

1   The breath in,

2   the pause,

3   the breath out, and

4   the pause before the cycle begins again.

Step 3: Now we have half of our 4/4 equation. To complete the exercise, we are going to focus our attention on the four stages of the breath and add a count so that each of the four stages lasts for four counts. For example, breathe in for a count of four, pause for a count of four, breathe out for a count of four, and pause for a count of four. Voilà! We have our 4/4 breath.

Good luck.

Why I meditated during pregnancy

Steph: During my pregnancy with Harvey, my hormones were all over the shop. Meditation helped me centre my thoughts and breathe through any feelings of stress or overwhelm. It was one of my favourite ways to stay grounded and connected to my little man. When launching KICBUMP, our pre- and postnatal program, it was important to me that we incorporate a series of relaxing meditations designed especially for new and expectant mums so they, too, could experience that sense of calm and clarity as they ride the emotional rollercoaster of motherhood.

Meg James helped me understand the benefits of meditation during pregnancy, so I thought it would be helpful to pass those on to you. Meditation can help you shift out of the body's 'fight-or-flight' response by lowering cortisol levels and re-engaging the body's parasympathetic nervous system, which controls a lot of important bodily functions. This not only helps to reduce stress but also leaves us feeling much calmer, centred and relaxed, which is incredibly beneficial for the growth and development of your baby.

Benefits of meditating during pregnancy

★ Reduces stress and anxiety

★ Lowers heart rate and blood pressure

★ Improves sleep quality

★ Connects you with your changing body

★ Deepens your connection with your baby

★ Enhances immunity

★ Reduces fears and enhances positive outlook for birth

First trimester

Meditation is most beneficial when practised daily; however, in early pregnancy you may struggle to find a state of calmness and peace if you're feeling nauseous or worried about the risk factors associated with the first trimester. Aim to practise three-to-five days per week. It doesn't have to be a long meditation to be beneficial either. Meg's motto for all of her students, especially mothers, is to practise 'small amounts, consistently'.

Second trimester

In the second trimester, it becomes easier to meditate comfortably again but, by this point, you'll start feeling movements and kicks from your baby, so this becomes an added source of distraction to work with.

Third trimester

By the third trimester, many women are incredibly uncomfortable in their bodies, not to mention nervous about the upcoming delivery and the life changes that arise with a new baby. You might even be so tired that you struggle to stay awake while meditating. These are all totally normal challenges to work with during pregnancy, so it's important not to let them deter you from your practice.

Fourth trimester

While it's harder to maintain your pre-baby meditation routine with a newborn, there are still plenty of ways you can weave the practice into your daily rhythm. For example, during the morning feed, you might like to take a few mindful breaths to centre yourself for the day. During baby's naptime you might recharge with a restful body scan meditation or a self-compassion practice to fill your cup back up. And during the last feed of the day, you might want to reflect on all the things that have gone well throughout that day, no matter how big or small.

Building a healthy habit is all about taking small steps consistently.

Let go of the things you cannot control, and focus on those that you can.

A BALANCED
MIND IS A STRONG
FOUNDATION
FOR A HEALTHY
BODY.

PART TWO

body

With social media comparison at our fingertips it's
no wonder that seven out of ten Australian women and
non-binary people between the ages of 18 and 30 have
experienced a lack of body confidence at some stage
in their life. This is a heartbreaking statistic, and one
that we are both a part of.

Thankfully, over the years, we've built up a toolbox
of tips, tools and habits to help us come out the other end
happier and healthier than ever. In this part of the book we
explore the damaging effects of diet culture, and open our
toolbox up in the hope of inspiring you with ways of
nurturing and nourishing your body.

It's time to stop chasing the 'perfect' body

The world we live in is constantly sending the message that personal value and self-worth are tied to the way our bodies look.

Laura: When we allow our worthiness to become intertwined by the number on the scales or on a clothing tag, a number that doesn't matter suddenly has the power to define self-worth and dictate how we feel. Too much time is spent worrying about the way our body will look at defining events in our lives rather than appreciating the special moments that those events bring to our lives. Dress size doesn't dictate if we are enough.

We are led to believe that a better life will come with a better body, and that a perfect life will be the reward for having a perfect body. The happiness at the end of the rainbow is supposedly waiting for us when we lose 'the last five'. This idea of perfection is amplified by apps such as Facetune, which morph and distort real proportions to present an idealised face and figure that are not achievable for 99.99 per cent of humans. But rather than see those versions for the unattainable goals they are, many people – especially women – waste valuable time, money and energy striving to be the 0.01 per cent.

Practical information about genetics and human biology is kicked to the curb as if they aren't the main reasons we look the way we do. Facts are tossed aside for fiction. We forget about the purpose of the body and that we need it. We forget that having the ability to move our bodies is a privilege, something we shouldn't take for granted. It's a subconscious freedom that doesn't come easily to people living with chronic pain and disability. Instead, we might treat our body horribly and with disrespect – forgetting to love it, care for it, or be grateful for what it does for us. We might trash it by spending years abusing it, depriving it of nutritious food or overworking it. We take advantage of its strength by pushing it to the limits. We have to fight against this way of behaving, and change the way we think about our bodies.

We must work hard to move away from the notion that the way a body looks matters or in any way defines what and who someone is worthy of. This can be done by reconnecting with the body and rebuilding a healthy relationship with it – one based on respect and love. Our body is with us for life. We only get one, so it's crucial that we feel at home and at peace inside it.

A lot of body-related pressure comes from social media, where many 'ideal' body types are showcased on various platforms. Certain body trends have come and gone, and, thankfully, several counter-movements have also sprung up around body positivity and embracing the body we've been given by nature. Countless theories and approaches have been shared about how to improve the relationship between the self and the body – whatever that body looks like. Everyone is different, and we each relate or connect with different things, so if one type of approach works best for you, that's awesome. It doesn't matter what journey or piece of advice you take; what matters is that you end up in a place where you feel at peace with your home (your body) and are able to respect and appreciate it for all of the incredible things it does for you.

A big part of our mission at KIC is to help people realise just this and to be proud of their body. After spending time (in real life and virtually) with thousands of people, most of them women, we learned some things that have helped us appreciate our bodies even more. ≫

Busting the smooth bikini line myth

KIC: While we're talking unattainable body/face goals, a perfectly smooth bikini line does not exist. If you choose to remove your body hair, contrary to the images you see on social media, it's actually bloody difficult to have a perfectly smooth, hairless bikini line. The reality is that ingrown hairs, cuts, red spots, shaving rashes or hairs that grow back almost as soon as you finish shaving are COMPLETELY normal. Don't get sucked in by the photoshopped images you see online.

6 body truths

1   **You are not your body.** Your body is a part of you, but it's absolutely not the whole of you.

2   **You do not need to 'love' every part of your body** – or any part of it, to be completely honest. We often confuse respect with love, but they are two very different things. There is a lot of privilege that comes with being able to love many parts of your body. If you are born into a body that fits the mould that society and the media deem 'the ideal', then by default it is easier to love your body. The pressure to look in the mirror and scream, 'OMG, I love my legs, my butt and my stomach!' can be too much. A far more realistic approach is to look in the mirror and focus on the many incredible things your body does for you. Flick back to page 40 if you want some examples.

3   **No one will stand up at your funeral and talk about your abs or thigh gap**. And if you think they might, please make new friends now so by the time you are 100 you can be remembered for something that actually matters.

4   **Your worth has nothing to do with your body.** Write down what truly matters to you and what you want to do with your life. We can guarantee you it will have nothing to do with your body.

5   **Weight doesn't dictate happiness.** It's time to stop weighing yourself – especially if you have a history of disordered eating, excessive exercising or any weight-related patterns that are unhealthy for your mind and/or your body. Eat well, move often, rest and look after your mind, not because of the number on your scales but because you want to look after yourself and feel good. That number rarely represents how healthy you are. If the scales don't serve you, get rid of them.

6   **You don't need to fit into those old jeans.** You know the ones. The pair that make you feel bad about yourself every time you see them in your cupboard. The sooner you throw those jeans out, the sooner you will stop telling yourself you are not good enough as you are now. You are enough.

People will remember you for

★   The way you made them feel

★   The joy and fulfilment you brought to their lives

★   The way you helped them through a really hard time

★   The shoulder you always offered them when they needed it

★   The way you always knew when they needed you

★   The support they always felt from you

★   The experiences you shared with them

★   The memories you created together

★   How much love you shared with them

★   A thousand other reasons that have absolutely nothing to do with your body!

TRY THIS

Keep a list of reasons people will remember you in a journal or in the Notes app on your phone. Keep adding to this list and reflect back on it whenever you need a friendly reminder of how special you are.

More amazing things about you that have nothing to do with your appearance

★ Your energy

★ Your drive

★ Your inner strength

★ Your laugh

★ Your greatest traits (e.g. kindness, compassion, sense of humour)

★ Your intelligence and knowledge

★ How you treat the people around you

Body positivity

I read a quote that really resonated with me: 'It's not learning how to love your body; it's unlearning how to hate it'.

Steph: The reason I love this quote so much is that it gets to something really important: nobody is *born* hating their body. Those negative habits and thought patterns are learned. Unfortunately, there will probably always be underlying pressure to look a certain way. Throughout history, there has always been an 'ideal body type'. That ideal has changed wildly to fit whatever values and standards society happened to celebrate during each particular era. Shouldn't this tell us that all bodies are beautifully unique? If your body type doesn't happen to be trending this year, so what? Why should you hate it? No matter what you do, you can't possibly look like someone with a totally different body shape, so why put yourself through the shitty journey of trying to?

As much as I understand the temptation to chase a body trend, I also understand when someone says they're just trying to look the way they used to because that was me. Growing up, I was super sporty and a little lean bean. I had visible abs from the time I was ten. And although 'abs' are commonly depicted as ideal (in this era at least), as a teenager I didn't really like my stomach. I envied my schoolmates with curves and felt like my muscular body was 'boyish'. Boys often bullied me for being flat-chested. I wouldn't say I truly struggled with my body image because this didn't change the way I looked at exercise or food at the time, but that soon changed.

I started modelling full-time when I was 18. At that point, I was an Australian size eight and had a very balanced view of exercise and dieting. I moved to the United States for a little while when I was 20 years old, and between the age of 18 and 20, I suppose you could say I developed a more adult-like figure. When reps from the US modelling agencies would measure me, they'd comment about how my measurements had increased since they signed me a year earlier. Being the young, driven model I was, I was determined to try and change that. They took my profile off their website and told me I would go back on when I lost weight. Only after that would they be proud to send me to castings and let me represent their agency. **Facepalm emoji.**

Prior to this experience, exercise had been something I did because I enjoyed it – something I did to stay healthy. But after hearing the ultimatum from the agents, I felt I had to get my measurements back down to where they were when I was a teenager. Exercise became a task, an obsession – something I had to force myself to do. I looked at food differently, too. I picked up binge-eating patterns and became overly careful about what I put into my body. Restricting foods that I loved became my new normal. Instead, I'd binge on whatever food I'd allow myself to eat right up until the point of feeling sick (sometimes even making myself sick). It was a horrible pattern and a horrible time. I was constantly thinking about food; I'd start planning what to eat for dinner while I was still having my breakfast (maybe even my second serving of breakfast).

Eventually, I did lose the inches my agency had asked for, only to hear that I still didn't have quite the right measurements. I was encouraged to keep going with my weight loss. You'd think I would have been happy to reach those goal measurements, right? But I wasn't. I was more insecure in my body than ever because now, all I could see were my 'flaws'. Flaws that I had learned to see – had been taught to see. To cut a long story short, it took coming home and surrounding myself with people who loved me for me and not for my measurements to 'unlearn' these horrible patterns of hateful self-talk and binge eating. It didn't happen overnight, either. Once learned, these negative lessons can be hard to shake. To this day, those old habits can creep up on me when I'm in a state of vulnerability. I'm just quicker at squashing them now.

you take care

No matter who you are, you've probably had or may still have insecurities about the way you look. That's normal. You don't have to love everything about yourself. WHO DOES? But with work, you can change a negative narrative and learn to be kinder to yourself. There's a common saying; *Treat yourself as you would treat a good friend.* And I think this is such an important message – in general, but especially when it comes to body positivity. Think about someone you love; you don't love them because of their looks, just as you don't hate them for the 'flaws' they see in themselves. That's not how relationships work, and it's not how our own relationship with our body should work, either. To me, being body positive doesn't necessarily mean accepting or learning to love my flaws; it means appreciating my body for what it's capable of and celebrating everything I do love about myself.

TRY THIS

Stand in front of a mirror. Let insecurities come up if they do, but be quick to counteract them with some kinder words. Tell yourself three things you're grateful for in your physical body. It could be as simple as saying you like your hair, your smile or that your arms allow you to carry your baby around. Once you start looking for things you do like, you'll see there's plenty to be grateful for. Sometimes, it just takes removing the noise and pressure of society to find them.

Acknowledge your body for how incredible it really is.

Accepting your body during pregnancy

Steph: When I was pregnant, one of the questions I kept getting asked again and again was, 'Are you worried you won't bounce back after you've had the baby?' Maybe because I'd never been pregnant before and I was so used to seeing that same pressure be applied to celebrity mums by the media, the phrase 'bounce back' didn't faze me. I started to question whether or not I was worried. Truth be told, I hadn't thought about how my body would look after birth prior to being asked. I was too busy being excited about being pregnant and fascinated by everything that my body was doing to create a human. Now that I have firsthand experience of pregnancy, birth and the wild highs and lows of the postpartum phase (aka the 'fourth trimester'), my view of this question is not so neutral. In fact, my take on that phrase is very much . . .

Screw the 'bounce back'

'Bounce back' – hearing these two words leaves me with my eyes rolling to the back of my head. There is sooo much pressure on women to look the way they did before having a baby, but why is that? And why do we even want that? I feel funny when someone says, 'You don't even look like you've had a baby'. I understand that person means well, but being pregnant and giving birth was a huge challenge that my body conquered. Don't take that accomplishment away from me by saying it's as if it never happened. Plus, I'm a mum now, and I'm proud to be recognised as one.

Why do we continue to comment on each other's weight or physical appearance like it's something to be congratulated for anyway? I mean, sure, if you know your friend has been getting back into exercise and wasn't quite feeling herself during that postpartum stage, then by all means, compliment her and tell her she's killing it. Tell her it's amazing to see how she's prioritising time to move her body and compliment her on her strength, not her weight or appearance. Some women will look similar to how they did prior to birth, and others won't. Neither is inferior or superior. In the same way that the body reacts when it hits puberty, changes are inevitable. The only reason these changes are perceived as negative is due to the many ways the media and society pressures women to always look their 'best'. I say your 'best' is however you look when you're your happiest self.

Welcome the changes – even if they're weird

In my first trimester and early into my second, my stomach started to bloat. This was a confusing time because, although I knew I was pregnant, it wasn't that obvious to other people. In one moment, I'd be sticking out my belly – trying to accentuate it so that it was more obvious that I was pregnant, but in another, I'd be trying to find clothes that hid the bump because it wasn't obvious enough yet. This really made me stop for a moment and think about where my relationship with my body was at. Why did I care if someone looked at me and wondered in their own mind if I was pregnant or not? First of all, it was highly unlikely anyone looking at me would be wondering that, and even if they were, did it matter either way?

This was a bit of a wake-up call for me because I was noticing that I was suddenly falling back into my old habit of caring too much about what other people thought of my physical appearance. That same habit had driven me down a horrible path of restrictive diets and excessive fitness routines in the past, and I wasn't going to let that happen again. I started reading more about the inner workings of the female body and learning about the incredible things that happen to it during pregnancy and after childbirth, and this helped me appreciate my body on a whole new level.

I can't write about the physical changes I experienced during pregnancy without sharing something else. I actually have a bit of a giggle about this these days, but I was quite hysterical when I first noticed it. I remember there being tears – a mixture of crying from laughter but also from embarrassment – when I noticed a few long brown hairs growing on my bum. And no, not pubic hairs. I'm talking hairs that were similar but growing in the centre of my bottom all the way down to the top of my thighs. This was NOT normal for me, and I suddenly developed an insecurity about my bum. I can't say I ever got to the point of 'loving' this change, but I did grow to accept it once I learned that weird and wonderful things like this happen because of the hormonal changes caused by pregnancy.

If you're currently pregnant and feeling insecure about your physical appearance now or what it may be postpartum, here's my best advice:

★ Read up on the incredible miracle of childbirth and pregnancy and celebrate what your body is capable of.

★ Ask yourself why it is that the 'dad bod' is so widely accepted and even celebrated while actual mums (i.e., the people who actually grew the baby) are pressured into feeling that they need to look the way they did before they became a mum? It's absolutely great that the dad bod is celebrated because every single body is amazing. We just need this standard to apply both ways. It's time to celebrate the 'mum bod'.

★ Head over to the mirror and cradle that belly of yours. If you're currently pregnant, appreciate that there's a little human being growing in there. How cool is that? And if you're cradling or touching your deflated belly, remember it was your baby's home for nine months. Remember, YOU GREW THAT TINY HUMAN that now keeps you up at night and makes you smile like nothing else. I find myself staring at my son while rubbing my belly because it was his first home. I was his first home.

★ Try your best not to fall into the comparison trap. Every woman's body is different and each experience of pregnancy and birth is different, so, of course, the changes to the physical body will also be different. Loving our body isn't always possible, but we should always be able to find things that we can appreciate it for.

Prep for the fourth trimester

The early weeks post birth are a rollercoaster to say the least, and these weeks following birth are known as 'the fourth trimester'. Speak to any mumma and they'll be able to reflect on that time and tell you about their ups and downs. And when listening to their stories, you'll notice a couple of themes start to creep in: there is so much we're not taught, and there are so many different ways those early postpartum days can go. You're not sent home after a birth without any help at all, so I'm not going to exaggerate the situation and say the midwives and doctors don't prep you at all, but there's only so much you can learn without experiencing it yourself. There's only so much your brain can hold onto after a marathon like birth.

You will hear a lot of parents say that when they brought their babies home they sat down and thought, *So, now what?* This is the moment where it really hits you. You are now responsible for keeping another human alive. They need you for absolutely everything, and there's something incredibly beautiful about that, but downright exhausting, too.

Know this: you are not alone if

★   Breastfeeding doesn't work out for you

★   You judge yourself for giving your baby a dummy

★   You cry over never having time for yourself anymore

★   You end up wearing adult diapers or period undies for longer than expected

★   You don't feel up to having sex, even after you've had clearance from your doctor

★   You go crazy from sleep deprivation and say things you don't mean to those you love

★   You suddenly find yourself overthinking and worrying about everything, even if you've never been that way inclined.

You're also not alone if you cannot relate to any of the examples on the previous page because, guess what? Just as pregnancies differ from person to person, so do our feelings after birth.

Self-care in the fourth trimester

One of the best ways to ignore the pressures from society is to tune out the noise and double down on self-care, because the only thing that truly matters in those crazy months after a baby arrives is their health, and yours.

Some things that helped get me through that fourth trimester

Surround yourself with other parents

And don't stop leaning on them for support. If no one around you has had babies, join a local mothers' group. I reach out to my mothers' group a couple of times a week even now, and my baby is almost 10 months old. You will learn quickly that you do some things differently, but you will also learn so much from each other's experiences. Not to mention there's a lot of emotional support that comes when you lean on people who can relate to you.

Take lots of sitz baths

Something I loved doing, not just for my mental health but also for my physical healing, was having a sitz bath. These are a lot like the usual bath that you would soak and wash yourself in, but typically shallower and in lukewarm water alone. Alternatively, you can add epsom salts or similar products recommended by your doctor. The water only needs to be up to your hips so that your perineum (area between your vulva and rectum) can soak. There are a number of benefits to sitz baths particularly for those who have had a vaginal birth. Sitz baths bring blood flow to the perineal area, helping to relax the muscles, reduce swelling and inflammation and promote further healing. Aside from all that, they also mean having a little time to yourself; time to sit/lie down and time to clean yourself without having to stand. I had a slight bladder prolapse after giving birth, so if I stood for too long overall throughout the day and wasn't careful, it would honestly feel like my insides would be falling out.

Say yes to help

I don't know what we are trying to prove when we try to do it all, but when you're at home with a newborn, please do not feel like you have to have it together. If friends or family reach out and ask if they can give you a hand with anything, say, 'Yes!'. If someone is coming over and asks if you need anything and you realise you're out of milk, say 'Actually, yes. Thank you. A bottle of milk would be great.'

Food prep and freeze

Use the weeks leading up to birth to prep as many meals as you can. Even if you have the time or the free hands to make a meal for yourself or your family in those early weeks after the baby comes, you may not have the energy or the brain capacity to think of what to make. I made big batches of a few KIC recipes, then divided them between containers and froze them prior to giving birth and I was so happy I did because I was so exhausted. My husband and I definitely ordered takeaway a fair bit in the early stages, but being able to also reach for those meals I'd frozen for nutritious and filling options when we didn't feel up to cooking really did help. On the following pages you'll find two of the recipes I batch-cooked and froze before having Harvey. They were easy to throw together and, wow, was I glad to have them in those hazy newborn days.

Chicken Cacciatore
Serves 2 (double the ingredients for more serves)

Steph: This has to be one of the simplest dinner recipes on the KIC app, but simple does not equal boring – this recipe is full of flavour. And the best thing about it is that whether you're making it in bulk to freeze or fresh for your family, it's quick, easy and nutritious.

250 g (9 oz) green beans
300 g (10½ oz) chicken breast (or boneless thighs*)
10 kalamata olives
2 garlic cloves
1 x 400 g (14 oz) tin crushed tomatoes
1 teaspoon dried oregano
Salt and pepper

1 Preheat oven to 180°C (350°F) and line a medium baking tray with baking paper. (Use a large tray if doubling the recipe.)

2 Trim the green beans. Place the chicken breasts or thighs, olives and beans in the baking tray.

3 Finely chop the garlic. Combine the garlic, tomatoes and oregano in a bowl and pour evenly over the chicken and veggies. Season with salt and pepper. Bake in the oven for 30–35 minutes, or until the chicken is cooked through.

*Note: whole chicken breasts may need more time in the oven than thighs.

Sweet Potato and Capsicum Spiced Soup
Serves 4

Steph: Regardless of the weather, when you're cooped up at home (which will be most of the time PP!), soup is a go-to comfort food.

300 g (10½ oz) cauliflower florets
300 g (10½ oz) sweet potato*
2 red capsicums (peppers)
½ brown onion
20 g (¾ oz) ginger
2 garlic cloves
1 red chilli
2 teaspoons extra virgin olive oil
2 teaspoons 5-spice powder
500 ml (2 cups) vegetable stock
500 ml (2 cups) coconut cream
1 tablespoon freshly squeezed lemon juice

*Note: You can peel these or leave the skin on for a more rustic flavour.

1 Roughly chop the cauliflower, sweet potato, red capsicum and onion. Finely chop the ginger, garlic and chilli.

2 Place the oil, onion, garlic and ginger in a large saucepan over a medium–high heat and sauté until the onion is slightly translucent. Add the remaining ingredients except for the coconut cream and lemon, and simmer until the sweet potato and cauliflower have softened.

3 Using a stick blender or blender, blitz until smooth and creamy. Serve with coconut cream and lemon juice to taste.

Tip: I left the coconut cream and lemon juice out until I defrosted each serving. Also, warning, soup is best enjoyed without a baby in your lap!

Anti 'before and after'

Fitness gurus and diet brands love these types of transformations. We don't. Let's unpack this controversial motivational tool.

Steph: Before I get into this chapter, let me start by saying that if you're someone who can look at transformation photos and only ever feel motivation, inspiration or positivity, you probably won't relate to a lot of what I'm about to say – and that's a bloody good thing! If you've taken your own 'before' and 'after' photos during your own health journey and found that helped you with motivation, then that's great. If, however, you find the 'before and after' trend leaves you feeling down about yourself or feeling the opposite of motivated, you definitely aren't alone.

I think the entire world needs a reminder that a 'healthy body type' can look a number of different ways. Someone being the leanest, skinniest or fittest physical specimen does not automatically mean that they are a better or happier person. Skinnier or leaner also doesn't equal healthier. Transformation photos suggest that there is something wrong with the 'before' photo when, many times, there may not be. Taking these 'before' photos can also be quite emotionally triggering for someone with body image issues and insecurities. I know in the past when I've taken my own 'before' in a moment of weakness, I have only studied my body even further for more changes I might want to see.

The transformations I stand for are measured by the smile on someone's face. When I see someone posting about their fitness journey and they're standing taller with more confidence in their 'after', I'm so happy for them, regardless of what they look like.

If you're starting a health journey and want to record some progress but feel triggered by looking at photos of yourself, then journal instead. Check in with yourself and write about the way you're feeling throughout your journey. You will be able to reflect on how you are changing and growing and see how far you get. Bodily systems – especially women's bodies with menstrual cycles – naturally ebb and flow. So it's completely natural for body shape or weight to fluctuate, even over the course of a month.

Confidence comes from within, and when your confidence isn't tied to what you look like, you'll be less interested in weighing yourself or comparing yourself to old photos because you won't actually care.

Sometimes, people who share their before and after photos are looking for external validation, but we don't always know what happened behind the scenes in order to bring about this physical change. For someone struggling with things like an eating disorder or exercise addiction, having strangers or friends tell them how good they look in this leaner or skinnier state can actually be damaging. When I was modelling full-time and going through my own struggles with disordered eating and over-exercising, my obsession with changing the way I looked was fuelled when friends or a modelling agent would comment on how good I was looking. Of course, on the flip side, for people who take a healthy, long-term and sustainable approach to improving their physical health, external validation is motivating and encouraging. It's just good to be mindful of our language when acknowledging physical changes in another person in case it does encourage them to continue an unhealthy habit.

Food is fuel, not the enemy

KIC: The majority of diet and weight-loss supplements are targeted at women, so it's no wonder that eating disorders and obesity are at an all-time high in Australia or that half of the adult population, male and female, is currently trying to lose weight. Toxic societal standards, mass marketing and social media have led us to believe that fad diets and quick fixes will help us feel our best when, in fact, they do so much more harm than good to our bodies.

If you've experimented with fad diets, you're certainly not alone. We've both been there and are fortunate to have come out the other side, but we are well aware that doing so is no easy feat. This is why we are so passionate about helping others overcome their negative relationships with food and dieting. To help us better understand why we should steer clear of fad diets, KIC's resident dietitian, Liv Morrison, explains what really goes on behind the scenes in our bodies when we fall into these fads.

Liv defines fad diets as any eating plan that promotes results or fast weight loss without scientific evidence to support those claims. Research shows that these diets do not work long term; the majority of people that lose weight regain it within a year, and less than twenty per cent of people can keep weight off for 2–5 years. After someone completes a fad diet, they typically regain any weight lost (and sometimes even more), ending up with poorer overall body composition than when they started. This negative cycle of diet, loss and then weight gain (hence the term 'yo-yo dieting') has significantly contributed to our obesity epidemic, which is also at an all-time high in Australia.

What happens to the body during a fad diet cycle?

★   The ability to burn calories decreases.

★   Lean muscle mass decreases.

★   Metabolism decreases.

★   There is an increased risk of future fat gain post-diet due to your body creating more fat cells to inhibit weight loss in the future.

The more times you lose and regain weight, the worse your body composition will get – meaning you'll have to eat fewer calories the next time you diet in order to lose the same amount of weight. With fad diets, you're embarking on a very vicious cycle.

At KIC, we're shining a light on intuitive eating, which is essentially a non-diet approach to eating. This has been a core belief of ours at KIC since day dot. This way of eating involves connecting with your body's cues, respecting hunger, responding to fullness and getting back in touch with what YOU actually feel like eating. Intuitive eating is not restrictive. There are no meal plans or calorie counting, just as there are no 'good' foods or 'bad' foods. You simply eat when you're hungry and stop when you're full.

This way of eating sounds sensible, even easy, but we appreciate that it's not always that straightforward. In all honesty, it's taken both of us years to overcome the negative relationships we've had with food in the past and reach a place where we can confidently and comfortably eat intuitively. But we are both living proof that it can be done.

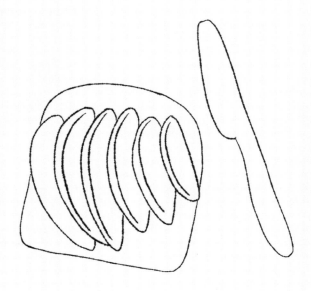

You don't need to drink celery juice and spend two hours in the gym to be 'healthy'

Laura: If you have an Instagram or TikTok account, chances are you've seen someone spruiking celery juice because #ItsSoHealthy and promising it will solve all of your problems. If you follow anyone like this and find posts like that triggering for you in any way, this is your sign to quietly unfollow. This type of toxic posting on social media is one of my least favourite parts about these platforms. It can be so damaging, and there is so little (if any) regulation around sharing of health information, so it's hard to tell what is, in fact, truthful and what is (politely) bullshit.

When I first got on social media about ten years ago, I got sucked into the world of toxic diet culture really quickly. The images of 'perfect' bodies, toxic diet messaging and a 'no excuses' mindset slid straight past all of my commonsense and biology knowledge. This horrible mindset continued for a few years until, through lots of growth and learning, I was able to make my way out of it.

Getting back to the balanced mindset I'd had for my whole childhood took a few years. It didn't happen overnight, and I'm grateful I was able to get back to a healthier place. Unfortunately, negative mindset is a trap so many people, especially young women, fall into on social media. According to The Butterfly Foundation, 15 per cent of women in Australia will experience an eating disorder. It is so much more common than we think it is. This is why it is so important to ensure that the relationship we have with our body, and health, is one centred on balance and sustainability, not deprivation and shame.

It's better to live
a happy life with
an imperfect diet
than an unhappy life
with a 'perfect' one.

Intuitive eating
Liv Morrison

KIC: We interviewed Liv on the KICPOD, and she shared some really valuable tips on how to get started. Here they are.

1   **Just start!** First things first, check in with how your body is feeling. Often, with diet culture and restriction, this is something that we fail to do. Ask yourself, What is my body wanting? How much food do I need?

2   **You will make mistakes, and that's okay.** Eating intuitively is not something you'll nail off the bat. It's all about being aware of how you're feeling before, during and after you eat. When you're getting started, it's completely normal to overeat. Listen to your body and let it tell you what it wants and when it's satisfied.

3   **Mindful eating techniques can help you understand where your body is at.** Rather than walking around or standing at the fridge, try sitting down while you eat and avoid distractions – such as the TV or scrolling through your phone – so you can concentrate on your food.

4   **Slow your pace.** If you're a fast eater, try placing your cutlery down and out of your hands between bites. Fully finish your mouthful before you get your next bite ready.

5   **Eat from a plate, not from a packet.** That way, your brain can more easily recognise what, and how much, you're consuming.

To be honest, we still do this all the time.

Reducing food guilt

KIC: Unfortunately, it's so common to feel guilt or shame around overconsumption or for eating certain 'bad' foods. We've all been there. One extremely powerful way to reduce food guilt is to allow yourself to eat intuitively with no restrictions. When we restrict certain foods, they become more appealing to us. We always want what we can't have, right? Overeating or binge eating generally happens after a period of restriction. By allowing ourselves to eat the foods we enjoy when we are hungry, the desire to binge is reduced – ultimately reducing our guilt.

There is a light at the end of the tunnel

Steph: As someone who has experienced binge eating and struggled with food guilt daily for years, I'm here to tell you that you can come out the other side. Finally, food is more to me than just calories and nutrients. It brings me happiness, particularly when it's shared with loved ones. I am now in a place where I can go out with friends and eat whatever I feel like and not feel guilty about it. I no longer allow myself to sit with feelings of food guilt because – at the end of the day – there are so many important things in life to worry about.

Like anything, this kind of mindset shift comes with practice. You're unlikely to wake up one day and no longer feel any guilt whatsoever around food. It's a journey with no perfect end destination. Don't let that demotivate you because you can get to a point in life where guilt no longer rules your day or your week. You may feel guilty for just a second but then forget about it just as quickly. Now that's progress.

Guilt around food
is a feeling that
has been learned.
It can be unlearned
with practice.

A day on our plate

KIC: Boy-oh-boy, do we hate this phrase. Apologies if you got excited when you saw this heading. Actually, we're not sorry, and here's why (spoiler alert): no one eats the exact same thing or the same way. Every. Single. Day. (Well, allegedly, Victoria Beckham does, but she hardly represents the 'average' woman.) When a public figure shares what an average day of eating looks like for them, they are usually putting their 'perfect day' forward for public consumption – they're likely not being completely honest about what they *actually* are eating on a regular day. The problem comes when their 'day on a plate' sets unrealistic expectations.

When reading or watching these 'menus', whether they're in a magazine or on TikTok, it's only normal for food guilt to start creeping in as we compare what we usually eat or have eaten that day to these (usually) unsustainable or overly restricted diets. During the early days of KIC, we were actually quite open about what we would eat throughout our days, but we quickly learned about the detrimental impact this can have on our community's relationship with food. Yes, we can show you what we ate today or yesterday, but tomorrow and the next day will be *completely* different. That's the beauty of intuitive eating. We can eat what we want when we want. How boring would it be to eat the exact same thing every day? So, next time you see a 'my day on a plate' feature, try not to read into that bullshit.

Periods, PMS and cravings

So, it's that time of the month and, along with bleeding, the majority of vulva owners will also experience some degree of premenstrual symptoms (aka PMS). These include bloating, cramps, pain, digestive issues, anxiety, depression, headaches, joint and muscle pain, breast tenderness, acne and breakouts, and cravings. Fun times, right? Thankfully, Liv Morrison, has pointed us in the direction of certain foods that can help boost our mood and reduce PMS.

When you start bleeding, your serotonin levels (happy hormones) are at their lowest, which can also cause sugar cravings and mood changes. You can proactively increase your serotonin levels by consuming foods containing tryptophan, which can be found in the likes of chicken, soybeans, tuna, nuts and bananas. Eating more of these foods during a period can help naturally boost mood. Magnesium levels also drop within the first day of a period, and this can lead to dehydration. Often, dehydration is confused with hunger, meaning you might eat more food when what you really need is water, so remember to keep hydrated.

On the flip side, high sugar intake, caffeine and alcohol can increase feelings of anxiety and depression, so it's best to limit these foods while you're menstruating. Make sure you eat protein and healthy carbs regularly throughout the day to decrease sugar cravings, consume plenty of colourful vegetables and fruits, and drink plenty of water to increase concentration, boost your mood and sustain your energy.

Things that can help to reduce PMS:

★ Exercising

★ Reducing your intake of high-salt foods, especially if you notice any puffiness

★ Staying hydrated

★ Practising relaxation techniques, such as yoga, meditation, massage or having a warm bath

★ Prioritising sleep

★ Avoiding too many refined sugars and opting for wholegrains and fresh fruit that are low in sugar

★ Acupuncture.

Work out *your* way

Ideally, exercise should be something you look forward to, not something you dread. It should make you feel good.

Steph: I think a lot of people avoid exercise entirely because they feel like it's supposed to look a certain way. It's like they've heard that if they're not running at a certain pace or lifting a certain weight or getting into a yoga pose perfectly, then there's no point even bothering. I get it. I've certainly been there. But those are huge misconceptions.

Exercise doesn't have to be a challenge or a competition. It's simply something you should do for yourself because of how good it makes *you* feel. Some people thrive on structure and routine when it comes to exercise, but not everyone can stick to a plan. It can be really demotivating when you get 'off track' with an exercise routine, so if you are someone who isn't naturally so structured, try taking a step back and loosening the reins a little. Find a routine that seems achievable for you, and don't worry about how it may stack up against someone else's routine. The number of days you exercise per week, the minutes or hours you train, and the type of exercise you do can and *should* look different from others because it's YOURS. What works for someone else might not work for you.

Something that helps me get back into a routine when I may have fallen out of one, is to look at the week ahead and plan which days and times I'd like to fit in a workout. What I don't do is choose what type of exercise that is. Personally, I like to see how I feel on the day, listen to my body and move it in a way that feels right at that time. That means I may only practise yoga and not do much else in a week because that's what my mind and body need. Other times, it means I'm smashing out runs or heavy strength sessions because I feel like pushing myself mentally and physically that week.

If you're someone who frequently says things like, 'I hate exercising', then you probably just haven't found the kind of exercise you enjoy yet. Your exercise could be rollerblading, it could be horseback riding, or it could be playing a team sport. What I'm getting at is this: exercise is important, but what kind of exercise and how frequently you do it each week really comes down to what makes YOU feel good. Don't let anyone else tell you otherwise.

Returning to exercise after a break

It's only normal that from time-to-time certain aspects of our lives will take a hit, we simply cannot do everything at once. When we are feeling stressed or overwhelmed, we tend to prioritise tasks that will please others, and looking after ourselves is pushed to the back burner. The ways in which we look after ourselves likely differ; however, moving the body is something most people recognise as 'self-care'.

Getting into a routine of regularly exercising can be really tough if you've been inactive for a while – for any reason. When I've been sick, injured, or even if I'm just on holiday and have decided to take a few weeks off exercising, I find it very difficult to snap back into the swing of things because that time off has broken a habit. Good habits can be hard to pick up but easy to lose. The thought of getting back into exercising after a long break can be seriously daunting, so if you're feeling overwhelmed, you are not alone.

Here are some little things that help me get back into an exercise routine. Feel free to give these a go. ≫

Top tips to get back into an exercise routine

Leave activewear by your bed the night before

Seeing it first thing in the morning reminds me of what my intentions were the night before. It also shortens the time it takes me to get ready for a workout as I can't procrastinate or distract myself by trying to decide what to wear.

Find a workout buddy

This doesn't mean that you do every workout together (though you can if you like), but it's nice to have a friend that holds you accountable. You can work out together, virtually or in person, or you can just check in with each other regularly and encourage each other to keep moving. I love being there for friends when they need a little extra motivation, and I love checking in with our KIC community when I'm lacking some myself.

Start small

When I've been out of a routine for a while, I know that I can't jump back into doing a KIC workout six days a week. Sometimes, in that first week back of being active, my only goal is to 'move my body every day'. That might include a two-kilometre walk or a ten-minute stretch. I just do what I can when I can, and I find that as the days go by, the motivation to push myself that little bit harder does come.

Take it slow

Don't run before you can walk. It takes time to rebuild strength and fitness. It's tempting to come in too hard and too fast, but not letting the body readjust could lead to potential injuries and also mean you wind up feeling discouraged. Try not to compare current fitness levels with past ones. Instead, set small, realistic goals suited to your current abilities. This will leave you feeling more accomplished and encouraged to keep moving.

Only plan exercise that you enjoy

I love trying new things and challenging myself by doing exercises I don't exactly enjoy from time to time, but when you're out of your routine, finding the motivation to do any kind of workout you aren't sure you'll enjoy can be really hard. My advice? Stick to the types of exercises that bring you joy in those early days.

Look ahead at your week and plan when you will exercise

Commit to your workouts as if they were an appointment you'd hate to miss. Once those slots are locked in, make sure you keep them free.

Follow a 'real-time' workout

Our KIC workouts are a perfect example of a real-time workout. They're virtual, but filmed in a way that you can follow along the entire workout with a trainer as if you're in a class at the gym. When I'm lacking motivation, I *need* a personal trainer talking me through every exercise and every rep, but I can't always fit a PT session into my schedule, so following along with a KIC workout at home for 20 minutes is the perfect way to have my PT at home with me.

Respect the body's need to rest

Without rest, the body cannot recover, this is especially true when we start using muscles we haven't engaged in a while. You'll feel so much better going into your next workout rested and not overworked.

Are you out of a routine right now? Know that YOU are in charge of that. It's easy to make excuses, but it's also easy to make minor lifestyle adjustments to fit exercise into your day. You just have to make that decision and commit.

Start with a routine and motivation will follow

Laura: When it comes to exercising, motivation simply doesn't show up sometimes, and that's completely fine. You don't need to wait for it to appear. More often than not, motivation arrives five minutes into a workout once those endorphins really start flowing. No one wakes up every day excited to exercise. It's all about developing a routine.

The tips that Steph has just shared are great for helping to establish a routine. One thing I'd add is to work out at a time that suits you. Personally, I have to exercise in the mornings because I don't have the energy after work. But if you're not a morning person, don't force yourself to get up early. Schedule exercise for the evening instead. Don't make things harder by working against your natural rhythms.

Switch up your mindset

The next time you're struggling to find motivation, instead of thinking, *I really should work out today*, try switching your mindset and thinking, *How lucky am I that I get to excercise today!* The ability to move our bodies is a blessing, and one that shouldn't be taken for granted. This mindset is something I discovered through running. For me, running is like meditation: I feel so alive, free and present in the moment. When I head off on my morning run, I'm often in a really positive headspace, so naturally I find I start thinking about the things that I'm grateful for, whether that's the beautiful weather, my supportive family or each and every one of our incredible KIC community members.

Something that always pops into my mind during a run is gratitude for actually being able to go on a run. Moving the body comes naturally to most of us, but there are so many people who are temporarily or permanently unable to do this. And some have never experienced this freedom. It's not just our physical capabilities that we can be grateful for; it's also important to acknowledge the privilege of having the time and financial freedom to be able to exercise, as this is also something that not everyone has access to.

Don't get me wrong, I haven't always had this mindset, and in all honesty, there are days where I lack motivation and think to myself,

I really should go for a run, but I just can't be bothered. We're all human. But when these thoughts pop up, I'm quick to remind myself how amazing I'll feel after I move my body and how lucky I am that I get to experience that feeling.

I think it's so important to exercise in a way that makes you happy, as this will help reduce those feelings of dread. In the past, my negative relationship with exercise meant I'd push my body to its absolute limit during each workout, and I'd wind up feeling absolutely exhausted afterwards. When I'd wake up to do it all over again, I'd dread it. Over time, I've learned that exercise can and should be enjoyable and that it doesn't need to take up hours in a day. It's all about finding a way of moving that best suits you.

Combating gym anxiety

KIC: If the thought of working out in a gym overwhelms you, you're certainly not alone. Whether you're approaching the gym for the first time or returning after some time off, gym anxiety will look and feel different for everyone. Perhaps you feel like your fitness levels and strength have reduced, your body has changed, your confidence to move around others is lacking, or you're worried that people will be watching and judging you as you work out. Regardless of what might be making you a little nervous about setting foot in the gym, it's important to remember that these thoughts are valid.

Top tips for combating gym anxiety
Have a plan

Not only will you be in and out faster, but you'll feel more confident knowing exactly what equipment you need and where you need to set up. Following a program like KIC is just like having a PT in your pocket. We have your back.

Use the resources available

Gym staff are there to help and to make our time at the gym better and more productive. Whether you've got a question about how the lockers work, what time classes run or how to use a piece of equipment correctly, ASK! This will immediately make you feel more in control and comfortable.

Pop a pair of headphones on

Music is such a good motivator, and it can really help to get you in the zone and tune out everyone else around you. When you focus on the song playing and the exercise at hand, there is very little space left to worry about those around you, which is often a trigger for many of us. If you do worry about others watching or judging you, try to remember that, more often than not, the one person that everyone's fixated on at the gym is themselves.

Lock in a gym buddy

Having a reliable gym buddy provides support and motivation, and this will help you walk in, move around and embrace the gym-going experience with confidence as you won't feel alone.

Don't overcommit

If you've gotten into a really good routine of exercising at home, let's say three to five times a week, aim to complete half of those workouts in a physical gym or studio and the rest from home. The beauty of online fitness programs like KIC is that you can literally roll out of bed and be done with a workout in 20 minutes. There's no commute or need to arrive early to secure your spot in the class, and you can do a session whenever you want, wherever you want. Complementing your gym workouts via online fitness will allow you to keep smashing your goals, leaving you with more time for life's demands.

Remember your why

By reminding yourself why you are there and taking time out to move your body, you'll be able to combat that natural instinct telling you to retreat. Remind yourself that you are there for YOU and nobody else. This time is going to benefit your physical and mental health, and you'll never regret a workout.*

*Well, actually, if you don't listen to your body, sometimes you might regret a workout. There are exceptions to every rule. Steph explains this on the next page.

You do you

The pandemic has definitely changed the way we work out. If you've fallen in love with the ease, comfort and routine of working out at home, there is absolutely no pressure to rush back to the gym. If you've proven to yourself that you can achieve incredible results from home with minimal equipment, we encourage you to continue to do what makes you happy.

Move to suit your mood

Steph: Something I've let go of over the years is the thinking that a workout needs to be super challenging and sweaty to be worth doing. In the past, if I woke up stressed and anxious about something and tired from lack of sleep, I'd still push myself to do some intense workout because I thought I needed to. That saying 'You will never regret a workout' became questionable in my eyes because these intense workouts would heighten my anxious or stressed emotions, and therefore, I would regret them.

The pressure to bring your A-game to every single workout is unhelpful because, in reality, that's simply not possible. Energy and motivation ebb and flow, and it's important to tune in and listen to your body and find a movement that complements how you're feeling. Some days you may feel a little flat or exhausted, and it's at times like these you really should be kind to yourself. Try introducing slow tempo movements, like a 20-minute walk around the block or a yoga or Pilates class. Even the shortest workouts can have a positive effect on your body and mind. Be okay with the fact that sometimes no movement at all is best. Rest is good; we *need* to rest. Taking time off is okay and is actually good for us. It is all about balance.

On days when I wake up feeling like Superwoman, I push myself and challenge myself with a strength or HIIT workout. Tune in to what your body wants and needs each day, and don't ignore it. Keep that relationship with exercise a positive one by keeping your body in line with your mind. You'll know five minutes into a workout if it's the right one to be doing that day. There are so many different ways that you can move your body, so it's all about finding a move to suit your mood.

Training around a menstrual cycle

KIC: Speaking of moving to suit your mood, have you ever wondered why some days you feel super strong in the gym, and others you feel like you can barely lift a finger let alone a weight? If you're a woman with a menstrual cycle, that might have something to do with it. Now, we're not just comparing the days you have your period with the days you don't. There's so much more to our cycles. Female bodies go through a magnitude of hormonal shifts, which are broken down to four phases (yes, four, not two!) each and every month, and it's crazy how many women have only the vaguest idea of what actually happens during their cycle.

To help explain the shifts in energy your body experiences throughout a menstrual cycle we asked Ashleigh Ormond, KIC's physio and women's health educator, to share her insights and the movements best suited for each phase.

Ash is a fount of knowledge when it comes to all things women's health, and we can't get enough of the experience, insights and good vibes she brings to the table. Ash is a physiotherapist, mindset coach, women's health educator, an absolute ray of sunshine and an incredible asset to the KIC team.

Before we dive in with Ash, it's important to keep in mind that hormonal contraceptives such as the oral contraceptive pill, IUD and Implanon work by suppressing ovulation, so you won't have the same hormonal fluctuations that you would on a natural cycle. Generally speaking, this means that people on hormonal contraceptives are unlikely to notice energy and mood changes throughout their cycle as a result of hormonal changes because their body is receiving a consistent dose of the contraceptive.

But, as you will learn, hormonal changes are just one factor that may influence your readiness to train. So even if you're on hormonal contraception, listening to your body and taking into account all of the factors that affect your performance is important when considering what type of exercise you'll do on any given day.

Take it away, Ash!

LIFE IS **BETTER** WHEN YOU GO WITH **THE FLOW!**

Period Power 101
Ashleigh Ormond

Follicular phase

Your follicular phase is the stage of your menstrual cycle when your body is preparing to release an egg. It runs from the first day of your period until ovulation, which is roughly the first two weeks if we think about an 'average' 28-day cycle (but note that not everyone's cycle is 28 days and a 'normal' period cycle could be anywhere from 21 to 35 days).

During this phase, estrogen levels are at their highest in order to stimulate follicle growth, which means you might notice a boost in your mood and energy. If that's the case, you might find yourself craving a HIIT workout and you could put the extra energy to good use with a weight-training or bootcamp-style session.

Ovulation

The second half of your follicular phase rolls into your ovulation phase. So, what's happening behind the scenes? Your high estrogen levels trigger your pituitary gland to release luteinising hormone (LH), which is what starts the ovulation process. Your ovary releases a mature egg that makes its way down the fallopian tube toward the uterus. If you're trying to conceive, this is when you'd hope for the egg to be fertilised by sperm, however we've learned that getting pregnant is not always that simple.

During this phase, your energy is at its peak thanks to high estrogen levels and increased levels of LH and follicle-stimulating hormone (FSH).

It's during this phase of your cycle that you'll likely be feeling your strongest. If so, this is the best time to lift heavy, push your run, and go for your personal best.

Be mindful, though. Despite feeling somewhat superhuman, you don't want to push yourself to the point of injury. It's important to listen to your body and take into consideration all of the other factors that impact performance. More on those below.

Luteal phase

The luteal phase is the last phase of the cycle *before* menstruation occurs. After the follicle releases its egg that month, it changes into the corpus luteum, which is essentially a mass of cells that forms in your ovary and produces the hormone progesterone. If you do get pregnant, your body starts producing human chorionic gonadotropin (HCG) – this is the hormone that pregnancy tests detect. It helps maintain the corpus luteum and keeps the uterus lining thick.

For the majority of women who don't get pregnant that month, the corpus luteum shrinks away and is reabsorbed. This leads to decreased levels of estrogen and progesterone, causing the onset of your period, which is the shedding of the uterus lining.

The luteal phase typically lasts 14 days (again, this is based on an average 28-day cycle and can vary from person to person). You may still have some energy left over from ovulation at the start of your luteal phase, but you may notice this starting to decline as you get closer to your period arriving. The peak in progesterone levels may also make you feel a little drowsy. Your body temperature increases, emotions run high and your body may not recover from exercise as efficiently.

Again, the key is listening to your body. If you do feel a little sluggish, you may find that low-impact options, such as Pilates or yoga, feel better to your body. You could also opt for low-intensity steady-state cardio, such as walking, cycling or swimming. You may notice that your usual workouts feel a little harder than usual during this phase, however, that doesn't mean your performance will be impacted. You can absolutely continue your usual workouts during this phase if you feel up to them. If need be, you can opt to slightly reduce the intensity.

Menstruation

Once your period arrives, you may be feeling pretty bleurgh and unmotivated, thanks to low levels of estrogen. BUT, if you do feel up to it, moving your body while on your period can have a lot of benefits, both physically and mentally.

For many menstruators, the first day or two of a period often comes with cramping, most often felt in the lower abdomen and lower back. Opting for a gentle yoga flow that focuses on opening through the hips and lumbar spine might help ease cramps by calming your nervous system and stretching the spots that feel tight.

If you are feeling up to it, this can actually be a good time to build strength thanks to relatively high testosterone during this phase. The follicular phase technically starts after the first day of your period, so you might notice your energy and motivation rising by day two or three.

Regardless of which phase of your menstrual cycle you are in, though, it's important to listen to your body. Your menstrual cycle is just one factor in how ready you feel to train on any given day, so take into account any other factors such as stress, how much sleep you had the night before, whether you drank alcohol the day before and your overall training load.

you take care

The breath test

Laura: The technique I'm about to share with you is something I've learned through a lot of trial and error (emphasis on error). It has helped me navigate what my body needs in each moment by guiding me on when to push myself, when to step back and when to do nothing at all.

Here's how it works: each morning, in the moments when I am deciding how I'm going to start my day (mornings before work are my me-time), I take a long, deep breath. My breath will either feel shallow, like I can't get enough air into my lungs, or deep – like my lungs are open and I can get air all the way down. In the latter feeling, breathing feels easy, and nine times out of ten, this means that if I feel open to moving my body, it will make me feel good. If I feel like I can't get the air in, this usually means I feel overwhelmed, and my cortisol levels are already high. In that state, rest and relaxation are what I need.

If you rely on movement for your mental health and self-care, it can be hard to opt for rest, but that's why it's so important to always check in with how you're feeling and do things that are good for your mind, but don't overtax your body. I've pushed through feelings of overwhelm while working out so many times, and each time I finish exhausted and the feeling of overwhelm is worse. It took years before I learned how to really connect with my body and trust myself enough to let go of that need to exercise intensely every day. This breath test has been something that has really helped me and, if you need it, I hope it can help you, too.

IT'S ABOUT PROGRESS NOT PERFECTION.

If you want big things, set smaller goals

This may be controversial, but I don't believe in resolutions. Every new year, some fresh societal pressure pops up for us to measure ourselves against. We make drastic resolutions in the hope that those will enhance our personal development, professional growth and/or overall health. But they rarely do because resolutions aren't goals – they are broader ideas. More like a promise you make to yourself. Goals, on the other hand, ARE specific targets – something tangible and real that you can aim at and keep your sights on.

When we set unrealistic expectations that will 'completely transform our lives', we're setting ourselves up for failure. There is a better way. Next time you're setting a new resolution, ask yourself if the behaviours and habits associated with it are ones you can comfortably and confidently continue with for the entire year. If the answer is no, I recommend revisiting that resolution.

I'm not saying don't aim for the stars – we are told to set huge, amazing goals, dream *BIG*, etc., and there are good things about dreaming big. The problem with this type of goal setting is that, while it is lovely to have big aspirations, we often forget the many, many steps in the middle, and we neglect to set smaller goals along the way. Then, without a roadmap to achieve that big goal, and with no checkpoints along the way, it becomes almost impossible *not* to give up. Imagine running a marathon without any checkpoints on the route to encourage you to keep going and fuel you until the next stop. You'd be running for hours on end with no idea of how much longer you had to go or how far you'd come. This is the same way I think about goal setting.

Break big goals down into smaller, achievable and measurable goals, and then reward yourself along the way. If you don't tick your small goal off when you had planned, you can just move the other checkpoints and adjust the timeline so you don't give up altogether. Set realistic goals you know and truly believe you can achieve.

One of the most common goals people set is 'to be healthier'. This is a wonderful goal. Looking after our bodies and minds is very important, but if you truly want to action this intention, you need to set some specific targets. What does 'be healthier' even mean to you anyway?

You might start by moving your body a couple of times a week, or drinking more water, or doing a five-minute breathing meditation once a week. These smaller goals will be simple to implement, realistic to achieve and they'll take you closer to that loftier goal of 'being healthy'. Let's try an example now.

Breaking down the bigger goal of 'being healthy'

Movement

★ Let's say you're a parent who works full-time and you can't currently fit exercise into your schedule. Setting a goal to work out six times a week for two hours each session probably isn't realistic (or fair on you). A better goal might be to exercise once a week or to walk more often. Don't underestimate walking – it absolutely can count as your form of movement.

★ Set yourself up for success in that weekly workout session by making things as easy as you can. If you don't know where to start, try doing some workouts at home and testing different types. There is actually an amazing app that has lots of different types of workouts, awesome trainers, and lots of options to suit you (cough, cough, KIC).

Mindfulness

★ As part of that big goal of being healthier, you may set a goal of practising mindfulness. Smaller goals around this might include practising daily gratitude in a journal or doing guided meditations a few times a week. Spending more time outside might also be a good goal, but again, make sure you specify what that will look like so you can tick it off as you progress.

Nutrition

★ You do not need to follow a diet to achieve the goal of being healthy. A more sustainable way to approach food might be to set some goals about how much water you drink, cooking more meals at home, eating more veggies, drinking less alcohol, etc. Again, just make sure you set specific goals. For example, 'I'm going to drink 2 litres of water a day.'

It's never too late to set a new goal. There's absolutely no difference between the first of January, Monday or tomorrow. Don't give up just because your year, month or week hasn't gone as planned. No matter what the date today, there are always another 12 months ahead of you to KIC your goals.

One last thing worth mentioning is that not all goals need to be big and meaningful. Okay, wait. There is one more thing: you do not *need* to set goals all the time if that doesn't work for you. Sometimes, we don't have the motivation, energy or inspiration to set goals, and that is okay. You don't *have* to set goals every year (or at all) to live a beautiful life. Take the pressure off. It's your life and your choice. You don't need permission to do what works for you.

7 things you can do for your mind and body right now

1 Drink a glass of water

2 Go for a walk

3 Do a yoga flow from home

4 Complete a guided meditation

5 Fill your fridge with nourishing food for the week

6 Make yourself a big cup of herbal tea

7 Take a nap

You don't *have* to set goals every year (or at all) to live a beautiful life.

Exercise during pregnancy

So you're growing a baby inside you and suddenly freaking out about what you can and cannot do. Totally normal!

Steph: Fitness is a huge part of my life. It makes me tick. When I found out I was pregnant, one of the first things I did was research which forms of exercise I could or couldn't do. One thing I realised pretty quickly was that Google was not the place to go for this kind of guidance. I found so much conflicting information and it left me confused and scared to do the wrong thing. Instead of relying only on what I had read online, I reached out to my personal trainer and my obstetrician, and I also met with a physio. But even after getting advice from the three of them, I have to confess the noise from the media and strangers online did confuse me at times.

This was the whole reason we introduced pre- and postnatal Pilates as well as educational pregnancy and postpartum content onto the KIC app. We wanted to have guided workouts that were safe to do during pregnancy, as well as postnatal sessions to help build the muscles in the pelvic floor and core back up prior to getting back into general exercise. KICBUMP (the name of our pre and postnatal program) is designed to empower women to keep prioritising strengthening and moving their bodies during and after pregnancy.

Motherhood, mental health and exercise

KIC: The road to parenthood is paved with some of the biggest changes a person is likely to ever experience. Their body, routine, relationships and (whether they like it or not) sleep patterns change in huge ways. It's completely normal to experience feelings of sadness or anxiety while trying to navigate this brand new way of life, not to mention the tidal wave of external pressure from social media, society and sometimes our very own family members as you're trying to do so. The reality is that one in five new mums and one in ten new dads will experience perinatal depression and anxiety. So, if you're feeling overwhelmed, know that your feelings are valid and that you are not alone.

Perinatal anxiety and depression are more than just the general ups and downs that come with parenthood. Some of the signs and symptoms include

★ Feeling sad or low, or crying without obvious reason

★ Persistent worry or fear about the health of your baby

★ Difficulty sleeping, even when your baby is sleeping

★ Withdrawing from friends and family

★ Feeling constantly tired or lacking energy

★ Finding it difficult to concentrate or remember

★ Abrupt mood swings

★ Panic attacks.

If you or someone you know are experiencing any of these for more than two weeks, please reach out and seek support from your local helpline. In Australia you can call the PANDA national helpline on 1300 726 306.

To help us better understand the benefits of exercising on mental health, we asked Ash Ormond (who you met on page 138) to weigh in.

WISE WORDS

How exercise benefits perinatal health
Ashleigh Ormond

Happy hormones

Exercise has been shown to be associated with increases in serotonin and endorphins, which are your body's 'happiness hormones'. Serotonin is the key hormone involved in stabilising mood and promoting feelings of wellbeing and happiness. Serotonin also plays a role in appetite and sleep, which are often impacted when our mental health declines. Endorphins, on the other hand, are a type of neurotransmitter or 'messenger', which can help alleviate pain and stress. In addition to the happy hormone boost, exercise also plays an important role in regulating our levels of stress hormones, such as adrenaline and cortisol, which are related to your body's fight-or-flight response. Excessive or prolonged periods of elevated levels of stress hormones can be detrimental to both your physical and mental health.

Energy boost

It might sound strange, but exercise can actually improve your energy levels, even when you're sleep deprived. A study published in the *Journal of Sleep Research* looked at the energy levels of people with insomnia. The study found that people who engaged in a minimum of 150 minutes of moderate-intensity exercise over the course of a week reported an increase in mood and reduction in insomnia symptoms. This equates to a daily 20—30 minute workout, run or fast-paced walk

Did someone say sleep?

It's no secret that sleep cycles are significantly impacted both during pregnancy and after the arrival of a little one. Exercise is known to improve sleep quality, alleviate daytime sleepiness and reduce sleep onset time, all of which equate to a more refreshing sleep.

You time

Exercise provides an opportunity for you to reconnect with yourself and your body. It gives your mind a break from whatever else is happening around you. Alternatively, joining a community (be it online or in real life) such as KICBUMP can provide an opportunity for important social connection as you're exercising with other mummas who understand the journey you're going through.

Strong mumma

New motherhood is a complex time that is further complicated by societal pressure and expectations. You're adjusting to a whole new way of life, and it's normal to feel overwhelmed by it all. Exercise provides an opportunity to regain your sense of control and accomplishment. When you're moving your body in a way that makes you feel good, you feel strong, confident, and more like yourself; it's a proven way to boost your self-esteem. You're here, you're doing it, and you're doing a great job.

You've got this, Mumma!

If you're feeling worried about exercising during pregnancy, Ash has also helped us pull together some tips that might help. ≫

WISE WORDS

6 steps to reduce your fear of exercising during pregnancy
Ashleigh Ormond

Step 1 **First and foremost, hold on to the fact that exercising is really beneficial for both you and your baby.**

Recent research from the Royal Australian New Zealand College of Obstetrics and Gynecology (RANZCOG) states that exercise during pregnancy is not only safe, but actually highly recommended for a multitude of reasons. It can help you improve sleep, promote muscle strength, boost your mood, enhance your energy and assist in the management of gestational diabetes and pregnancy-related aches and pains. Roll out your mat and reap those benefits.

Step 2 **Aim to be physically active on most days, and preferably every day of the week.**

We're not talking about long and sweaty workouts every day, but it is recommended that we move our bodies on average for 30 minutes per day, aiming to accumulate 150–300 minutes of moderate-intensity physical activity each week. Our KICBUMP program recommends two strengthening exercises per week on non-consecutive days, along with stretching and daily walks – so long as you have the all-clear to do so from your healthcare professional.

Step 3 **Whether it be in person or online, ease your way in with guided exercises.**

Having an expert with you every step of the way will boost your confidence. One-on-one prenatal Pilates classes can be expensive, so if you're looking for an affordable option, we recommend giving KICBUMP a go. Our Pilates instructor, Christina Traychevska, was pregnant at the time she recorded these workouts, so you're working out with an expert who truly understands the modifications your body needs during pregnancy. When you're ready, our postnatal program can also help you with recovery and return to exercise postpartum.

Step 4 **Move to suit your mood.**

You've probably guessed by now that this is one of our favourite tips – pregnant or not. If you feel that your body is craving something slow and nurturing, try yoga or a gentle walk, especially later in your pregnancy. And if you have a boost of energy, put those pregnancy hormones to good use with some higher energy strength or low-impact sessions. Listening to your body is always vital, but especially when you're pregnant.

Step 5 **Connect with other new and expectant mums.**

A community can be so encouraging and supportive – make sure you join our KICBUMP Facebook Community, it's such an inclusive, safe place for mums to connect.

Step 6 **Most importantly, find comfort and confidence by speaking with your own trusted health professionals.**

As tempting as it may be, don't go digging with Dr Google. At the end of the day, you know your body better than anyone else. If something doesn't feel right, it's time to stop.

Health check (this is your reminder)

KIC: Life admin . . . It can be an absolute drain sometimes. But when we're looking at our to-do list, there are some things that we have to be prioritised. Can you spot which one rises to the top in this list?

★ Dry cleaners

★ Post office

★ Book a skin check

★ Pay bills

★ Supermarket

If you answered, 'Door number three', then DING, DING, DING! Looking after our health is so important, and no matter how busy we get, health has to be taken seriously. Regular health checks allow us to keep on top of our health and act quickly if there are any signs of change. More often than not, the longer you leave something health-related, the worse it's going to get, right? So, take this as your friendly reminder to ...

☐ **Check your skin.** Sadly, Australia has the highest rate of skin cancer in the world. Approximately 81,000 Australians missed their annual skin checks throughout 2020–2021 as a result of the pandemic. No matter what time of the year it is, don't forget to book your skin check.

☐ **Book a dentist appointment.** How long has this one been on your to-do list? This one tends to slide down the list of priorities. Pick up the phone and book yourself in.

- ☐ **Book your cervical screening test.** In Australia, the pap test has been replaced with a new cervical screening test to help reduce illness and fatalities from cervical cancer. It's recommended that women and people with a cervix aged 25 to 74 years of age have a cervical screening test every five years.

- ☐ **Go for an STI check:** How long has it been since you've had one of these? If you are sexually active, it's recommended that you get tested for chlamydia every year between the ages of 15 and 29. Chlamydia is really common but doesn't always show symptoms. If you are at risk of other sexually transmissible diseases, such as HIV/AIDS or herpes, you should ask your doctor about further testing.

- ☐ **Check your breasts.** Sadly, one in seven women will develop breast cancer. It's the fourth leading cause of death in Australia. But early detection can make all the difference. Every month, two or three days after your period, you should be checking your breasts for any abnormalities or lumps. There are so many good videos explaining how to do this on YouTube so watch a couple to get the key moves down, then make it part of your shower routine. Simply grab some shower gel and start massaging.

The importance of rest

Rest allows time for our mind, body and spirit to recover and rejuvenate. It's not optional, it's essential.

Laura: Spending endless weeks in lockdown taught me many things about myself. I know that I thrive in my fast-paced routine because filling my day is what really makes me tick, but stopping to rest is incredibly important. When I set aside time to pause, reflect and rejuvenate, the positive impact it has on my body never fails to surprise me. I catch myself thinking, *I need to do this more often.*

Resting not only helps the body combat stress and relax, it recharges our batteries so we're ready to go when it's time to move our body and harness brain power. I've come to realise that my life is actually worse when I don't rest. The stresses of day-to-day life slowly build up, and before I know it, something that wouldn't ordinarily bug me or cause me to feel overwhelmed sends me off the deep end.

Getting comfortable with the idea of resting and taking time for yourself can be hard. Hustle culture glamorises 'the grind' and tells us to keep pushing, to achieve more and be better. I don't deny that there are fantastic things to strive for, but I also think it's super important that we remove this type of pressure (especially from the content we absorb on social media). Just because you see someone smashing out intense morning workouts doesn't mean you have to do the same.

In the interest of complete transparency, setting aside time to rest is something that I have struggled with (and still do). Deep down, I know that rest is what my body craves, but I can't help but put pressure on myself by thinking about the productive things that I 'could and should' be doing during that rest time. This is a thought pattern that I'm actively trying to change, by reminding myself of the benefits I've just outlined.

I am learning to listen to my body and be kind and gentle rather than power through on autopilot. I'm trying to be better about giving my body and mind whatever they need on that particular day. Because that's the thing; the time I need to rest fluctuates depending on so many internal and external factors, including how much sleep I've had the night before, any stresses I'm carrying, recent exercise exertion and the competing demands from my work or social life. Rest is sacred and personal. What I need and what you need will be different. So, make sure to make rest all about YOU, and try not to compare yourself to the way others 'rest'. I encourage you to be confident in owning your rest.

Rest and exercise

Since exercise is a huge part of who I am and also one of the things that brings our KIC community together, I want to highlight the importance of rest when it comes to moving our bodies. In my early twenties, I often neglected rest. I'd push myself to work out consistently, oblivious to the fact that I was doing my body more harm than good. Now, when I think of rest in relation to exercise, the term 'recovery' comes to mind. Rest is a vital part of not only recovering from your previous workout, but also preparing you to maximise the next one. For me, recovery looks like:

★ A proper cool down and *actually* stretching

★ Consuming something wholesome and nutritious

★ Rehydrating

★ REST

★ A good night's sleep.

Take a nap

First, I want to confirm that the type of naps I'm referring to here are those heavenly Sunday afternoon 'I have no plans for 90-minutes' type of naps. I'm not talking about the 15-minute power nap you try to squeeze in between work and a dinner commitment. I find power naps can be useful when I am horrendously tired and can't keep my eyes open, but they often leave me feeling like I have been hit by a bus.

Those wonderful Sunday-type of naps were something I deprived myself of for years. Why? Because I felt guilty for not being productive 24/7 and for 'wasting' time. Instead, I'd spend that time scrolling on social media (definitely not productive). Give yourself permission to have a nap or binge an entire season of *Grey's Anatomy* in one day, or go and sit on the beach and read a book for as long as you feel like. Let go of the pressure to be productive, and feel comforted by knowing that it's in these moments of calm we create for ourselves that we are able to truly be present and enjoy a sense of stillness we may not have felt for a very, very long time.

Get a better night's sleep

KIC: Why is it that on the nights we really need a good sleep, our bodies and brains have other plans? Perhaps you've spent the night tossing and turning, trying to get to get comfortable or you've woken up in the middle of the night battling with your monkey mind. There's honestly nothing worse than a bad night's sleep.

Sound familiar? You're not alone, because between 33 and 45 per cent of Australian adults don't get enough good-quality sleep. The negative effects of widespread sleep deprivation impact us over a range of day-to-day symptoms, such as fatigue, low mood, daytime drowsiness, impaired work and study performance, and long-term health issues, such as poor immune function, type 2 diabetes, high blood pressure and heart disease.

The blissful benefits of sleep meditation

KIC's meditation expert, Meg James, shared a lot of great information about the many benefits of introducing sleep meditations to a nightly routine. It helps ease the journey into sleep and improve the quality of that sleep, making for a healthier, happier, more well-rested you.

Meg explains that healthy, restorative sleep has more to do with the quality of your rest than the number of hours you're asleep. When your mind is busy worrying about a problem, going over the details of your to-do list or anxiously anticipating a night of interrupted sleep with young children, it becomes difficult for the body to settle into the state of restfulness required to drift off to sleep. Meditations for sleep are specific, guided experiences that help you to not only let go of the happenings of the day, but also invoke your body's natural sleep aid: the relaxation response. This helps to quiet the mind, calm the nervous system and settle the body in preparation for a truly restful night.

Sleep meditations can be practised either just before bedtime or used to create the internal conditions required for you to drift off with ease when you wake in the middle of the night. Some of our favourite and most effective meditations for sleep are on page 91.

If you wake up in the night, it's likely that racing thoughts and an endless stream of worry is contributing to disturbing your sleep and keeping you awake. This is totally normal, as things often seem worse in the middle of the night than they do in the light of day. Refocusing the mind on gratitude will help steer it away from this negative cycle.

The fact that Aussies don't get enough good-quality sleep leads to an array of both physical and mental health problems. Regardless of whether you're someone who has trouble falling or staying asleep, sleep meditation is a highly effective tool for calming the mind, settling the body and providing the optimum conditions for a restorative night's sleep.

7-step routine for a better night's sleep
Olivia Arezzolo

KIC: We interviewed one of Australia's most trusted sleep experts, Olivia Arezzolo, on the KICPOD, and she was generous enough to share her signature seven-step research-backed bedtime routine to achieve a better night's sleep.

1 **Block out blue light**

   We're exposed to blue light through our mobile phones, laptops and even the TV. Pretty much every device that we use to wind down. A study showed that even the most basic room light can suppress melatonin (the sleepy hormone) by as much as 71 per cent. That's huge! Less melatonin means you'll find it harder to fall and stay asleep. If you are using your devices in the evening, it's important to block out the blue light for at least two hours before bed by wearing blue light blocking glasses.

2 **Use lavender**

   A clinical trial found lavender oil capsules improved sleep quality by 45 per cent, and reduced anxiety by 59 per cent.

3 **Set a goodnight alarm on your phone**

   1 hour before your bedtime you should have a pre-set alarm labelled 'Sleep better'. This is your signal to disconnect from all tech. Those who use a phone in the hour before bed are 48 per cent more likely to take longer than an hour to fall asleep.

4 **Have a shower**

   We love any excuse for an evening shower. The drop in your core body temperature as you emerge from a steamy shower into a cooler bathroom is a cue for melatonin synthesis to take place, which releases those sleepy hormones.

5   Take a magnesium-based sleep supplement

It's been shown to reduce anxiety by 31 per cent. We love that.

6   Meditate or read

A trial found that participants who meditated were able to fall asleep 18 minutes faster – from 39 minutes to 21 minutes. We are big fans of blissful sleep meditations, like the ones on page 91. Reading a good book is another fantastic way to unwind at night

7   Wear an eye mask

This will protect you from any sleep-sabotaging blue light while you sleep.

Olivia makes a point of saying that getting a good night's sleep is not about doing one thing in this routine, it's about doing all of them consistently for at least seven days to see the best results. If you find yourself feeling overwhelmed at the thought of implementing them all at once, start with the easiest one, and build up to incorporating the others. Sleep tight.

Stop trying to fix something that isn't broken. Your body doesn't need a transformation, it just needs to be cared for.

IT'S NOT
ABOUT HOW
YOU LOOK,
IT'S ABOUT HOW
YOU FEEL.

connection

As humans we innately want to feel a part of
something. We want to feel connected and we
want to feel heard. This final part of the book
explores the many ways in which we connect with
those around us. We share our lessons on nurturing
existing relationships, establishing new ones and
strengthening the most important relationship
in our lives: the one we have with ourselves.

Finding connection at work

The average person spends a third of their life at work. Finding ways to make this time meaningful is essential to living a good life.

Laura: Like most Australians, around half of my waking weekday hours are spent at work. And when I'm not at work, I'm likely still thinking about work or doing work. Finding balance and connection within a workplace as well as with the way you work is a major stepping stone on your way to making your life work for you. Workplaces are changing, and careers and working hours are more flexible than they've ever been, so if things aren't feeling aligned for you on the work front, there's every reason to believe you can tweak your situation and achieve a happier, more balanced worklife.

Steph and I feel so incredibly grateful to wake up and get to work at our own company every day, where our purpose is to help people live healthier and happier lives. This work has given us some incredible opportunities and taken us to where we are today, and while there has definitely been an element of luck, we have also grabbed each opportunity with both hands and given it all we have. If someone had tapped us on the shoulder at the time we released our first e-book together (the first phase of KIC) to tell us what KIC would become, we would have probably laughed and said, 'No way'. It is truly beyond our wildest dreams and, while we do not regret any part of the journey because it has led us to where we are now, one thing we would go back and tell ourselves at the beginning is to dream big, and then go bigger!

We've been so lucky to have found the partnership we have, and to achieve all we have together makes every success ten times as special. This doesn't, of course, mean our 'dream' roles are 100 per cent fun or full of challenging activities that we love every second of every day. Every role – even dream jobs – includes tasks you may not love, but if the connection with the purpose of your work and fulfillment is there, and if you have a great group of colleagues, clients and support around you, it makes that job a lot easier to enjoy.

Don't assume something is unattainable

How many times have you thought about a particular person, job or experience and thought, *Wow, I would absolutely love to do/be/try that, but it isn't within reach for me*? Making yourself small or not trying new things because of a fear of failure or being embarrassed means you stay in your comfort zone. Think back to a time you put yourself in a box that meant that you could not achieve something? When did you last convince yourself you couldn't do something? What did you not try or put yourself forward for because you didn't feel completely qualified? Did you put it on someone else and say something like, 'Well, that person is extra special and I am not, so I can't try that thing'? Or did you put it down to bad timing, and say 'I will try that next year'?

One of my biggest learnings has been that when we put something off and do not believe in ourselves, we will never do that thing. Saying, 'One day' convinces the mind that we aren't letting ourselves down, but deep down we know that we are. You have to believe in you. I know we've said this multiple times already in this book, but I will repeat it because it is so important: you are responsible for believing in yourself. No one else will do it for you.

If there's one thing we would go back and tell ourselves at the beginning, it's to dream big, and then go bigger!

Please don't wait for someone else to give you permission to do/be or try that thing – you may be waiting your whole life. You have two choices (pick whichever option you are the most likely to convince your mind of):

1 **You are, in fact, special.**	**2** **No one is special.**

Whichever way you look at it, there's no reason for you *not* to take your shot. Either you're special, so it will work out, or no one is special, so why shouldn't it work out for you?

I have been very lucky in my life to have met some incredible and influential people. Something they all have in common is that they are human. They are imperfect, not particularly 'special' and do not have superpowers. What they *do* have is grit, determination and a take-control mindset that allows them to believe that they are worthy. Most importantly, they are each very clear on their personal values.

Imagine you are walking into a job interview. You are very nervous, and when the person interviewing you asks you why they should give you the job, you freeze and think, *Oh my goodness, does this mean they know I'm an imposter? How can I convince them that I'm the right person? The other candidates are so amazing. I should probably give up now.* Self-doubt takes over, and suddenly the person interviewing you – someone who has never met you before – realises that you do not believe in your own ability to take on this job. Consequently, they do not believe in you.

Self-doubt. It is absolutely natural, but the successful people I know don't let it cripple their dreams. Instead, they use it to fuel their desire to never stop learning and growing. You are the author of your story. You, darling, get to decide what you are capable of. Don't be afraid of the ceiling. It does not exist for you.

You are never too old to change direction

From a young age, many of us get the message that we should know exactly what we want to do for the rest of our life the second we finish high school. And if we don't, then we must pursue whatever career we've decided on at that moment and continue with it, even if we had no idea what we wanted from life at the time. One of the most common questions I'm asked by younger people is whether they are too old to study – and the people asking me this are not old at all. (What is 'old' anyway?)

Societal norms are there if you want to follow them, but they are completely optional. At the end of your life, I highly doubt there will be anyone checking which boxes you ticked off and whether you ticked them off in the 'right' order. You will not regret making a change to a career something you love or have more passion for. Of course, other circumstances including financial, family, caring commitments, etc. may make changing directions hard – and some people won't always have the option. But, if the only thing holding you back is worrying about your age or that your journey isn't living up to your best friend's or someone you follow online, you can let that go. Give yourself permission to change. Your life is not set by anyone, except you. You get to decide the order of events, and when and if you study. Don't forget this.

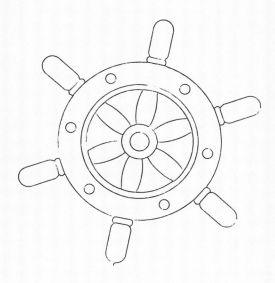

Self-confidence

Laura: Sounds simple enough, doesn't it? You just need to trust yourself. I mean, we know that building trust with others can be hard, but surely building trust within ourselves should be easy, right? Unfortunately, not. It is much harder.

So, what exactly does it mean to trust our abilities, qualities and judgement? Let's break each of those elements down and work through them one at a time.

> **Self-confidence:** *(noun)* **A feeling of trust in one's abilities, qualities and judgement.**

1 Belief in your own abilities

Believing in your own abilities and where they can take you isn't limited to what you do for work. Abilities can encompass anything you love doing, whether that's a favourite hobby or something that comes naturally to you. When you believe in these abilities, you know that you can deliver if someone asks something of you at work or in your personal life. For example, if you are offered a promotion at work, you need to believe in your ability to take it on (and you should). If you want to start running, and you are able, but you have never really done it before, you must believe you can be a runner, and that you can do it.

You can believe in your own ability to try things out, and this doesn't mean you need to master new things every time; you just need to feel confident that you will try your best, and that your best will be enough. Even if everyone around you believes (or does not believe) in your abilities, you will not find your confidence here until you believe in them yourself. If you have people around you who make you feel small and do not believe in your abilities, try and stay as far away from them as possible. If you can't do that, then make them small in your mind and do not listen to what they say.

I once worked with someone who, after a while, left me feeling absolutely incapable of anything. This didn't happen overnight, and I didn't see any problems coming until I ended up in a heap, questioning everything about myself. When doing a task at work, I was terrified of doing it wrong, and I started to believe that I was so incapable that I would probably do it wrong. Everything I attempted took ten times longer than it should have because I would check for mistakes so many times.

What was worse than all the checking and self-doubt were all the things I just didn't try at all during this time. When you don't believe in your ability to do things, the scariest thing is actually doing anything new as you do not want to again be reminded that you, well, 'suck'. This was the most anxious period of my life.

I spent quite a few months feeling this way until I finally had a light-bulb moment: the person who put me in this spot was absolutely not coming to save me. The only person who could do that was me. I realised that while I did not agree with the way this person acted or their values, that it wasn't their fault I was feeling this way. I took responsibility for the fact that I (albeit subconsciously) had allowed them to change the way I felt about myself and my abilities. I had let go of something I should have been in control of.

You may think I'm being harsh by blaming myself for losing confidence in my abilities – especially if you are in the thick of something similar right now. But the truth is, it's easier to blame other people when we lose confidence. They may be part of what causes a lapse in confidence, but if we don't take responsibility for our own feelings and beliefs, we will not be able to get on top of them and find our confidence again. Without taking back control, we'll stay stuck in our comfort zone (which we have made smaller), and will miss out on experiencing the best parts of life or ourselves. ≫

To get through this tough time I revisited my values and did some personal work around letting go of others' judgements. I did this by listening and reading, and I remembered that two of the most important things to me are growth and learning. If I stayed stuck in the spot I was in at that moment, I would be preventing myself from growing or learning. So, I did the only thing I knew how to do to make me believe in my abilities again: I put myself out there again. I started by jumping into a shallow pool, and I swam. I then went deeper and deeper and pushed further outside my comfort zone until I felt like me again and, most importantly, until I *believed* in myself again.

I learned a few important lessons from this experience.

★ Don't put your value in the hands of anyone except you.

★ There are many 'right' ways of doing things. Just because you aren't doing something the same as someone else doesn't mean you aren't doing it 'right'.

★ There will always be people in your life who will not believe in you. All you can do is make sure that you have the right tools in your belt to ensure that you don't let those people penetrate your belief in yourself.

★ People who make you doubt your own abilities should never be your teachers.

2   Belief in your qualities

Your qualities are the things that make you, you. Your honesty, for example, or integrity, kind heart, drive, loyalty – your ability to make people laugh, etc. The thing about qualities is that there's no one universal list of qualities that everyone agrees makes a 'good' person. And it's lucky that's the case or we'd all be clones of each other and the world would be a very boring place. Belief in your qualities is about knowing that you have everything you need inside of you right now. You are 'enough' as you are.

Repeat after me: I am unique, and I am worthy of love, deep relationships – both romantic and platonic – of new experiences, and of being valued by those around me. I am worthy of finding fulfilment in my career and feeling good about myself.

You are worthy of each of these things, and so much more, as you are. Right in this very moment.

I believe that someone with good intentions is a good person (in most cases, anyway). Therefore, questioning every part of yourself in order to work out if you deserve to feel confident in who you are is futile. You simply, just do.

3   Faith in your own judgement

This one is a big one, as being confident in this area is how we are able to make decisions about our lives, for us. If we don't have faith in our own judgement, we run the risk of living our lives for others rather than ourselves. We might spend hours speaking to people, asking their opinions on the big decisions we need to make in our life. We might try to find those answers by reading books, listening to podcasts or googling. But the truth is the only person who knows what to do is *you*. Deep down, if you reduce all the noise around you, you have the answer. You just need to trust yourself.

If you listen to the likes of Oprah and Glennon Doyle, who are both incredible thought leaders when it comes to trusting your judgement and owning the decisions in your life, you may have heard them talk about the importance of clarity and stillness – how you need to be able to go deep and make important decisions yourself. In an interview on the *We are supported by* . . . podcast, Oprah likened the decision-making process to buying shoes. If you know that you like a pair of shoes, then you should just buy them. You don't need to ask your friend if *they* like them, because they aren't the ones who'll be wearing them. And you don't need to ask your friend if *they* like them because you want to make sure that they'll still like *you* if you wear them. Hearing her put it this way made me realise how much we self-sabotage our lives when we make decisions based on what others *like* or what they think we should do. Each of us only gets one, beautiful life. Live your life for you. Not somebody else.

Another thing I find helpful when I'm faced with big decisions is reminding myself that despite not always making perfect decisions, I do not regret anything because everything I've done has led me here. Of course, there are regrettable bad decisions (like breaking the law), but most of the time, even if a decision does not feel 'right' to begin with because you are unsure of the outcome, it will teach you things about life and yourself. Once you can feel comfort and be at peace with the fact that you are always learning and growing, big decisions aren't so scary after all, and you absolutely can trust your own judgement.

Why are there more male than female leaders?

Laura: As I type these words, you are more likely to become the CEO of an ASX Top 200 company if your name is Andrew, than if it's Laura, Steph or any other female name. While women make up 51 per cent of the Australian workforce, they make up only 19 per cent of CEO positions, 32.5 per cent of key management positions, 33 per cent of board members and 18 per cent of board chairs (aka the majority of key decision making and leadership roles are held by men). Sadly, I am not typing this in 1950. It's 2022 at time of writing. Navigating the world of business, a world that is still very male-dominated, has been challenging because I've felt like I've had to prove myself in almost every moment. It's as if, because of my gender, I am not really meant to be in the room.

It's well documented (thanks in a large part to Sheryl Sandberg, who we'll discuss on page 179) that women have to work a hell of a lot harder to get a seat at the table than men. There are fewer seats for us and, on some boards, there are none at all. The only conclusion would seem to be that we aren't there because we aren't qualified for those roles, but that's not true. Women aren't less equipped for these top roles. In fact, many would argue that women are actually *better* equipped. Emotional intelligence (EQ) is a very important factor in successful leadership, and in a study completed by the Johnson & Johnson Consumer and Personal Care Group, women scored higher on empathy, interpersonal relationships and social responsibility, and were found by their peers to have higher levels of self-awareness, have better communication skills and be better than their male counterparts at developing others. All of these traits are extremely important in being a great leader.

I've worked with some wonderful businessmen, but I also know that there are some out there who believe the reason for this huge imbalance is that women don't want to be there or that they'd prefer to stay at home with their kids. Some men believe women don't aspire to big roles the way their male colleagues do. But these are not the main reasons why there are fewer women in boardrooms. The real reason we aren't represented equally is because we start *behind* men.

Imagine you're running a race that laps around a running track, and when you start your race you realise that some people are already 10 or 20 laps into their race. You're running right alongside them, but in reality they're way ahead, and it's tough to catch up. Well, the corporate world is structured a lot like that, with (most) women starting their race way behind, making it almost impossible for them to cross the finish line before those who started earlier.

The motherhood penalty

Without a doubt, one of the biggest factors in inequality in leadership roles is the fact that women are the ones who bear children. The assumption that a woman will eventually leave a job to have a baby is not something a man has to deal with as he's climbing the career ladder. Becoming a mum means women risk missing out on promotions, career growth and don't go back to full-time work or don't re-enter the workforce at all – sometimes due to prohibitive childcare costs. When deciding which parent (in heterosexual relationships) will go back to work after a baby is born, the default decision is the person making the most money, which – when we add the gender pay gap to the mix – is likely to be the man.

This means that five or ten years down the track, when and if the woman decides to return to the workforce, they'll be starting back where they were five or ten years ago (or even further behind), while the dad has had those years to continue progressing in his career. Women also do not accrue superannuation (employer contributions to retirement funds) while they are taking on the very important role of being the primary carer, which is not something their husband/partner is sacrificing if he is the one remaining full-time at work. This dramatic gap in retirement savings is one of the major reasons women over 55 are Australia's fastest-growing homeless population. This is why it is so important to fight for equality both in society and within our own personal relationships.

Closing this gap

There's no law that says you have to assume the gender roles of the past. Each of us has the power to shape our future within our own home. In my relationship with my husband, Dalton, equality is something we speak about often. Right now, our careers are very important to both of us, and as CEOs of our respective companies we are both very open about what our expectations will be when we start trying to get pregnant. I don't know what our circumstances will be when we hopefully have children, but if it happens while we both have demanding roles, we both expect to make sacrifices (aside from the fact that only one of us can actually grow the baby). We've made a promise to each other that we will not assume that either one of us is going to take on more or less simply because of our gender.

How can you be the change?

Don't let the stats deter you. You can be the change because you are capable and worthy of every success. If you come up against a ceiling and find that it won't lift or break no matter how hard you push against it, don't take that as a sign that you aren't strong enough. Take it as a sign that you need to enter a new room, or create your own.

To expect extraordinary results, we must put in extraordinary effort

We live in an 'Uber-fied' world. If we want something quick, we can get it. A burrito, a cocktail, a date, a new pair of shoes, someone to fix the broken dishwasher . . . You better believe we have also translated this instant way of life to how we feel about ourselves. If we feel down, we can post an image on social media and instantly get 'likes' to validate the fact that people like us. (Or do they just like our new haircut? I guess we don't know.)

This way of life, while very convenient and with many positives, also has some seriously negative negatives. When I reflect on how this way of life has altered my perception, I think the main thing is the gap between how long we think things *should* take in this instant world, and how long they actually do. We are so laser focused on the end result that we forget to find moments of joy along the way. And if we don't get what we want quickly, we're likely to give up and move on to the next instant validation/gratification hit. I'm guilty of this behaviour, but I've realised that the things I really work hard for – the things I put the hours in to achieve – are where I find the most fulfilment. I also completely acknowledge that it is a privilege to be able to work hard and find fulfilment in that work. This is not the case for everyone – or even most people.

What really helps me when I am in the middle of a process that feels like it is taking forever, or what helps me get back up after I've stumbled on the way to a goal, is to reflect on things I've done in the past that took a very long time and a lot of hard work, but that I am very grateful to have achieved.

Next time you find yourself paralysed by the prospect of starting some super-daunting project, write a list like this for yourself and stick it somewhere where you'll see it often so you can remember that you *can* do hard things.

A few 'hard things' from my list

★ Studying for 12 hours a day for about five weeks straight before my final year (VCE) exams and getting into my degree

★ Finishing my degree (even if it took me nine years)

★ Creating a blog, which was mainly work content that I produced for free for a few years

★ Doing my first keynote speech, even though I was extremely nervous that it would go horribly and that the person who booked me would regret it. (PS, it went great, and I now love doing them.)

As great as it feels to chase down a goal, there's a fine line between working hard and constantly 'hustling'.

How I deprogrammed my 'hustle' mindset

Laura: Hustle. I've had a very complicated relationship with this word over the past five years, and so – I feel – has the internet. About three years ago, the concept of 'the hustle' – the idea that someone should constantly be striving towards success and goals – became something that was highly glamorised. It was sold as something we should all strive for, as if busyness was a stamp representing our worthiness for success. I used to feel a strong desire to share all the ways I was 'hustling' behind the scenes – the way you absolutely have to when you are pursuing something beyond your ordinary. Now, however, I feel differently. I spent many years talking about how busy I was, like it was some sort of competition, but instead of feeling accomplished I felt highly strung, as if I was always in fight-or-flight mode. Something had to change.

So, over the past couple of years, I've changed the way I talk about busyness in order to shift my mindset. I no longer call it 'hustle', I simply call it working towards the goals and vision I have for myself and our company. I choose to put in long hours and place work before a lot of things in my life not because of #hustleculture, but because work makes me feel connected to my purpose. And heck, yes, I *am* busy, but, my goodness, there are way more important things to talk about with the people in my life than how busy I am.

I promise you; nobody wins the hustle competition. You could spend your whole life being 'busy', and not ever get anything meaningful done. This mindset switch has coincided with me maturing and understanding that I am worthy without anyone else's validation. I'm working hard enough to deserve everything I have achieved. I feel at peace with who I am, and my value. I'm very grateful to no longer feel the need to justify my life to others in order to feel validated.

Don't avoid difficult conversations

KIC: Sheryl Sandberg, long-serving COO of Facebook (now Meta) until her resignation in June 2022 authored two bestselling books: *Lean In,* which sparked an entire movement, and *Plan B*, a memoir about losing her husband, Dave, to a heart attack in 2015. In an interview with Oprah, Sheryl talked about how many of her close friends stopped calling her two weeks after Dave's death. In the years that followed, Sheryl was able to process her grief and eventually talk to those friends about that difficult time. Through that, she learned that many of them had avoided her because they simply didn't know what to say and they didn't want to have a difficult conversation. Isn't that so sad?

In our interview with Deni Todorovič, they spoke about coming out as non-binary – an identity they finally felt was truly them. After coming out, they also noticed that some of the people in their life started to avoid them, and likely for the same reasons that Sheryl's friends had avoided her after Dave's death: they were so worried about saying the wrong thing that they thought it would be better not to say anything at all. But both Deni and Sheryl would have welcomed having these difficult conversations rather than feeling shut out or isolated.

In a completely different context, when we reflect on our KIC journey, there is truly no way we would be where we are today if we had avoided the difficult conversations. From a business perspective, these conversations have challenged us, challenged the people around us (in a good way) and have stopped us from settling for less than we believe we can achieve. They are never easy, and sometimes they don't feel like they will bring growth afterwards as you are consumed by anxious thoughts, but we have never had a tough conversation that we regret. In fact, we usually find we wish we'd had it sooner.

When we avoid difficult conversations or situations in our personal lives or relationships because we aren't sure what the 'right' thing to say is, we risk losing important connections, or hurting people we love who just want to know we are there for them.

Never apologise for being you

The overuse of the word 'sorry' is another issue that, unfortunately, is commonly highlighted among women. Sorry is a very important word, and when used in the right context for the right reasons, it is a way of expressing regret and accountability for our wrongdoings. However, we do not ever need to be sorry for simply existing or asking a question. After all, asking questions is how we learn. Over-apologising at work, at home, and in other areas of our life for things that don't need an apology can lead others to take us less seriously in a work environment or even take advantage of us. It's also tied to lower self-esteem and puts us at risk for taking the fall for things that aren't our fault.

There's no need to be sorry for taking up space, having a seat at the table or speaking up in a meeting. If you find yourself automatically apologising for things you shouldn't, it's time to retrain your brain. Learning when to say sorry is a skill, and if this is a word that you identify you overuse, it's something you'll actively have to train yourself out of doing. Next time you feel that word is about to come out of your mouth, ask yourself why you are saying it and if whatever you are about to apologise for is something that warrants it. Are you actually at fault for whatever has happened or are you saying sorry because things feel uncomfortable and you want the discomfort to go away? Are you using the apology as a way to take the blame off another person and make them feel more comfortable, even though you aren't at fault? Are you underestimating yourself by saying sorry?

When we are trying new things, especially in the workplace, a big part of this testing and learning process is figuring out what does or doesn't work. It's trial and error, and mistakes are a valuable part of this process. If they are made in this context, by all means take accountability but rather than apologising, talk about the learnings you've taken from the experience, and how you might approach the task differently next time.

Stop using the world 'just'

There is evidence that women, in particular, use the word 'just' a little more than necessary. Why? To make ourselves smaller and because it feels like a good way to tone down the intensity or assertiveness of whatever we are about to say. Why? Because of the gender bias around what is considered to be likeable for both men and women and what we expect from a 'good' woman, vs. a 'good' man. The gender stereotype of a 'good woman' is someone who is caring, warm and selfless. The gender stereotype of a 'good man' is someone who is decisive, assertive and ambitious. As women, we feel the need to overuse words like 'just' in order to be liked, to help others feel more comfortable. We don't want to be seen as 'too ambitious,' or 'too confident.' If, as women, we display the same qualities that are considered positive in our male counterparts, we are automatically classified as bossy, feisty, selfish, opinionated and unlikeable.

At work, this leads to a huge disadvantage for women as the qualities that are considered to be those of a 'good' leader are those seen as typically 'male'. This is why we need to continually question our gender bias and rewire our brains on what we expect from different genders because human beings exhibit human behaviour. Just as it is normal for a male to be caring and warm without being regarded as 'weak' or be penalised for it; it is also normal for women to have drive. Therefore, it should be considered perfectly normal for a woman to display that ambition rather than have to hide it for fear of being disliked or disapproved of by others.

Through our KIC community we've been so lucky to have spoken to many incredible people. And one thing that makes us so sad is when they use this word when describing what they do, what they study, where they live, who they live with or any other fact about their life. It's as if they feel that those things aren't worthy of being said so they put the word 'just' in there. 'I'm just an assistant', or 'I'm just a mum'.

The thing is, when we use the word this way, we are subconsciously telling ourselves (and others) that where we are at in life right now is not good enough compared to those around us. As if we are less worthy of having pride in our job or existing if it doesn't fit the societal norm of 'excellence.' Repeat after us, 'I am worthy, and I am allowed to be proud of and own what I do and who I am'. Next time someone asks you a question you would normally answer with the word 'just', tell them the answer and be damn proud of it.

If overusing the word 'just' is something you struggle with (and it is very normal/common if you do), we recommend going back to the values section on page 54, and making sure you work through the exercises on page 56 and 57. Hopefully, after doing those, it will become clear that status, job titles and so many things we feel insecure about do not actually matter. There are so many more important things.

Ad-'just' your emails

Before hitting send on an email, re-read it to see if you've used the word 'just'. *I'm just checking to see if you got my last message*, or *I just wondered if you'd finished the report I asked for last week.* Does the word 'just' really need to be included or are you trying not to come off as too assertive? If it doesn't need to be there, take it out.

It's not who you are that holds you back, it's who you think you're not.

Returning to work as a mum

Steph: It's fitting that, at the time of writing this, I am in my first month of returning to work (almost full-time). As anyone who runs their own business knows, it's almost impossible to completely switch off, so I haven't had the standard 'maternity leave' experience. I certainly could have had it. It's not like Laura forced me to work. In fact, she has constantly reassured me that as long as I am open with her about my workload, I'm good to take all the time that I need, and I'm incredibly grateful to her for that. But when you love what you do, how can you go on leave? There are some who might ask, 'Well, if you love spending time with your baby so much, how can you want to work?', but those people can bugger off with that undermining question. The answer to both is this: motherhood is a new title. It's a new hat you're wearing, but it doesn't have to be the only hat. You can love being a parent AND love your job at the same time.

One of my favourite Oprah quotes, and one that has been repeated by many incredible women is 'You can have it all. Just not all at once.' I'm close to printing this quote out and putting it in a frame on my desk so I see it often enough that it sinks deep into my psyche and I start to live by it.

Whether you have to return to work or you're choosing to return to work, it is not easy. I've been doing everything I can to psych myself up for jumping back into the deep end. I've been doing bits and pieces of work since Harvey was only a few weeks old, but now I'm working more hours, both from home and from the office, and I've also taken back some of the responsibilities and tasks I offloaded to other team members in this break. I'm as nervous as I am excited about being a working mum, and I think the nerves about work only come from being out of practice. What excites me is the thought of having time to myself, time for challenges and time for doing what I love and making a difference in people's lives.

Tips to help you transition from maternity leave to work

Something that is becoming very clear to me is that it's quite hard to 'wing it' at work when you have a baby. My confidence level at work has already increased by being more organised and structured with my working week. Below are some of the tips I'm trying to follow myself as I transition from maternity leave to working mum.

Set boundaries and priorities

When you're trying to balance mum life with work, time with friends, self-care, etc., something has to give. Work out what your priorities are and then set some boundaries for yourself so you can keep your cup full. I've learned that I need to allow myself time each week for zero plans, so that I have time to recharge and give myself some love. Without that downtime, I cannot be my best self as a mother or a team member at work.

Create a base schedule

I've set my working hours and I've set my family time hours. Of course, not every week will play out perfectly, but at least this way, I can be 100 per cent present when I'm at home with my little one and not feel guilty about not being at work. When I'm at work, I have the space I need to be committed and engaged to whatever we're doing without feeling guilty for not being at home, most of the time.

Cut yourself some slack

This is easier said than done, but let's stop setting ourselves impossible targets, like being 100 per cent excellent at everything we do. Motherhood is all-consuming, and it does change us, so set realistic expectations for yourself when it comes to work.

Be open with your work colleagues

Whether you're an employee or an employer, it's important that the people you work with are aware of where you are. My mum took a year off from work when she had me, and when she returned, she felt really able and confident in taking her old workload back on. But she felt like she had to keep assuring the team around her that she was okay as they had assumed she would be struggling. On the flip side, I've had to be very open with Laura and the team about where I'm at and how much I can take on because, at points, I have certainly jumped in too deep, too quickly and overwhelmed myself in the process. This hasn't come from external pressure – only my own. I needed to be honest with myself and my team. And as an employer, I would hope that members of my team would feel comfortable to be open and honest with me about their needs or expectations when returning to work.

Have physical to-do lists

Sleep deprivation mixed with having a mini human being on your mind all the time often results in forgetfulness. This was one of the biggest barriers for me when it came to the idea of returning to work because I found myself forgetting things daily. I started writing to-do lists, keeping track of appointments and jotting down notes throughout the day – either on a physical notepad or on the Notes app on my phone, and I find this really helps me to stay on top of things. Try using one of these each day to keep your thoughts in one place.

Whether you're returning to work full-time or part-time as a mum, I take my hat off to you. It isn't easy, and whichever decision you make, you are doing amazing things for yourself and your family. Whether it was your choice/preference or not to return to work, I hope you're okay and I hope you thrive at work knowing that you're a superhero for juggling it all. And if you have a partner or there's another carer in your child's life, remember that it's not your job to do everything. Often, as mothers, we feel like we need to have everything sorted. That we need to be the one who remembers the appointments, does the grocery shopping, makes the lunches, etc. Remember, you do not need to do everything yourself. It's okay to speak up and ask others to help and to share the load. And if you are a mum going solo and doing it all, you are my hero.

Remember, you do not need to do everything yourself. It's okay to speak up and ask others to help and to share the load.

BE **KIND**
TO **YOURSELF**.
THERE'S ONLY
SO MUCH YOU
CAN DO.

Networking

Steph: So many of the exciting things I've experienced have come from putting myself out there and making connections. I wouldn't be where I am today without networking. Laura and I met through modelling, and if it weren't for the connections we made on those jobs, we wouldn't have found the sponsors who funded our original e-book, *Keep It Clean!* Now that we're business owners, we're constantly meeting new people and reaching out so we can continue to learn and grow. One thing I've learned is to treat everyone with respect, regardless of their job title or how little or how well you know them. Treat everyone equally. When you feel like the smallest person in the room and one of the 'most important' people in the room shows you care and attention, it can do wonders for your confidence.

There's a quote I love from Will Smith's book, *Will*. His grandma used to tell him, 'Be nice to everybody you pass on your way up, coz you might have to pass them again on your way down'. This quote is attributed to several people, but whoever came up with it definitely got it right. I think it's a fantastic reminder to be kind to everyone along the way.

If you're not the networking type, I really encourage you to put yourself out there and attend some social events that you may have avoided in the past due to not knowing anyone there. You never know who you're going to meet. In business, you often hear the saying, It's not what you know, it's who you know. And while that isn't entirely true, it is true that knowing the right people can do wonders for your business, your career development and your self-development in general. You might end up meeting someone who becomes an incredible mentor and helps you through some of the toughest business/life decisions you'll ever face. You might go out and meet someone who connects you to a friend who is hiring for the exact job you've been looking for. Connections are everything in business, but they aren't likely to fall into your lap. You have to go looking for them and be open to finding them.

You'll never know if you never ask

Laura: I used to think that the only way to network was to attend
an event with 100 people and exchange business cards and emails.
If the thought of navigating a room with that many strangers scares you,
that's perfectly okay. Me too! Thankfully, I can assure you that this is
absolutely NOT the only way to network. Like most things in life, there
are many ways of achieving the same outcome.

When I think of where I've made the most meaningful connections
in my own life – ones that have truly helped me in my career and in
what we do at KIC – they have all come about in intimate settings.
The wonderful mentors in my life arrived after I reached out, accepted
help and then showed up. This can feel scary, but so can missing out
on incredible connections because you're too stuck in a comfort zone.

In my experience, one of the scariest things about networking and
asking for help is the 'asking' part. That initial reach out, when I put the
words down in an email and hit send, is hard. Turning up to the coffee
or lunch date after that connection has agreed to meet is also tough –
the urge to pull out at the last minute always comes up because of a fear
I won't know what to say or ask. But the old saying always rings true:
If you never ask, you'll never get. Don't fear reaching out. People are
(usually) willing to help but you have to ask first.

Don't make life choices to impress an ex

Laura: There's someone I've known since childhood that I continually
seek validation from even now. I never get the validation I'm looking for,
but this hasn't stopped me from striving for it. I know, deep down, that
I will never get it, and I don't know why I feel I need it so badly,
especially since we have grown into such different people.

Don't make decisions in your life so an ex-friend will think you are
worthy. They may have played a part in your past, but you can't let
them dictate your future. A sad truth is they have most likely moved
on from the bond you once shared. Now it's your turn to do the same.
It is healthy to move on. People will flow in and out of your life. Give
yourself permission to let go.

Money

Why are we writing about money in a book about self-care? Because being empowered and taking control of your own finances is so important, especially if you're a woman.

KIC: We've already touched on some of the reasons why this is the case, and we'll get into more detail on those in a minute. While the old adage 'money can't buy happiness' rings true, we can't ignore the security and peace of mind that money can provide.

Financial stress, especially debt, can have a crippling effect on a person's mental health. It can also have a negative effect on sleep and cause strain on relationships, so it's not surprising that tackling a negative financial situation is something that can have a hugely positive impact on a person's overall health. When we improve our financial literacy and get on top of our finances, it helps us to improve our 'financial fitness', which is super important to our overall wellness. Money pays for the things we need and value and it offers a safeguard as much as possible for unforeseen circumstances we find ourselves in (like losing a job).

Knowing that you have the funds to look after yourself, and the people you care about provides so much peace of mind. Having a healthy bank balance also gives you more choices and freedom. Freedom to leave a job that doesn't fulfill you, change direction in your career, start your own business, experience more of the world, take a break from work or retire. For women, it can also mean having the freedom to leave a relationship that isn't working (though in cases of domestic abuse it isn't always as simple as just leaving).

One woman who we have had the pleasure of meeting throughout our journey is Victoria Devine, founder of the number 1 business, money and finance podcast in Australia, *She's on the Money*. Victoria is on a mission to improve financial literacy for women, and is making an incredible impact. In an interview we did on our podcast ('Savings, Tips, Money Values and Afterpay'), Victoria introduced us to some great tips and tools to use when we think about money, including understanding our money story and money values.

What's a money story?

Laura: A money story is a narrative we tell ourselves about our own relationship with money. It is based on experiences with money throughout our lives, and the feelings and beliefs we've developed about it. Our money story is formed by the role money played in our life when we were growing up and how money made us feel. Whether we associate it with stress or opportunity, or abundance or scarcity will all inform the story.

Really understanding this has helped me understand the way I feel about money, and helped me understand myself better, too. When I think about my experiences with money when I was younger I remember feelings of fear, worry and lots of arguing (it was one of the reasons my parents separated). There was also embarrassment for having less than a lot of my friends (something I have since learned does not matter.) I also remember being really scared of credit cards (probably a good thing), and always being worried that something bad could happen that would mean we'd have to use our emergency family savings account, and what then? Despite these fears, we absolutely had enough, and I absolutely acknowledge my privilege in the childhood I had, and that I had a safe and loving home.

Financially, my ambitions have always been quite big, and until reflecting on my money story, I hadn't worked out why this was.

Now, I can see that those thoughts of fear and worry are what drove me from quite a young age to create financial security for myself, and to do all I could to prevent myself from financial worry and stress. It's probably why I hung on so tightly to every single opportunity my career has afforded me, and why I worked hard to create more opportunities for myself. I put myself out there, and while I do put some of my success down to luck, and also the privilege of being a white woman, I have created a situation for myself financially where money is not scarce, and I *know* that I have enough.

I do not take my financial security for granted for one second. I always dreamed of having it, and now that I do it feels different than I thought it would. When I really dig deep, I feel an immense amount of gratitude, but I also feel guilty and uncomfortable about it. I often ask myself, *Why me?* I know I've worked hard, but I also know there are people who work hard their whole lives and never experience financial security. The truth is, I don't really know how to feel about it.

The relationship each of us has with money is such a complicated thing. Not having money can feel uncomfortable. Having money can feel uncomfortable. Talking about money can feel uncomfortable, but it is so important that we do. Women, especially, *need* to talk about money because having enough of it gives us choices, freedom and options. It empowers us to leave places or situations we don't want to be, like a job we hate or a shared house we don't feel safe in. Having a backup savings account means we are able to choose to pursue a dream or make life changes we wouldn't be able to when living paycheck to paycheck. It means when we are old and grey, and our bodies are failing us we don't have to work a 40-hour week and can step down or away from work as we have the savings to do so. There is a lot of shame around money and wanting to earn or have more money, and there should be absolutely no shame in creating more freedom for your life by becoming more empowered with your finances.

Victoria explains that to understand your own money story, you must take time to write it out, and really dig deep. Think back to memories or experiences that may have shaped how you feel about money. What sort of money conversations did you hear growing up? Only *you* know your story, and only you have the power to take control and write the rest of it.

Identifying your money values

Money values are the point at which our financial choices intersect with an internal value system (which we talked about on page 54). These are the things that are the most important to us. A lot of us don't ever really think about values when it comes to money, and this can lead to us feeling unhappy and unsatisfied when making purchase decisions. When we create a life based on choices that aren't in line with our inner value system, this can have a big effect on our mental health and emotions. Psychologists refer to this as cognitive dissonance.

For example, if a person really values their health and their family, but they are spending their money on takeaway food and impulse clothing purchases, then their spending is not aligned with their core values. In the above example, that person may be hoping that their purchases will make them feel good, but they won't because they are not the things that are the most important to them.

Identifying and then writing down your money values is a great exercise to do because then you can check in with your spending habits and see if they reflect the things you really care about.

Examples of some different money values

- ★ Health
- ★ Connection (family and friends)
- ★ Travel
- ★ Giving back (charity)
- ★ Education
- ★ Self-development
- ★ Independence
- ★ Security
- ★ Experiences
- ★ Passions

Tip: Once you know what your money values are, spend according to them. Having this list makes spending decisions so much easier. If you value travel or life experiences highly, then you shouldn't feel guilty about spending your money on those things. However, it may make it easier to decide if you really *need* that new handbag. You can have more than one money value of course, but be clear with yourself about what they are.

Taking control of your money

Money is the cause of so many problems in the world, but having it can also prevent many of the problems that women, in particular, face. Financial abuse is one of these, and while it does affect all genders, women are much more likely to be victims. Financial abuse occurs when one person uses financial means to control another by controlling their access to money. When we don't have access to money or control over our finances, freedom of choice is taken away from us. This is why it is so important to take control of our own finances from our late teens.

A common thread of discussion I find around financial matters is that they are 'too complicated' and 'too hard'. It's easier to close your eyes and hope your card doesn't get declined than it is to check your bank balance or transaction statement before hitting the shops (especially if you don't actually want to know how much you are spending). If this is something you sometimes do or do often, don't worry. It is absolutely something you can get on top of.

Finding financial matters daunting is pretty normal because most of us come out of school with only the most basic level of financial literacy. We simply are not taught enough – or in many cases anything at all – about how to manage our finances in the real world. This is why it's up to us to take control and empower ourselves with the information and tools we need to manage our money. The sooner we do this, the better. It's easy to put this off and wait until we are earning more money, or for a time when we don't have so many expenses to start saving or paying off debt, but the time to start is NOW. Like most things in life, the sooner you start, the sooner you will get ahead.

In the episode we recorded with Victoria Devine on the *KICPOD*, she explained that a really great, easy place to start is by doing a bank account audit. Here's how.

How to do a bank account audit

1   Print out your bank account statements. If you have multiple accounts, print all statements out and work through them one at a time. I know this can feel scary, but it is important.

2   Highlight your expenses using different colours for different categories: one colour for necessities, such as car registration, rent, groceries, and another colour for expenses or 'discretionary spending', such as going out for dinner, alcohol, clothes shopping, etc.

3   Next, write down how much money goes into your account each month from your salary or investments, etc. In another column, write down how much is going out.

4   Look at how much money is going in, and how much is going out. Ideally, and in order to save, more money should be coming in than coming out. Then look at any debts you have – are you able to put a plan together to pay these off with the amount of money you have left over each month? If this isn't the case, and it feels overwhelming – this is where it would be good to seek some extra help from a professional.

5   From here, you can work out how much you can realistically save, set saving goals that align with your money values and create a budget that works for you.

Tip: Start saving for retirement today

Laura: Another really quick way to make sure you are setting yourself up for financial freedom in the future is to take control of your retirement account (in Australia, this investment account is known as your 'superannuation' aka super). The gender pay gap (among other factors, including the motherhood penalty we discussed on page 176) makes a significant impact on super for women, and it is why it is so important that we stay on top of it early, and keep it front of mind. Currently, in Australia, women retire with 42 per cent less super than men.

Make sure all of your super is in one super account because if you have more than one super, you are wasting your money on extra account fees. Make sure you have the best super account for you. In Victoria's book, *She's on the Money*, there's a fantastic guide to this and much more. There are plenty of financial resources available now, especially for women, and it is up to us to take control and empower ourselves with knowledge so the money stories we write for ourselves are positive ones.

It doesn't need to be all or nothing

KIC: We often speak about the 'all or nothing' mindset when it comes to health and fitness. Even though it's not a balanced or useful approach, this mindset often creeps its way into other areas of our lives, too. Like our approach to money. If the thought of taking control of your finances is daunting, we get it. It can be overwhelming, and the word 'budget' might sound like a huge scary thing that equals living off canned baked beans and never buying anything exciting ever again. But really, a budget is as simple as understanding what is coming into and out of your bank account, and working out if it aligns with your values around money.

You don't have to be an Excel or maths wizard, or have done a 20-week budgeting course to get started, either. Just like it's okay to start small with a health and fitness journey, the same is true for a financial journey. And just like a health journey, each money journey is different. Just because one type of budget works for your friend doesn't mean it will work for you. You've probably got different expenses, money values and levels of income. Find something that works for you, and empower yourself with the information you need to understand and take control of your finances.

Helpful money mindset tips

★ How much you have does not make you more or less worthy.

★ You (almost) always have the ability to change your money story and take back control.

★ Your retirement savings are really important. Make sure you know which fund you are with, and that they have a good return history with their clients.

★ Don't let anyone take away your power to earn money.

★ There will always be people with less or more money than you.

★ Using Afterpay or a similar payment option means you'll have to pay a certain amount of money four times. Will you still want to be paying for this item in four weeks or four months from now? Will it still bring you joy? Do you really need it?

★ Don't wait for your next pay rise to take control of your finances. Start now.

Victoria has shared some of her favourite money resources with us. Turn to page 249 if you're ready to dig in and take control of your money once and for all.

Connecting online and IRL

In a connected world, possessing the ability to unplug and share an analogue moment with loved ones is an essential life skill.

KIC: We have never been more (literally) connected, nor have we been less (figuratively) connected. We catch up with friends in real life, and even though we're experiencing real connection at the time, we feel compelled to seek out digital connection with others at the same time. There's so much more to this life than scrolling through a world that is not very real at all. As humans, we crave and need social and in-person connection, and if the pandemic has taught us anything, it's that loneliness cannot be fixed with FaceTime or Zoom. The only fix is real-life connection. We need to hug our loved ones more, have meaningful conversations and break this addiction to our phones. You never truly know what you are missing until you look up from the screen and see it through the lens of the present. There is so much power in being present in the moment, don't scroll it away.

Making your social media a safe space

Steph: I consider myself lucky to have gone through my teenage years without Instagram. Sure, we had Myspace and MSN Messenger, but the likes of Instagram and TikTok are another kettle of fish. If I'd had these apps when I was a teenager, naivety would've led me to believe that everything I saw online was real. Though, to be fair, age isn't always the biggest factor when it comes to social media being a dangerous and misleading place. Your own headspace and relationship with yourself play a huge part in how you use social media and how it, in turn, will affect you. There are a lot of ideas in this book around how you can work on your own relationship with yourself. And as part of that, let's chat about making social media (if you choose to be on it) a much safer and enjoyable place. Because even those with an incredible relationship with themselves can find it a horrible place to be.

Do your best to avoid comparing yourself to others. However, this is easier said than done. The online comparison trap hits from every angle. I find myself falling into the comparison trap when I've lost confidence in myself in certain areas. I used to be really insecure about my physical appearance, and I would compare my body to the bodies of people I followed online. These days, my insecurities are mostly career related, so I find I compare myself to where others are at in their careers. Unfortunately, comparison is just a part of life. We can get better at managing it, though, and we can also do our best to avoid it. Next time you find that you're comparing yourself to someone online, please remember that what you are seeing is likely not the full picture. Not only is the type of content people share curated, but often it's edited. Thankfully, on Instagram stories you can now see when a filter is being used, but within someone's feed you have no idea what kind of effort or editing has gone into every image. On top of that, Instagram is a highlight reel. Even the people who keep it pretty raw and relatable online will have struggles they won't share, and that's their prerogative.

Curate your experience

Remember, YOU ARE IN CONTROL of your social media. It's your choice to be on Instagram. It's your choice to have a public or private account. It's your choice to follow the people you do. It's your choice how much time you spend scrolling. There are certain things out of your control, for example, trolls or how someone else acts online. But you have the power to block, mute and restrict the people you interact with.

How do you feel when you're scrolling through your feed? Are there any accounts that make you feel bad about yourself? Unfollow or block them, or – if you're worried about someone finding out you've unfollowed them – mute them. Instead, follow more people who bring you joy. And consider what you are using social media for. Do you spend time online for fun? Inspiration? Entertainment? Whatever it is, follow more of the accounts that tick those boxes.

Own your feed

Now it's time to get another thing straight: your profile/feed is YOURS. Post whatever you like and don't stress over how much engagement it gets. You're never going to please everyone, and that's okay. Outside of being considerate to the world around you, of course, don't worry about what anyone else thinks of the content you decide to share. Your likes, comments and followers do not define you as a person. They do not prove your level of worthiness or coolness. You do you.

Finally, if you feel like you've done everything you can to make your social media a safe place, but there's still something about it that gets you down, here's our big tip:

Spend less time online

Limit your use of your favourite apps or take extended breaks that are days or even weeks long. Remember, that while it's fun, helpful and a form of connecting with others, it can also be consuming. Real life is where the party's at.

Tip: Social media reality check

★ Remember, what you see online is a highlight reel

★ Quit comparing yourself to others online

★ YOU decide who you follow

★ YOU can unfollow, block or mute accounts that make you feel bad about yourself

★ It's up to you if you keep your profile public or private. If it's private, it's up to you who follows you

★ Follow accounts that bring you joy, education or inspiration

★ Post whatever YOU want on your own feed

★ Limit your use and take breaks when you need to

Gifts do not equal love

Laura: Gift-giving (and then making that public) has become about public validation. At this point, it almost feels like we're all in a competition for who 'gives' the best. (Or is it who receives the best?) This, for me, is one of the hardest parts about social media.

When I think back to my childhood, I remember how – at the start of each school year – we'd be reunited with our classmates after the Christmas holidays and the comparison of gifts would begin. I remember one particular year so clearly. My sisters and I were always given a gift each from Santa. They were small but awesome gifts that we were happy to get and proud to show off. On the first day back at school, my classmates would start talking about their gifts and comparing them innocently, the way seven-year-olds do. I'd listen to everyone describe the multiple large gifts they unwrapped the month before. Some kids even brought in pictures of their trees to compare, and in some of them you couldn't see the floor underneath the tree for all the presents.

After hearing about everyone else's gifts, my one gift from Santa suddenly felt very small. I was no longer proud of it. In fact, I felt the opposite: ashamed. When my turn came, I said that I had forgotten what I'd been given. Comparison robbed all the joy that I'd had about my Christmas. Not because anyone took that awesome gift I loved away from me, but because of what others had received.

Luckily, this comparison was really only an issue for me once a year as a child, but now social media exposes us to this type of thing nearly every day. Gifts are special, but they are not an accurate indication of how much someone loves you. We all value very different things and are in different financial positions. If you are scrolling through your newsfeed and start to feel sad or envious that someone has more than you, or that they have a partner who gives them more expensive presents, a bigger engagement ring, etc., remind yourself again and again that gifts do not equal love. They *never* equal love. The most important things in life cannot be wrapped because they are not found in any shop (and definitely not in a designer or jewellery shop).

you take care

Choose kindness. It's good for you, too.

KIC: It is a special thing to care for someone, to be cared for, to give generously and help others, and have others offer a hand to you. Kindness is truly an amazing thing to experience, and it's something we all have the power to feel. It is a feeling/act that is so beautiful to receive, and even more so to give to others.

Being kind is a choice – one that is a conscious choice for some and subconscious for others. Not everyone chooses to be kind, and you may not always choose to be kind for whatever reason. But if you think back to moments where you have consciously chosen to be kind to another person, you would be able to remember that warm, fuzzy feeling inside.

According to the incredible research by the Random Acts of Kindness Foundation (yes – that exists), the 'warm and fuzzy feeling' we're referring to comes from the boost in your serotonin levels and the release of endorphins and production of oxytocin (the love hormone). Acting with kindness towards others doesn't only positively impact them, it can also impact you positively.

It's been proven that acting with kindness can reduce levels of anxiety, stress and depression. The hormone oxytocin causes the release of a chemical called nitric oxide, which dilates the blood vessels and in turn, lowers blood pressure as well.

We are not born kind or unkind. These behaviours can be taught. And once you practise kindness and witness the benefits for yourself, it's an easy choice to make. If you are kind to someone and that isn't reciprocated, know that this is not on you. And when we do something nice for someone, it should be without expectation of praise or reward – a selfless act of consideration towards others.

> **Kindness:** *(noun)* The quality of being generous, helpful, caring about other people.

We can't control how others live their lives nor their values, but we can control our own. If someone is not being kind to you, they may have things going on in their life that you aren't aware of, and they may be unable to separate their emotions from how they are with you.

Kindness can be shown in a number of different ways. It is also not scarce or something we will run out of. The supply within us is infinite. Here are some examples of small acts of kindness you can show another that may end up making their day.

★ Let someone go in front of you in the line to get a coffee if they seem rushed or stressed

★ Help someone pick up their belongings if they've dropped their bag

★ Offer to babysit a friend's child for an hour if you know they're in need of a break

★ Smile at a stranger

★ Help an elderly person to cross a road or offer your seat to them on the bus

★ Check in on a friend going through a hard time

★ Pay someone a compliment

★ Cook dinner for your partner/family tonight

★ Text one of your friends and tell them how much you appreciate them

★ Email a work colleague and tell them something they are really good at

Showing kindness does not make someone weak, and it's not something that we should fear doing. It makes us strong. If you need any more reason to be kind, remember that anyone, at any time, can be fighting a battle you know nothing about.

you take care

Kind people are magnets

Steph: Do you have people in your life who you crave time with because they just make you feel so good? When I see positivity and kindness radiating from someone, I am instantly drawn to them. When I surround myself with people who are thoughtful, supportive and kind I feel on top of the world. This encourages me to pay it forward and be a positive light to those around me, too.

Of course, I'm not always a happy-go-lucky person. It takes a certain kind of angel to be able to put their own struggles aside and still be a positive light to anyone that they pass all day/every day. But no matter what is going on in our own lives, it's important to be mindful of those around us, and to release the kind of energy we wish to receive back. A simple and somewhat obvious way to do this is to think about what you're about to say or do, and try and imagine how it would feel to be on the receiving end. Simply thinking about how our words or actions can affect others is the best way to avoid being unkind.

Tip: Kindness is contagious, but so is meanness. If you find yourself spending time with someone who is constantly unkind to you or to others and you feel yourself picking up on their habits, call them out on it or spend less time with them and stay true to your values.

Friendship

When it comes to friendship, quality should always come before quantity.

KIC: Why do you think friends exist? What is it about your friends that you like? Why do you choose to have them in your life? Is it because they fill you with joy? Is it because they encourage you to do great things? Is it because they support you, entertain you, love you?

In high school, there's an unspoken pressure to have the most friends. Your friends are almost decided for you because you end up hanging out with people in the same class, or people who are friends of other friends. In adulthood, you slowly become more conscious and careful about who your friends are. You realise that you don't necessarily have to be friends with someone because you work or study with them.

It's important to ask yourself questions like the ones above because if you can't answer what it is you like about a certain friend or what good things they bring to your life, it's time to question why you are still friends with them. It may sound harsh, but the reality is most of us don't have enough time in our lives to work, exercise, study, chill and see those close to us, let alone spend time with 'friends' who don't lift us up.

They say you start to pick up on the habits and characteristics of those people you spend the most time with, so if you're spreading yourself thin by trying to hang out with everyone and anyone, you may be finding it hard to define who you really are and who you want to be.

you take care

We're not saying your friends have to be perfect or only have characteristics or interests that align with yours; we're saying that it's worth looking at how you feel about yourself and your life after hanging out with certain people. Do you leave your catch-ups with them feeling . . .

joyful   anxious
proud   upset
relaxed *or* demotivated
motivated   unsure

If it's the latter, we're not saying drop that person as a friend, but maybe evaluate how much time you're spending with them. It's probably time better spent with other friends, or with yourself in a bath. The people in your life who bring you the most joy should get the most time with you.

Making friends as an adult

Steph: The concept of making a new friend is an odd one, isn't it? But it's really no different from finding a romantic partner. You have to put yourself out there, and that's not always an easy thing to do. The most important thing when trying to make friends is to stay true to yourself. Don't try to be someone you're not when you're trying to make a new friend because the likelihood of that friendship lasting isn't high. Look for friends who align with your core values or who have similar interests and be prepared to put time and effort into that relationship.

Some of the most beautiful friendships I've seen formed are through our KIC community. Whether virtually, through our Facebook community, or at an event, we see women connecting over a common interest in healthy living and it's so lovely to see these friendships blossom.

If you feel awkward or alone in admitting you want to make a friend as an adult, please don't. You're not the only one, and there are plenty of fish in the sea who would be lucky to be your friend.

Spark new friendships by

★ Leading with kindness and curiosity when meeting new people

★ Reaching out to friends of friends

★ Joining friendship apps

★ Heading out to community events that interest you. Don't be afraid to go alone.

The only risk you run when putting yourself out there is that you'll meet people who aren't your cup of tea. If that's the case, then you only end up where you started anyway. You've got nothing to lose, but lots of potential friends to gain.

Go on, gorgeous. They'll be lucky to have you.

Expectations and friendships

Laura: Some of the biggest challenges I've faced, while navigating platonic and romantic relationships, are due to the standards and expectations I expect those in my life to live up to. As someone who has very high expectations of herself, I often find myself falling into the trap of expecting the same of others, and I've found that this has a sabotaging effect on my relationships and my mindset.

It's so easy to fall into the trap of expecting perfectionism from ourselves and those around us, but with high expectations comes a high level of let-down when we don't feel our expectations are met. This is something I've had to work through over time and slowly let go of. One thing that's really helped me work through this is remembering that we all have different versions of perfection based on our value system. The idea of 'perfect' is not the same for each of us, and therefore it is impossible to live up to another person's standard of perfection.

For example, punctuality may be important to you. Being on time means you respect and value other people's time, and so you do everything you can to make sure you are never late. But one thing that might *not* be high up in your list of personal values is time away from your phone. You might think nothing of replying to texts while with your friends, and you might often spend time in their presence attending to notifications. If you have a friend who values quality time and being present, they might find it disrespectful when you whip out your phone during dinner. Perhaps this same friend is always late for things because being on time isn't important to them. They don't notice when others are late, or worry about being on time themselves.

So, now we have two people – both with differing values and definitions of 'perfection', and different expectations of themselves and their friends. In this example, if both people put their expectations onto each other, they will almost always be let down. Without communicating what's important to them, neither of them will know they are letting the other down as they have differing expectations. I remind myself of this example often, and I find it helps me let go of worries I don't need in my mind, and focus on the important things in my relationships. Strong relationships and connections are hard to come by, so when they do, try not to sweat so much of the small stuff.

Tip: If you ever feel disrespected by a friend, it is important to let them know. And if you constantly feel you have to sacrifice your value system to please them or make them feel comfortable then you may need to ask yourself if this friendship is serving you. There's a big difference between being okay with someone being five minutes late, and someone treating you badly.

Navigating friendships at different life stages

Steph: Once you hit your thirties, the assumption tends to be that the people around you at this point will always be around you. The idea that friendships come and go feels like something you only had to worry about during your teens and twenties. But since we each arrive at big life stages at different times, friendships will still come and go, so any you want to keep need to be nurtured and cared for in order to thrive.

I'll use my friendship with Laura as an example. For a while, we were at the exact same stage in life. It was easy to catch up, make time for each other and relate to one another. But at the moment, we're at slightly different stages in life. I use the word 'slightly' because there is still so much that we do have in common, but the biggest changes are that I'm a mother now and Laura, well, she's the CEO of our company and absolutely smashing it in her career.

Our love and support for each other has not faded, and our friendship is still thriving because we both make an effort to be there for each other and check in constantly. But big life changes, such as becoming a parent, moving overseas or working hard towards a career goal, can sometimes set us apart from our friends. Catch-ups become few and far between because your schedules no longer line up perfectly the way they once did.

With a lot of my friends, I honestly feel like a burden at times because my new schedule can make catching up difficult. Outside of inviting them over, we have to work things around getting a sitter for Harvey. It's not impossible to make plans, but it does take effort, and it takes patience from our friends, too. Good friends will never stop checking in or inviting you out even if you've had to say 'no' many times in a row. Good friends, although they may not always be able to relate, should be able to understand and be flexible with where you're at, as long as you're flexible, too. Friendship is a two-way street, like any relationship. You both have to make an effort and water the grass if you want it to stay green.

The in-between life stage

To add another layer to the mix, we wanted to acknowledge another life stage – the one where you may be ready to start a family but still waiting for your dreams to come true. When you're trying to conceive, struggling with infertility or have been through a heartbreaking pregnancy loss, spending time with friends and their little ones can be really difficult.

At this time of life, you should be your number-one priority. It's so important to check in and be aware of your emotions. No matter what the occasion, whether it's a coffee catch-up, baby shower, barbecue or birthday party, if you're feeling vulnerable it's always okay to say 'no'. Be open and honest with your friends and explain that you'll see them when you're in a stronger frame of mind. They will understand. On the flip side, spending time with friends who don't have baby-making on their radar can be a great 'escape' and help take your mind off the stresses of starting a family. Whether these are friends, work colleagues or family members, the change in conversation can be like a breath of fresh air.

 TRY THIS

The power of listening

Do you ever find yourself having conversations where you're not fully listening to what someone's saying because you're focusing on what you're going to say next? Next time you catch up with a friend, ask them a question and really sit back and listen to their response. Put your experiences, advice and contributions aside and give them your undivided attention. It's harder than it sounds, but you'll be surprised by how much information you absorb and how much better you connect.

Unsolicited advice during pregnancy

Steph: One thing no one prepares you for when you're pregnant is the influx of unwarranted advice. It tends to centre around what you should/ shouldn't be eating, whether you should/shouldn't be working, which type of exercises you should avoid, what your birth plan should/shouldn't be . . . the list goes on and on and the advice comes at you from all directions. Whether it's your family, co-workers, friends (even those who haven't been pregnant or had a baby themselves), the advice floods in.

The most confusing thing is that a lot of the time all the advice is contradictory. A newly pregnant woman quickly picks up that there are many ways to do things because everybody's experience with pregnancy is completely different. Women are all different and each baby is unique, so how can we be expected to follow one singular set of advice or have the same experience as everyone else?

To help clear things up and make an educated decision on all of the areas you actually *want* advice on, reach out to your trusted health professional, talk it through with them and then make a call that feels right to you.

Think twice before offering 'helpful' advice

If you're reading this and feeling like you may have been guilty of offering unsolicited advice in the past, don't feel bad. Everyone has different ideas about what's appropriate to share and what's not. But unless your friend or relative has asked for advice or your opinion on something, think twice before sharing it. Even when you do, be mindful of the language you use when doing so. Try to frame it in a way that is free of value judgements. Steer away from saying things like, 'I'd never do that.', 'You need to do this', or 'You shouldn't be doing that'.

'Have you had your baby yet?'

A time when I felt most confused and uneasy from unsolicited advice was when my due date was approaching and there was no sign of labour. If I had a dollar for every time someone messaged me, *Is he here yet?* in the weeks leading up to Harvey's birth . . . I mean, honestly, it was as if people thought we wouldn't tell them when he had arrived. But even if he had arrived and we hadn't told you yet . . . be patient and let us tell you.

My advice to anyone who has a friend nearing their due date is to be patient and cautious with the language you use when talking to them. Some people are completely chilled out and have all the patience in the world for their bub to come, but others (like me) can start feeling really anxious and overwhelmed towards the end of their pregnancy. Just think, if you feel like they've been pregnant forever and *you* just can't wait to meet the baby, imagine how they must feel.

Along with that question, I also started getting everyone's 'tips and tricks' to 'induce labour' from home. I got sucked in by it all and honestly tried everything. Having people tell you that something '100 per cent works' but then have it not work for you is irritating. I completely lost patience and started to become incredibly emotional thinking there was something wrong with me because none of these 'sure things' was working. I look back now and think how silly it was to let all of that consume me. It took so much time and energy away from just being excited about meeting our baby.

It's easy to feel overwhelmed by all of the noise. In the end, what helped me was smiling and nodding along when the people who I knew weren't the ones I should be listening to gave me their advice. If I ever needed another opinion, I'd engage with those I *did* trust. People mean well when they share advice, but it doesn't always come across that way. It's up to you if and how you take what they say on board. If anyone judges you for your 'birth plan' because it's not what they would do, try to ignore them. They should know better than to cast judgement on such a personal moment.

The best piece of advice I got was, 'You do you. You know what's best for you.'

Miscarriage: Screw the stigma, I'm talking about it

Nicole Maycroft

'I had a miscarriage.' Something that I never thought I was going to hear come out of my mouth. When I found out I was pregnant, even though I had heard about the upsetting fact that one in four pregnancies end in miscarriage, I didn't think that I would be that one . . . Twice. During my pregnancies, I always questioned the unspoken rule that you 'shouldn't tell many people until you're over that 12-week hump'. I always thought, *Why should I wait to tell my friends the most exciting news, 'just in case' when, in fact, I would want, and more importantly need, their support if anything were to happen?* Which, unfortunately, in my case, it did.

My heart breaks for any woman and her partner who have to go through this, no matter what stage of pregnancy they're at. There is nothing anyone can say to make things better. It's such a shitty thing to go through. Just remember that you are not alone, and it wasn't your fault.

I know that every circumstance is unique, but I thought it might be helpful to share some of the things that got me through the hardest days:

Talk about it

The more I spoke about it, the easier it was to digest and process what had happened. It's so important to find your support group, whether it be your parents, friends or partner. Openly talking about your experience can really help.

Social media detox

No doubt with the excitement of your pregnancy you started to follow pregnancy and baby-related Instagram pages and profiles. Seeing this content along with pregnancy announcements, bump updates or baby arrivals can be really triggering, so it's important to take a step back as you grieve. When you're comfortable to jump back on, you can unfollow or mute any accounts that may upset you, or ask a friend to do this on your behalf if you need. One thing that caught me by surprise after both of my miscarriages, was logging back into my pregnancy app when we were ready to start trying again and seeing notifications about how far along my pregnancy 'would've' been. If you feel up to it, reset your profile so you're not struck with this unwanted surprise like I was.

See a psychologist

For some reason, during a time where my body and mind needed to be nurtured, I was quite hard on myself for not being my 'normal happy self.' My psychologist helped me understand that my feelings were valid, and that I had actually been through something horrible and that it's completely normal to grieve.

Be open and transparent with your managers and work colleagues

You may not need to tell your entire team, but it's helpful to inform those who work closely with you so they can help you manage your workload and support you. Being open with work means that you won't have to pretend that everything is sunshine and rainbows. Putting on a front can be really exhausting, and you don't need that added pressure right now.

Try meditation and yoga

I wasn't up to this in the early stages, but about two weeks after my dilation and curretage (D&C), I introduced exercise back into my routine. I found slow, mindful movements were what my body was craving. After miscarrying, especially the first time, my anxiety was through the roof so taking the time to nurture my body and mind was really important.

Journalling

Similar to talking about your experience, writing can help you to process your thoughts. When you're comfortable with looking back on what you have written, you'll be proud of what you have overcome. Trust me, it does get easier, it just takes time.

How to support a loved one who has experienced a miscarriage

Just be there

Whether it be in person or over the phone, your friend is going to need you. I know confronting something so devastating might feel uncomfortable, but please don't avoid the situation. Showing up is what matters the most.

Check in regularly

A key thing to remember is that grief doesn't go away overnight. It's so important to regularly check in with your friend. It doesn't take much, just a simple message like *I'm thinking of you*. They may not respond, but when you're heartbroken, it's so nice to know that others care about you.

Send love from afar

It doesn't have to be a grand gesture – even a handwritten card would mean the world right now. My favourite surprise was a bunch of sunflowers; they made me smile each time I saw them, which can be a rarity in the early days of miscarrying.

Avoid silver linings

I understand that the following comments come from a good place, but trust me, offering silver linings isn't helpful. Do your best to avoid saying things such as

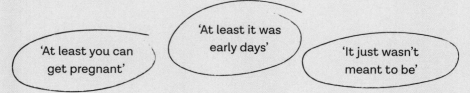

'At least you can get pregnant'

'At least it was early days'

'It just wasn't meant to be'

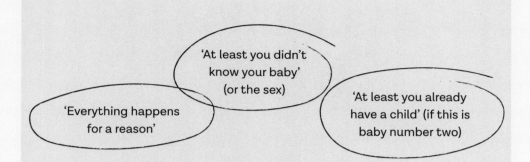

'At least you didn't know your baby' (or the sex)

'Everything happens for a reason'

'At least you already have a child' (if this is baby number two)

Instead, you could acknowledge their pain and heartbreak by saying things such as

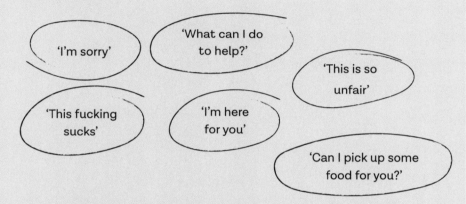

'I'm sorry'

'What can I do to help?'

'This is so unfair'

'This fucking sucks'

'I'm here for you'

'Can I pick up some food for you?'

The sad reality is that, eventually, we're all likely to know someone who has experienced a miscarriage or been close to someone who has. Yet, for some reason, the topic is still considered taboo. I'm incredibly passionate about sharing my story to help break the stigma, build awareness and ultimately show others that they are not alone. I'm so grateful to have had the opportunity to share my story with Steph on the KICPOD. If you'd like to go back and listen, it's episode #124 KICBUMP: 'Miscarriage: Screw the stigma, Nicole's talking about it'.

Let's talk about sex, baby

Talking to sexperts has taught us that we need to speak up to unlock a healthy, fulfilling and pleasurable sex life.

KIC: The two of us are extremely fortunate to each be in supportive relationships where we feel comfortable having open, honest conversations about sex with our partners. However, we haven't always had the confidence to speak up about what we want in the bedroom. Even when you're in a loving relationship, this can be uncomfortable and often quite difficult.

Lucy Wark is the founder of NORMAL, a sexual wellness and sex education company behind the free online sex education course *The Modern Guide to Sex*. During an empowering episode of the *KICPOD* ('Let's talk about modern sex, baby') Lucy and Georgia Grace, NORMAL'S in-house certified sex coach, talked us through how sexual communication is a skill – one most of us are never taught. There are societal expectations that you should just 'know' how to pleasure your sexual partner, and that you shouldn't have to tell them what you like. The reality is, no matter our gender identity or sexual orientation, being a good lover is a skill that is learned, and the best way to do that is via communication.

Whether you're wanting to talk about a vulnerability or a desire to try different sex positions or toys in the bedroom, have a threesome or watch porn together – whatever you wish to explore, Lucy and Georgia suggest waiting for a time that feels safe to bring this up with your partner. That might be while you're out on a walk or before you have dinner, but not when you're both at your most vulnerable, i.e. before, during or after sex. If you're not sure how to bring up these conversations, you could always mention this book or the podcast, and say, 'I've heard about this thing called sexual communication, and I think it's important to work through this together so we can both find ways that we can make our sex even better.'

The sex-ed we wish we received

The type of sex education being pioneered by people like Lucy and Georgia is revolutionary, and so necessary. When the two of us think back to the sex-ed we had in schools, we get flashbacks of extremely awkward and very limited conversations led by a maths teacher about contraception, pregnancy and STIs. If your school was a little more advanced, then maybe, just maybe, you were taught to put a condom on a banana.

There was a lot left out of the material we were taught, and what we learned didn't leave us feeling equipped for real-life sexual connection. Yet unfortunately, in the ten plus years since we left school, not much has changed. Lucy and Georgia shared their valuable insight into the information they believe is missing from the current sex education curriculum, and they backed this up with some eye-opening statistics from their own research.

Georgia is passionate about the fact that sex-ed should be sex-positive and shame-free. She believes students should feel informed and empowered with information that's relevant to their sexual orientation, while having the ability to learn in an environment where they feel safe and comfortable, during their own time – ideally online. More often than not, sex-ed is taught by people who haven't received the right sex education themselves, so of course they feel awkward teaching this subject. The fact that a generation of digital natives is still being taught about sex by teachers unqualified in this subject, and in a classroom setting, is mind boggling.

In a survey of over 1000 Australians of all ages, NORMAL set out to better understand the nation's thoughts on sex, sexuality and pleasure. They asked about the sex education respondents had received at school and found that, even within the Gen Z demographic, less than one in ten people had had education with any mention of LGBTQIA+ sex or people. Unsurprisingly, this resulted in members of this community feeling like they are not seen – something that needs to change immediately. Only one in three recent graduates said they'd learned about discussing consent with their partners and only one in ten had been educated about the differences between the type of sex depicted in porn and real sex. The bar seriously needs to be raised.

Sexual confidence

Even the most sexually confident person has days when they feel a bit *meh*. Working on sexual confidence is often a lifelong practice. If you've ever felt as though your confidence is lacking, you're not alone. Recently, NORMAL did a nationwide survey and found confidence was the single biggest issue for most people around sex. So, to help boost our confidence in the bedroom, we picked the very qualified brains of Georgia Grace.

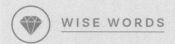

Sexual confidence
Georgia Grace

Sexual confidence means different things to different people. For some, it can be feeling present in the moment, being connected to their body and another person's, feeling comfortable to ask for what they want, experiencing equal access to pleasure, asking to try something new or being able to fully release into pleasure. And it doesn't just begin and end in the bedroom. It can also be about how a person engages with their partner on a daily basis, how they speak to themselves about their body, how much pleasure they allow themselves to experience, how often they rest or how they date or flirt. It isn't just one thing; it is many.

Since sexual confidence is incredibly individual, rather than giving you a rigid definition of what it should feel like, it's more useful to figure what it looks like for you. Let's pause and work through this together.

Sexual confidence check-in. Ask yourself

★ When do I feel most sexually confident?

★ How comfortable do I feel in asking for what I want?

★ What's getting in the way of me feeling sexually confident?

★ What has informed how I feel about my body? (Examine social, cultural, religious and political influences.)

★ What does a fulfilling sex life mean for me?

If you don't feel like going into this now, these prompts may be useful to discuss with someone, or when you're alone and in the right frame of mind to journal or mentally work through these questions.

Sexual confidence *continued*

Building sexual confidence with yourself

Building sexual confidence on your own is often an ongoing process but it's also a good foundation for building confidence and intimacy with sexual partners. Here are a few other things to consider when it comes to feeling confident with others.

Prioritise pleasure on a daily basis

This can be something as simple as bringing awareness to your senses as you sip tea, taking an extra few minutes to moisturise with your favourite body oil, or setting aside time each week for self-pleasure.

Ctrl, alt, delete harmful messages

Examine and challenge anything that is sex-negative, body shaming or doing you more harm than good. Actively seek out sex-positive resources, messages or practitioners. There's so much good stuff out there.

Sex-positive affirmations

Yes, these can feel awkward at first, and they can also feel a bit fluffy, but I've found these to be radically useful for my clients. When we engage in new behaviours, thoughts and activities (for example, around our bodies or our sexual confidence), we can hack the brain and rewire not-so-useful thought processes and habits. Become aware of negative self-talk, challenge it and swap it out for something like 'I am really fucking sexy', 'I deserve pleasure' and 'I am sensual and confident'.

Solo sex is sex

You don't need to be in a relationship to have a rocking sex life. Value self-pleasure as a valid, healthy and important part of a fulfilling sex life. Solo sex is one of the best ways to learn about your body and pleasure.

Building sexual confidence with others

Once you've built a good foundation with yourself, you can build confidence and intimacy with sexual partners. Here's how.

Ask for what you want

Many people struggle to ask for what they want during sex for a range of reasons. It could be that they don't know what they want or that they feel too vulnerable to voice their desires. They might feel like vocalising those desires is an entirely new language. Sexual communication is a skill, and, like any skill, you'll need to practise often to get good at it. If you identify this as an area you need to work on, it may be useful to flick back a page and explore the questions on self-confidence.

Hear a 'no'

It can really suck hearing a no, especially if you feel vulnerable asking for something. However, if someone isn't into something, instead of taking their no personally, making them feel bad or going on the attack, try saying, 'Thank you'. This shows them that you respect their boundaries and openness. It communicates that you've heard them and it's also a way to see a boundary as useful and constructive information rather than a rejection.

Create the context for sexual confidence

What do you and your partner need to each feel confident during sex? Is it a space free from distraction? Having enough time to build arousal? Locking the door or turning up your fave sex playlist? Explore what you need to create a context that feels safe and sexy.

Body image, shame and confidence come up regularly in my sessions – mostly because a lot of people don't know where to start. I've dedicated a whole topic to this in NORMAL's free online video course, 'The Modern Guide to Sex'. It has a huge amount of information and resources to support you in building your sexual confidence. The online sex-ed course is currently inspiring people in over 40 countries around the world. Get amongst it! **itsnormal.com**

Love

KIC: Whether you're single, dating or married, the way you show and receive love may be completely different to your partners and peers. Different personalities have different needs. In order to strengthen any relationship, romantic or platonic, we need to not only understand our personal wants and needs, but also become aware of our loved one's desires, too.

Perhaps you've heard of the book, *The 5 Love Languages* by Gary Chapman. Maybe you've already completed the quiz, thought about doing it or perhaps this is brand new information. Either way, Chapman's philosophy is that there are five love languages, and that by 'learning to recognise these preferences in yourself and in your loved ones, you can learn to identify the root of your conflicts, connect more profoundly, and truly begin to grow closer'.

The 5 Love Languages are:

1 **Quality time:** If this is your love language, then having your partner be there and be present is the thing that makes you feel truly special and loved. We're talking TV off, phones down, spending beautiful, uninterrupted, quality time together.

2 **Acts of service:** Anything someone does to ease the burden of responsibilities weighing on you speaks volumes. The words, 'Let me do that for you' mean the world. It might be cleaning your car, putting away your washing –simply taking initiative and completing a task on your behalf is the best way for someone to show you that they care.

3 **Words of affirmation:** Compliments, praise and hearing, 'I love you' mean the world to you. Kind, encouraging and positive words are what make you thrive.

4 **Physical touch:** Despite its name, this love language isn't all about touch in the bedroom; it's also about those spontaneous hugs, holding hands and thoughtful arm touches that make you feel loved and cared for.

5   **Receiving gifts:** This is the most misunderstood of the five love languages. It may sound materialistic, but gift giving isn't just about presents. In fact, it's not the price tag that you cherish, it's the care, effort or thought that went into the gift. Hearing 'I saw this and thought of you' is music to your ears.

Our love languages

Steph: Josh and I are so similar when it comes to our love language. Quality time is the number one priority for both of us. But even though we share the same values, we still need to make a conscious effort. It's funny we'll both be on our phones in bed or on the couch, and as soon as one of us puts our phone down, we'll tell the other to get off their phone so we can chat, even though we were *just* doing the same thing. Ha! We've recently set some boundaries around not having our phones in bed so that we can wind down and actually be present with each other. It's honestly been such a positive change to our routine. It's all about understanding what means the most to your partner, being proactive and consciously making an effort to show them that you care.

Laura: Dalt and I show and feel love in slightly different ways. Acts of service definitely mean the most to me. We both live such busy, active lives, so anytime Dalt takes time out of his day to do something for me like bringing me a coffee in bed or cleaning my car, it makes me feel so loved and supported. Dalt is more like Steph and Josh: quality time is what he cherishes most. Nights on the couch, phones down with a glass of red wine, cuddling up to our dogs make him incredibly happy.

What are your love languages? If you have a partner, what are theirs? Take the 5 Love Languages quiz at 5lovelanguages.com

Relationship comparison

KIC: As we've touched on a few times by now, comparison is honestly the thief of joy. We've just explored how people show love in so many different ways, so we know that every relationship is unique. With that in mind, it's sensible to say that we need to learn to stop comparing our own relationships to others. However, we are also fully aware that this is a lot easier said than done.

It's completely normal for relationships to go through highs and lows, and when we're stuck in a love rut we tend to compare ourselves to others even more. Whether we're catching up with another loved up couple in person or seeing romantic posts online, it's important to remember that we are witnessing a mere glimmer of that relationship.

Just because a relationship seems all sunshine and rainbows to you, doesn't mean that's really the case. We've spoken about Instagram being a highlight reel. Well, think about it: chances are you've never shared a fight with a partner on your feed, so why would anyone else? The same way you might put on a brave face when you go out for dinner after bickering in the car on the way there, every relationship has its own baggage. You honestly never know what's going on behind closed doors.

Subconsciously, we believe that the grass is greener on the other side, when in reality, grass is greener where you water it. If you find yourself making comparisons, try to stop yourself and switch your mindset to focus on the beautiful things that make your relationship unique. You may look at a relationship where one person is being showered with gifts and physical affection, but those things could be making up for a lack of quality time together, or not lifting a finger around the house. Focus on *your* love language and what's important to you and your partner. Think of the memories you have together and remember that if you do have any concerns, open communication is the best medicine.

Knowing when to end it

If you read this title and your heart sank because you've been tossing this thought around lately, perhaps you're hoping we'll have answers that will help. Unfortunately, we simply don't have them. Only you and your partner know the ins and outs and the struggles and strengths of your relationship. Only you will know whether and when it's time to move on. As heartbreaking as it is, people drift apart. If you're feeling really sad because this is happening to you, know that the feelings of sadness are temporary and that you will get through the goodbye if that's what needs to happen.

When it comes to romantic relationships it's almost impossible for a couple to be aligned on absolutely everything, but it is important that their core values are aligned. As we grow, mature and are exposed to new life experiences, our wants, needs and desires shift. When this isn't happening in sync with a partner, that can cause strain and heartbreak.

If you find yourself searching high and low for signs to show you whether or not they are 'the one', perhaps deep down you've already answered this for yourself. Only you know.

To parent or not to parent? That is the question.

Laura: The topic of parenthood often goes hand-in-hand with relationships. Some couples find themselves brought together by a child unexpectedly, while others plan for that adventure together. But before talking about motherhood and fertility windows, it's important to acknowledge that being a parent isn't a prerequisite for being an accomplished, together adult. There is so much societal pressure to follow a certain path in life, but the most beautiful thing about life is that YOU get to choose how yours looks. You can create your own path, and the path you take, no matter which elements you decide to include, or the order in which you tackle them, will not make you any less or more worthy of happiness or having a life you love. If the prospect of parenthood excites you, then read on. If not, feel free to skip to page 234.

The wild and wacky road to motherhood

KIC: It wouldn't be right to launch into a section on motherhood without discussing the wild, emotional and sometimes heartbreaking journey it takes to get there. Motherhood is a miracle that some of you may have already been blessed by. Perhaps you're striving to achieve it now, or not quite ready yet but eager to educate yourself to find out if it's the right choice for you, in which case, kudos to you! We believe equipping yourself with knowledge before you decide to embark on the journey to motherhood is so empowering.

Many heterosexual couples find that having a baby isn't as easy as they have been led to believe. Having sex doesn't always result in a pregnancy, and the window in a woman's cycle when she is likely to conceive is actually very narrow, and even then there's no guarantee. And starting a family when you're a member of the LGBTQIA+ community can often require even more emotional, physical and financial stress. No matter what your sexual orientation or gender identity, there are hurdles to overcome, such as infertility, IVF, surrogacy, adoption, miscarriage and stillbirth. So many paths for those dreaming of the same miracle.

Weighing up the fertility window

Laura: One of the hardest things about the twenties and thirties (for me, anyway) is having to confront the inescapable biological reality that fertility decreases with age. The years when a woman is most able/likely to conceive are known as the 'fertility window'. When I searched this term online, the first article that came up reported that the 'optimum' time to conceive is 30.5 years old. That same article also advised that women have far fewer eggs after the age of 35, but that if they wait longer and have children later (I guess the author meant past the 'optimum' age of 30.5) the positives might be that they might have more patience and more money saved up.

We spend our younger years fearing pregnancy, and believing there is a 100 per cent chance of falling pregnant if we don't use protection. Then, in our twenties we learn that this is absolutely not a certainty. Far from it. Instead, we find out about the 25 per cent chance of miscarriage, and that not everyone is physically able to have children. For those who are able to conceive, it turns out that there are only a certain number of 'fertile years' to do so. This new information forces us to consider our parenthood plans at an age when many of us still feel unsure of what our plans will be. This 'fertility window' is something I worry/think about often. I know that I'm not ready right now, but what if I wait too long and miss my window and then wish I'd started earlier?

I always thought I would have children or be pregnant by the time I was 30. I'm not sure why, but that was always the number for me. Maybe it's because when I was younger that seemed like the age when people were really 'adults'. Maybe it's because any movies I watched growing up about 30-year-old women dealt with this topic, and these expectations have been subconsciously sitting in my head ever since. Perhaps it's down to the negative narrative around being an 'old' parent and the way society tells us that we should want to be a 'young' mum. What is a young parent anyway? Aren't we only as old as we feel? I also wonder if we feel we need to have our 'shit' together by 30, and having everything together includes a plan to start a family.

When I speak to parents about how they decided on the right time to have their children, everyone's answer is so different. Some say there's never a right time, so don't wait for one. Others say they would do anything to wind back the clock and start trying earlier, as they struggled to conceive, and it took them years to fall pregnant. Some say they wished they'd had their kids earlier so they could enjoy more time with them as grown-ups. But then other people have also told me they wish they'd waited longer before becoming a parent, as they feel they gave away the best years of their life or that having kids early in life prevented them from establishing themselves in their career. I think, in having these discussions, while I absolutely didn't get the answer I was looking for (which deep down I knew didn't exist), I did learn one thing: the 'right time' is different for everyone.

As I write this, I'm approaching my 30th birthday, and while I do feel scared of waiting too long to have a baby, I also feel petrified of the thought of becoming a parent in the near future. Sacrificing the ability to make spontaneous plans, or sleep through the night doesn't feel like something I'm ready to do. But then I feel guilty for being selfish – shouldn't I want to sacrifice those things to become a mother?

I feel scared that if I were to have a child now I would not feel as though I have done enough or given enough in my career before kids, but I'm also almost equally afraid of the guilt I know I will feel if I put career before family, wait too long and then struggle to conceive. I feel scared that I will lose myself and forget who I am by having a child, but equally scared that I will not understand or realise my true purpose until I become a mother. I feel scared I will not enjoy swapping dinners with friends for kids' birthday parties or trips to the park. What if I don't like the park?

If I were to really dig deep right now and ask myself why I am not ready, I think the answers would be a combination of the worries I've just shared – especially after the experience of losing myself and my purpose in 2020 (pg 10). I guess I'm only just starting to feel like myself again now. I'm excited, motivated and driven again, and I want to make sure that when Dalton and I decide the time is right for us, it isn't because we are trying to fill a void or because we are wanting a 'change', but because we are ready to become parents. We hope to have children, but I don't know how fertile I am or how fertile my husband is.

We'll have to wait and see.

Trying isn't always the 'fun' part

Steph: If you're in a heterosexual relationship, once you've made the decision that motherhood is for you, it's time to start 'trying'. Whether you're currently trying to conceive or fortunate to already be a mumma (in which case you can look back and potentially relate), you may agree that trying to have a baby isn't always as fun as it sounds. Don't get me wrong; yes, it encourages you and your partner to connect on a deeper level, have sex on a regular basis and strive for the same beautiful goal but, in all honesty, it can be emotionally draining. If I had a dollar for the number of times people said, 'Bet you're having fun' or 'Josh must be loving it', seriously. (By the way, this is such a dated, misogynistic statement. Who said I'm not enjoying all the sex?) But as much as sex is enjoyable, I wouldn't necessarily call the process of trying 'fun'. It really can take its toll, on both of you.

Josh and I were extremely lucky to fall pregnant with Harvey within three months of trying. I know that for many couples, this isn't the case. It can often take several months or even years before you're blessed with a miracle. It's important to remember that every experience is unique, and that your feelings are relevant and valid – whatever you are going through.

'Trying' feels like being on a constant emotional rollercoaster. After finishing your period, you feel excited and hopeful that this month will be the month. You watch your period-tracking app like a hawk, calculate your most fertile days and have sex as much as possible during those days. Once you finish ovulating, you wait until your period is due and if you're anything like me, you over-analyse every ache, pain and flinch in your body, thinking, *Maybe that's a sign of pregnancy.* If your period is a day or two late, you start thinking, Could it be? Then, you take a test. Three minutes later you're either on the highest of highs when you see those two lines, or you're riding that rollercoaster back down the hill, to start again the next month.

How to be kind to yourself while trying
Don't place too much pressure on yourself
I know this can be easier said than done, but if you're exhausted and not quite up to having sex one night, there's absolutely no need to push yourself. There's always tomorrow, and listening to your body and mind, and resting when you need to is so much more important.

Understand that your partner needs rest, too
Sometimes, your partner will be exhausted, stressed from work or simply isn't in the mood. This can be frustrating, (trust me, I totally get it), but remember, this is an emotional time for them, too. Do your best to respect how they're feeling and be open with your communication.

Find ways to connect outside of the bedroom

When you're trying to get pregnant, it can feel like the romance has been taken out of love-making. When sex is scheduled, sometimes it can start to feel like a chore rather than a spontaneous sign of affection, and that's normal. It's important to set aside time to connect with your partner and celebrate your relationship away from the bedroom because the fact that you're ready and wanting to start a family is really exciting. Whether it's a date night, a weekend away, a long walk or simply having dinner without the TV on, make sure you find time to reconnect and take the focus off baby-making for a while.

Prioritise and celebrate YOU

It takes a lot of strength to pick yourself up after disappointment. It may not feel like it, but you are so much stronger than you realise. It's important to make the time to celebrate all you are doing. Whether that means sipping on a margarita or two, pouring a hot bath or booking yourself in for a blissful massage, treat yourself to the things that make you smile, because you deserve it.

Schedule sex

After a long, stressful day, sex might be the last thing on your mind. I know this might sound a bit clinical but if you allocate time during the day to have sex, not only will you have more energy to connect with your partner, but you're less likely to put it off. Ticking this off reduces the chance that you'll wake up the next day feeling the 'We should've had sex last night' worries.

Major milestones are wonderful, but don't forget to find happiness in the little things along the way.

Setting healthy boundaries

Establishing healthy boundaries is empowering. We find it's a strength, not a weakness.

KIC: Award-winning life coach, Sahar Andrade explains that boundaries create trust and build healthy interpersonal and professional relationships. When you put healthy boundaries in place, even if some people don't like what you do, they will likely still respect you for standing up for what you believe in. When your boundaries are respected, you are more likely to feel heard, validated and appreciated. But most of all, when you set boundaries, you are less likely to be taken for granted by either your loved ones or your colleagues and supervisors.

It is not selfish, rude, pushy or self-centred to make these requests. Boundaries demonstrate that you understand your value and know what your priorities are. When you share these boundaries, you're making sure that others do as well. Some people feel the need to please others, often without realising that by saying 'yes' to everything, they are also saying 'no' to something else that might be equally important to them. It is about you creating the space and time for you to flourish and achieve your career goals and your life dreams.

Boundaries in your work life

It's so easy to fall into bad habits at work, switch between tasks or get dragged into unnecessary meetings. Before you know it, working late on the regular and over weekends is your new normal. If you want to make sure you are striking the right 'balance' between work and health and you want to leave the office on time while getting all your projects done or getting that promotion, you're going to need to set and implement boundaries that work for you.

We thought we'd share some of the ways we encourage our KIC team to prioritise their workloads. These tips are geared towards people who work in an office environment, because that's what we have experience with, but we encourage you to think about some boundaries that you could personally implement or suggest that are relevant to your workplace.

How we encourage our KIC team to set boundaries in the workplace

Turn off notifications on your laptop or computer

This will allow you to fully focus on the task at hand. A quick check of your incoming email may seem harmless, but did you know that it takes on average 23 minutes and 15 seconds to get back to a task after a distraction?

Turn off notifications on your phone

If you need to have your emails set up on your personal phone, having your notifications switched off will allow you to also 'switch off' at night and on weekends.

Don't respond straight away

If you're jumping onto your laptop to draft a reply as soon as an email hits your inbox, people will start to expect that you'll always respond in an instant when the reality is that's just not possible all the time. Plus, more often than not, when you're responding to someone's email, you're prioritising *their* task over your own. Unless the matter is urgent, take your time, prioritise YOUR most important tasks and then get back to them.

Block out a meeting-free day

This is something we've recently implemented at KIC. Meetings are vital when it comes to collaborating and strategising, but they can eat up so much time. We've found our meeting-free days extremely helpful and productive. Blocking out an entire day may be something that's out of your control, and if that's the case, consider if you could bring this up with your manager as a suggestion to help boost both your productivity and theirs.

Eat lunch away from your desk

This is easier said than done, we know. But it's important to give yourself time to rest, recharge and move your body so you can take on the afternoon with energy and enthusiasm.

Work smarter, not harder

There will be days where you'll need to put in an extra hour or so, but if you're having to stay late on the regular, it's probably time to reassess the way you work. Think about things you can cull, combine or cancel to ensure you're not having to spend more of your own personal time working.

Boundaries in your social life

When it comes to our social lives, we've all had those times where we could quite happily cancel that dinner or coffee catch-up and stay rugged up on the couch. We're only human. However, we've found that having realistic boundaries in place can reduce our temptation to cancel. If there's one good thing to come out of the pandemic, it's the realisation that slowing down is necessary. The hours in our weekends are so precious, and it's important to make time to rest and re-energise.

Here we set boundaries in our social life

Learn to say, 'no'

When it comes to social occasions, you are your number-one priority, and it is always okay to turn down an invite. Don't be afraid to be upfront and tell your friends the truth, whether it's, 'I'm too tired', 'I've had a massive week', 'I've got too much on that weekend' or 'I'm just not feeling up to it'. Try committing to one social event per day, or even per weekend so you can save your energy for that one occasion, allowing you to be fully present with that person or group of people. When we over-commit, we set ourselves up for exhaustion.

Be upfront with how much time you have available

Just because you're already there, doesn't mean you can't say 'no' to the extra glass of wine or another hour of conversation. Make sure you allow yourself enough time to rest and recharge afterwards.

Get to know your own personal capacity

The amount of socialising you can handle might be completely different to friends', partner's or family's. Just because one person thrives off back-to-back catch-ups doesn't mean you have to tag along for the entire ride. Check in with yourself before, during and after each occasion and take note of how you're feeling emotionally. You'll start to learn how much you can actually commit to and when it's time to say no. It's all about understanding and acknowledging your own personal capacity, and setting boundaries based on this.

Block out 'me-time'

Just like having a meeting-free day at work, it's important to block out time for you to do the things that fill your cup. Perhaps you love spending Friday night on the couch with takeaway after a long week or you value your Sunday afternoons reading your book in the sun. Allocate time to prioritise YOU and suggest alternative dates or times if someone tries to schedule plans that conflict with your me-time.

Be honest

Not only with those around you, but also with yourself. If going out for dinner on a work night is too much for you, there's absolutely no point or need for you to commit.

It is okay to cancel

If you're feeling overwhelmed or exhausted, listen to your body and know that it's not the end of the world if you don't go out. For some reason, we feel like we need to come up with a good excuse to cancel, like 'My car broke down' or 'I'm working late'. We're all guilty of this. But be open with your friends and tell them how you're feeling. If they're true friends, they'll understand.

Tip: In saying all of this, do try to remember the power of human connection. You could be feeling flat or anxious and as soon as you give your friend a big hug, you could really start to feel happy and alive.

Boundaries in your love life

When we personally think of setting boundaries, our initial instinct is to think about creating space from external factors and connections, but it's just as important to set boundaries with those closest to you. When it comes to a partner, being clear with your boundaries can help you minimise conflict and maintain a healthy, happy relationship.

How we set boundaries in our romantic life
Ask for space

When you feel your fuse getting shorter, whether you're tired, stressed, frustrated or whatever the reason may be, speak up if you need to be alone. Run yourself a bath, head to your bedroom to read a book or take yourself out for a walk in the fresh air. Don't be afraid to do what's best for you. When you're craving time alone, it's important to lean into these signs. Both of you will be better off, trust us.

Don't overcommit

As we learned on page 237, our capacities and limitations are unique to each of us, therefore what you can handle over the space of a weekend will likely differ from what your partner can. Understand that it's okay to say 'no' when your partner suggests activities that aren't going to fill your cup!

Listen

Remember that just as you'd like your partner to respect your boundaries, it's important for you to understand and respect theirs. It takes two to tango.

Redefining what self-care means to you

When we think about self-care, our minds automatically picture warm baths, massages and meditation . . .

Laura: But actually, I've come to learn that self-care can be much deeper than this. It can look completely different because what works for one person may not work for another. It's all about implementing behaviours that promote *your* overall health.

A not-so-typical self-care activity I've recently discovered is setting aside time on a Sunday so I can plan my week ahead. I know a long walk on the beach sounds a lot more relaxing – and trust me, I make time for this too – but I've found that allocating time to plan and prepare makes a world of difference as I enter the next working week. I've now made this non-negotiable. Think about what makes you happy, energised, organised and calm – and actively make time to prioritise YOU.

Self-care: *(noun)* **The practice of taking an active role in protecting one's own well-being and happiness, in particular during periods of stress.**

Some not-so-typical self-care activities

★ **Plan your week on a Sunday** so you can feel calm and focused on Monday.

★ **Fill your car up with petrol in the evening** so your future self doesn't have to deal with that task first thing in the morning.

★ **Doing a big supermarket shop on a Sunday** and prepping your lunches so you can eat wholesome, delicious food throughout the week. This saves you money and multiple trips to the supermarket. If you've had a really big week, get your groceries delivered to save yourself the time and effort.

★ **Opt for a morning walk over an at-home or gym workout** if you know you're facing a busy day at work. This means you can prioritise getting 30 to 60 minutes of fresh air before you're tied to your desk all day.

★ **Put your personal appointments and work commitments into the same calendar** so you don't double book yourself.

★ **Schedule dinners with friends during the week**, especially if you're living alone or working from home. This will help you to stay connected and break up your week.

★ **Spend time alone on the weekend rather than filling it up** with activities. Remember that saying 'no' to someone means saying 'yes' to yourself.

Self-love

KIC: When we think about romantic love, we fully expect our relationships to have ups and downs, twists and turns, good times and bad. Yet when it comes to loving ourselves, there's an expectation that we 'should' love ourselves all of the time. The reality is, it's not possible to wake up every day in love with who you are, how you're feeling or what you look like. Self-acceptance on the other hand, is a feeling that we should aim to come close to every day. Practising regular, small steps of self-love and acceptance should leave you feeling content, and ready to take on anything just as you are. It's all about developing your personal self-love recipe towards a happier, healthier and more confident you.

A peek inside our self-love toolbox

★ **Consume content that fills your cup.** It might be getting lost in a book, listening to your favourite podcast or zoning out to a blissful playlist. Make sure you put your phone down and make time for content that fills you with joy.

★ **Get out in nature.** Take yourself out of the house, and head to the beach, the park or go on a bush walk. Breathe in the fresh air. There's something about getting out in nature that makes us feel grateful, alive and reconnected with ourselves.

★ **Say self-love affirmations.** Repeat to yourself: 'I am strong. I am loved. I believe in myself.' Affirmations are short and sweet, yet extremely powerful and can set you up with a positive mindset. Find an affirmation that resonates with you, then repeat it in your mind or repeat it out loud to remind yourself just how incredible you are.

★ **Move your body.** When you make time to exercise, you're proving to yourself that you're prioritising your body and mind over anything else. Now that is self-love!

★ **Run a hot bath.** Light a candle, pour in some bath salts and don't bring your phone int the room.

- ★ **Shift your mindset.** Celebrate differences and appreciate uniqueness instead of comparing and trying to be the same as someone else. Try to steer clear of anyone that triggers any self-doubt or negative comparison.

- ★ **Surround yourself with good people.** Friends who embrace uniqueness and celebrate you as you are will inspire you to be the best version of yourself.

- ★ **Show yourself physical love and be open to masturbation.** Our bodies are made to be pleasured and explored. Get to know yourself and learn what gets you off and what makes you tick. If you don't have a vibrator, treat yourself to one (trust us).

Nurturing your relationship with yourself

Laura: The most important relationship you will ever be in, over your entire life, is the one with yourself. The most amazing thing about this relationship is that you don't need to worry that this person will not call you back, or that they'll let you down, since she/he/they is you. And the sad thing is that some people live their entire life without ever realising how important this relationship truly is, when it has been there all along.

Just as we invest time and effort into relationships with friends and loved ones, we need to be proactive about doing the same with ourselves. Learning to be comfortable in your own presence can be difficult, especially if you're dependent on your close group of friends or partner. Our challenge to you is to take yourself out on a date. This may sound weird, but trust us. Treat yourself to a nice breakfast or coffee at a cafe, turn off your phone and be present with yourself. Sit there and people watch, brainstorm, set yourself goals. Use this time to focus on YOU. As you become more comfortable with yourself, your confidence will start to shine through.

The relationship you have with yourself is the foundation for all intimate relationships. If you're open, honest and kind to yourself, you'll be able to be the same way with others. You know the saying: *Treat others how you'd like to be treated?* Now's the time to switch this around and focus on treating yourself the same way you would treat your BFF. We are our own harshest critics. Some of the things we've said to ourselves would never even come to mind when talking to or thinking about a friend. It's time to learn to be kinder to ourselves. Next time you find yourself speaking negatively to yourself, switch up the narrative and treat yourself with the same compassion that you would show a friend.

We hope that this book has reminded you of how truly capable you are, and how much control you have over your life.

We can't always control what happens around us, but we can control how much we believe in ourselves, and what we are capable of.

You have every single thing you need right now to be worthy of love, acceptance and success. You deserve to feel fulfilled and full of joy. You are enough just as you are, and we hope that the words in this book will be a reminder for you whenever you need to hear exactly that.

Notes

Mind

22   In a world where so many of us feel pressured to be everything: Deni Todorovič interview with Laura Henshaw and Steph Claire Smith, *KICPOD*, podcast audio, November 17, 2021. keepitcleaner.com/episode-119-navigating-insecurity-and-learning-to-love-your-own-skin-with-style-by-deni

28   Dear Mama, I see you: Emma Heaphy, 'Know this', *Dear Motherhood*, Your Books, Wellington, New Zealand, 2021, p. 51.

30   She defines shame as 'the intensely painful feeling or experience': Brené Brown, *Atlas of the Heart*, Publisher, City, 2021, p. 137.

36   Great post-break-up tips: Kath Ebbs, 'Heartbreak Club', *Conversations with Kath*, podcast audio, Jan 18, 2022. podcasts.apple.com/au/podcast/heartbreak-club-moving-on/id1562605646?i=10005360591023

48   In fact, social comparison theory is a scientific concept used by psychologists: Kendra Cherry, 'Social Comparison Theory in Psychology, verywellmind.com, September 19, 2020. verywellmind.com/what-is-the-social-comparison-process-2795872

49 There is an amazing interview Oprah did: Oprah Winfrey interview with Kristen Bell and Monica Padman, *We are supported by ...*, podcast audio, July 7, 2021. armchairexpertpod.com/pods/oprah-winfrey

——It's the crush of conformity from one side and competition from the other: Brené Brown, ibid.

54   He says that good values are 'evidence-based, constructive and controllable': Mark Manson, *The Subtle Art of Not Giving a F*ck* HarperOne, New York, 2016, p. 86.

58   Beyond Blue reports that one in four people in Australia will experience anxiety in their lifetime: Beyond Blue, 'ABS National Survey of Mental Health and Wellbeing: Summary of Results, 2007', 2008, p. 27.

66   Name your worry story: Dr Jodie Lowinger, *The Mind Strength Method: Four steps to curb anxiety, conquer worry and build resilience*, Murdoch Books, Sydney, 2021, p. 47.

78   In his Ted Talk on Imposter Syndrome: Mike Cannon-Brookes, 'Imposter Syndrome', TEDxSydney 2017, video, Aug 2, 2017. youtube.com/watch?v=zNBmHXS3A6I

——Research has found that there are some personality traits that contribute to: Arlin Cunic, 'What is Imposter Syndrome?' *verywellmind.com*, May 23, 2022. verywellmind.com/imposter-syndrome-and-social-anxiety-disorder-4156469

Body

120 'The majority of diet and weight-loss supplements are targeted at women': Women's Health And Beauty Supplements Market Report, Grand View Research, 2016–2020. grandviewresearch.com/industry-analysis/women-health-beauty-supplements-market

——Research shows that these diets do not work long term: KD Hall and S Kahan, 'Maintenance of Lost Weight and Long-Term Management of Obesity' *Med Clin North Am*, 2018, vol 102, no. 11, pp. 183-197. doi.org/10.1016/j.mcna.2017.08.012

122 According to the Butterfly Foundation, 15 per cent of women in Australia: Butterfly Foundation, 'The reality of eating disorders in Australia', Sydney, 2020. butterfly.org.au/wp-content/uploads/2020/12/The-reality-of-eating-disorders-in-Australia-2020.pdf

124 We interviewed Liv on our KICPOD, and she shared some really valuable tips on how to get started: Liv Morrison interview with Laura Henshaw and Steph Claire Smith, podcast audio, *KICPOD*, Feb 22, 2022. keepitcleaner.com/episode-133-gut-health-overcoming-guilt-building-a-positive-relationship-with-food

150 The study found that people who engaged in a minimum of 150 minutes of moderate-intensity exercise: I Hartescu et al., 'Increased physical activity improves sleep and mood outcomes in inactive people with insomnia: a randomized controlled trial', *Journal of Sleep Research*, 2015, vol 24, no. 5, pp. 526–534, doi.org/10.1111/jsr.12297

154 Sadly, Australia has the highest rate of skin cancer in the world. Approximately 81,000 Australians missed their: Cancer Australia, 2020. *'National and jurisdictional data on the impact of COVID-19 on medical services and procedures in Australia: Breast, colorectal, lung, prostate and skin cancers'*, Surry Hills, NSW.

155 It's recommended that women and people with a cervix aged between 25 and 74 year: Department of Health and Aged care, National Cervical Screening Program. health.gov.au/initiatives-and-programs/national-cervical-screening-program

——If you are sexually active, it's recommended that you should get tested for: Better Health Channel, 'Regular health checks'. betterhealth.vic.gov.au/health/servicesandsupport/regular-health-checks

——Sadly, one in seven women will develop breast cancer. It's the fourth leading cause of death in Australia: National Breast Cancer Foundation, 'Breast Cancer Stats'. nbcf.org.au/about-breast-cancer/breast-cancer-stats/

158 Because between 33 and 45 per cent of Australian adults don't get enough good-quality sleep: R Adams et al., '2016 Sleep Health Survey of Australian Adults', University of Adelaide, 2017.

160 We interviewed one of Australia's most trusted sleep experts: Olivia Arezzolo interview with Laura Henshaw and Steph Claire Smith, *KICPOD*, podcast audio, Jun 23, 2021. keepitcleaner. com/episode-98-7-steps-to-a-better-nights-sleep-with-australias-1-sleep-expert/

——A clinical trial found lavender oil capsules improved sleep quality by 45 per cent: S. Kasper et al., 'Silexan, an orally administered Lavandula oil preparation, is effective in the treatment of 'subsyndromal' anxiety disorder: a randomized, double-blind, placebo controlled trial', *Int. Clin. Psychopharmacol*, 2010, vol 25, no. 5, pp. 277–87, doi.org/10.1097/YIC.0b013e32833b3242.

——Those who use a phone in the hour before bed are 48 per cent more likely to take longer: Agent France-Press, 'Teenagers sleep less when they have more computer screen time says study', *The Guardian*, 2015. theguardian.com/technology/2015/feb/03/teenagers-sleep-less-when-they-have-more-computer-screen-time-says-study

161 A clinical trial found magnesium could reduce anxiety by 31 per cent: NB Boyle et al., 'The Effects of Magnesium Supplementation on Subjective Anxiety and Stress-A Systematic Review', *Nutrients*, 2017, vol 9, no. 5, p. 429, doi.org/10.3390/nu9050429

——A recent trial found that participants who meditated were able to fall asleep 18 minutes faster: JC Ong et al., 'Combining mindfulness meditation with cognitive-behavior therapy for insomnia: a treatment-development study', *Behav Ther.*, 2008, vol 39, no. 2, pp. 171–82, doi.org/10.1016/j.beth.2007.07.002

Connection

166 Like most Australians, around half of my waking weekday hours are spent at work.: Rebecca Cassells, *Happy workers: How satisfied are Australians at work?*, Curtin University & mwah, April 2017. bcec.edu.au/publications/happy-workers-how-satisfied-are-australians-at-work/

170 Self-confidence *(noun)* A feeling of trust ...: 'Self-confidence', *Lexico (Oxford English Dictionary)*, 2022. lexico.com/definition/self-confidence

173 In her interview on *We are supported by* ...: Oprah likened the decision-making process to buying shoes.'; Oprah Winfrey interview with Kristen Bell and Monica Padman, ibid.

174 While women make up 51 per cent of the Australian workforce, they make up only 19 per cent of CEO positions ...: Workplace Gender Equality Agency, 'Women in leadership'. wgea.gov.au/women-in-leadership

175 Emotional intelligence (EQ) is a very important factor in successful leadership and in a study completed by ...: K Cavallo and D Brienza, 'Emotional competence and leadership excellence at Johnson & Johnson', *Europe's Journal of Psychology*, 2006, vol 2, no. 1, doi.org/10.5964/EJOP.V2I1.313

176 This dramatic gap in retirement savings is one of the major reasons women over 55 are …:Australian Human Rights Commission, '2019 Older Women's Risk of Homelessness: Background Paper exploring a growing problem', April 2019. humanrights.gov.au/our-work/age-discrimination/publications/older-womens-risk-homelessness-background-paper-2019

179 In an interview with Oprah, Sheryl talked about how many of her close friends stopped calling her …: Sheryl Sandberg interview with Oprah Winfrey, Oprah's Super Soul Conversations, podcast audio, August 8, 2017. super-soul.simplecast.com/episodes/sheryl-sandberg-how-to-build-resilience-and-find-joy-after-loss-ugxhawjs

—— In our interview with Deni Todorovič, they spoke about coming out as non-binary …: Deni Todorovič interview, ibid.

188 His grandma used to tell him, 'Be nice to everybody you pass on your way up …: Will Smith and Mark Manson, *Will*, Penguin Press, New York, 2021, p. 111.

191 In an interview we did on our podcast ('Savings, Tips, Money Values and Afterpay') …: Victoria Devine interview with Laura Henshaw and Steph Claire Smith, *KICPOD*, podcast audio, May 12, 2021. keepitcleaner.com/episode-92-savings-tips-money-values-and-afterpay/

194 Financial abuse is one of these, and while it does affect all genders, women are much more likely to be victims.: Women & Money, 'What is financial abuse?' *womenandnoney.org.au*. womenandmoney.org.au/what-is-financial-abuse/

196 Currently, in Australia, women retire with 42 per cent less super than men.: Australian Super, 'The gender super gap: How gender inequality affects superannuation', *australiansuper.com*, Jun 24, 2020. australiansuper.com/superannuation/superannuation-articles/2020/02/gender-equality-and-your-super

203 Kindness (noun) The quality of being generous …: 'Kindness', *Lexico (Oxford English Dictionary)*, 2022. lexico.com/definition/kindness

—— It's been proven that acting with kindness can reduce levels of anxiety …: Random Acts of Kindness Foundation, 'The science of kindness', *randomactsofkindness.org*. randomactsofkindness.org/the-science-of-kindness

220 'They asked about the sex education respondents had received at school and found that …: NORMAL, 'Normal's Big Australian Sex Survey', *itsnormal.com*. itsnormal.com/pages/big-sex-survey

224 The 5 Love Languages are …: Gary Chapman, *The Five Love Languages*, Northfield (Moody Publishers), Chicago, IL, 1992.

228 When I searched this term online, the first article that came up reported that the 'optimum' time to conceive is 30.5 years old.: Stephanie Wason, 'When can you get pregnant and what's the best age to have a baby?', *healthline.com*, June 6, 2018. healthline.com/health/womens-health/childbearing-age

234 Award-winning life coach, Sahar Andrade explains that boundaries create …: Sarhar Andrade, 'The importance of setting healthy boundaries', *Forbes.com*, July 1, 2021. forbes.com/sites/forbescoachescouncil/2021/07/01/the-importance-of-setting-healthy-boundaries/?sh=69cfabae56e4

235 A quick check of your incoming email may seem harmless, but did you know that it takes on average …: G Mark et al., 'The Cost of Interrupted Work: More Speed and Stress', Conference paper, April 6, 2008, doi.org/10.1145/1357054.1357072.

240 Self-care: *(noun)* The practice of taking an active role …': 'Self-care', *Lexico (Oxford English Dictionary)*, 2022. lexico.com/definition/self-care

Resources

Beyond Blue

If you're experiencing feelings of anxiety or depression we encourage you to reach out to the wonderfully supportive team at Beyond Blue.
beyondblue.org.au

If you feel that you're struggling with your relationship with food and want to seek help, a great place to start is at the Butterfly foundation.
butterfly.org.au/get-support/helpline

Victoria Devine's top money resources

YourSuper comparison tool

This is a new tool created by the ATO and it's absolutely fantastic for helping you review your superannuation. Up until now, the only super comparison tools available existed to make a profit and didn't put our communities in the best possible position as the results really depended on which super fund was paying the most amount of money to appear first in the search!

The YourSuper comparison tool helps you to compare MySuper products and pick a fund that aligns to your personal values and needs. We love that.
ato.gov.au/YourSuper-Comparison-Tool

Money Smart

Money Smart is the holy grail of information because it's non-biased and not product-related. It is government-run and includes free calculators and tips to help you take control of your financial life. It's a great place to start for anyone at any age.
moneysmart.gov.au

Budget Template

The free basic budget template on my website will help you get started on your financial wellness journey. If you want to take control of your money, the first step is knowing exactly where it's going!
shesonthemoney.com.au/downloadspage

Thanks

Thank you from the bottom of our hearts for the support you've shown us by reading this book. Through all that we do at Keep it Cleaner, our greatest achievement of all is being able to support you and to help you realise your true potential.

We want to start off with a big thank you to one very special woman: Nicole Maycroft. Nic has supported us in the writing of this book, and we are so lucky to work alongside her at Keep it Cleaner. Nic, this book would not have been possible without you, and we are forever grateful.

KIC has opened doors to some of the most magical opportunities – things we never could've dreamed of. The people we've met, the conversations we've had and the lessons we've learned have been invaluable in shaping our lives. It's something we'll never take for granted.

To Danny Kennedy, thank you for being there since day one. It's hard to put into words how much you've taught us. Our community appreciates your expertise, advice and banter just as much as we do, and we are so lucky to have you as a core part of the KIC journey.

Ash Ormond, your knowledge and passion for women's health never fails to amaze us. We admire the way you put your hand up for any opportunity to empower and educate our community. This means the absolute world to us.

To the woman with one of the most soothing voices on the planet, Meg James. Your meditations have brought us some much-needed stillness and creativity throughout the process of writing this book. Likewise, Jamie Strathairn, your words, wisdom and yoga flows have kept us calm and grounded. Thank you for allowing us to pass on your knowledge, it's simply too good to keep to ourselves.

Liv Morrison, for speaking up about the damaging effects of diet culture. You've taught us so much about the power of intuitive eating and we are incredibly grateful for everything you do to help educate our community.

To Georgia Grace and Lucy Wark for voicing the conversations we should be having in high school. We are in awe of your work in the sexual education space and are thankful to share a taste of that within these pages.

Amid guiding the birthing of many beautiful babies, thank you to Dr Bronwyn Hamilton for opening our eyes to the raw realities of the journey to motherhood. And to Emma Heaphy, thank you for capturing the thoughts of many new mums on paper. You're a beautiful mother and writer, and we're thankful for the opportunity to share your raw and wonderful words with our readers.

To Victoria Devine, you've helped so many women understand the importance of financial literacy – the two of us included. Thank you for being so open with your advice.

For the nights we struggled to switch our busy brains off, the fact that we were able to get enough sleep was testament to Olivia Arezzolo. Olivia, your 7-step sleep routine worked a treat and we're so grateful to share this with our community.

Kath Ebbs, we can't thank you enough for being so open and vulnerable with our community. Your interview on the KICPOD resonated with so many. Thanks as well for reminding us of the magic that music and dancing can have on our mental health.

To the ray of sunshine, Deni Todorovič, for teaching us to be okay with 'the ish'. We keep your advice in our back pockets for whenever we need to be reminded. Thank you for being you.

And Jane Morrow, Justin Wolfers and Sarah Odgers from Murdoch Books, thank you for believing in us and the success of this book. A big thank you to our editor, Katie Bosher, for cheering us on, correcting our grammar and challenging our ideas. Thanks as well to Jacqui Porter at Northwood Green for the beautiful design and illustrations.

Steph's shoutouts: A gigantic thank you to my incredible life partner, husband, baby daddy and friend, Josh, for being so supportive of me and my career, and encouraging me to continue to work hard. You keep me grounded, sane and watching you nail it as a dad brings me so much joy. And Mum, I know you'll likely be reading this book as you're the most supportive person I know. Thank you for all that you do for me, and for making me the mother I am today.

Laura's shoutouts:
To Dalton, thank you for being my rock - for your unconditional love and support through everything I do. And to my mum, thank you for sharing your strength with me. I believe I can do anything because of you.

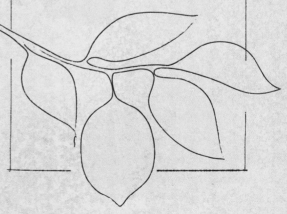

Index

you take care

you take care

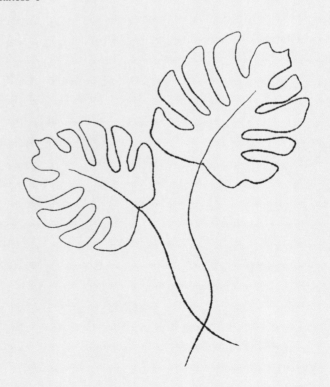

Published in 2023 by Murdoch Books, an imprint of Allen & Unwin

Murdoch Books Australia
Cammeraygal Country
83 Alexander Street
Crows Nest NSW 2065
Phone: +61 (0)2 8425 0100
murdochbooks.com.au
info@murdochbooks.com.au

Murdoch Books UK
Ormond House
26–27 Boswell Street
London WC1N 3JZ
Phone: +44 (0) 20 8785 5995
murdochbooks.co.uk
info@murdochbooks.co.uk

For corporate orders and custom publishing,
contact our business development team at
salesenquiries@murdochbooks.com.au

Publisher: Jane Morrow
Editorial Manager: Justin Wolfers
Design Manager: Sarah Odgers
Designer and Illustrator: Northwood Green
Editor: Katie Bosher
Production Director: Lou Playfair

Text © Laura Henshaw and Stephanie Miller 2023
The moral right of the author has been asserted.
Design © Murdoch Books 2023
Photography page 7 © Keep it Cleaner 2023,
by Marten Ascenzo

*Murdoch Books acknowledges the Traditional
Owners of the Country on which we live and work.
We pay our respects to all Aboriginal and Torres
Strait Islander Elders, past and present.*

ISBN 9 781 92261 641 8

 A catalogue record for this
book is available from the
National Library of Australia

A catalogue record for this book is available from
the British Library

Colour reproduction by Splitting Image Colour
Studio Pty Ltd, Clayton, Victoria
Printed by C&C Offset Printing Co. Ltd., China

DISCLAIMER: The content presented in this
book is meant for inspiration and informational
purposes only. The purchaser of this book
understands that the authors are not medical
professionals, and the information contained
within this book is not intended to replace
medical advice or to be relied upon to treat,
cure or prevent any disease, illness or medical
condition. It is understood that you will seek full
medical clearance by a licensed physician before
making any changes mentioned in this book.
The author and publisher claim no responsibility
to any person or entity for any liability, loss or
damage caused or alleged to be caused directly
or indirectly as a result of the use, application or
interpretation of the material in this book.

10 9 8 7 6 5 4 3 2 1